about the authors

PAUL ANTHONY

Paul Anthony is a woodworking author and teacher living in Riegelsville, Pennsylvania. He is the author of *Smart Workshop Solutions* and edits the Tricks of the Trade column for *Popular Woodworking* magazine.

LONNIE BIRD

Lonnie runs the Lonnie Bird School of Fine Woodworking in Dandridge, Tennessee; is the author of six books, including *The Complete Illustrated Guide to Using Handtools*; and is a contributing editor to *Fine Woodworking* magazine.

GRAHAM BLACKBURN

Graham is a furniture maker and author of 18 books on woodworking and home building, including *Traditional Woodworking Handtools* and *Traditional Woodworking Techniques*. He also is the publisher of the *Woodworking in Action* DVD-based magazine.

DAVID CHARLESWORTH

David teaches courses in making fine furniture from his shop in Devon, England, and is the author of the three-volume set of books titled *Furniture-Making Techniques*. He also has four DVDs produced by Lie-Nielsen Toolworks on sharpening, tuning and using traditional hand tools.

ADAM CHERUBINI

Adam builds reproduction furniture using the tools and techniques of the 18th century. He demonstrates his crafts at Pennsbury Manor in Bucks County, Pennsylvania, on Historic Trades Days and is a contributing editor to *Popular Woodworking* magazine.

SCOTT GIBSON

Scott, author of *The Workshop*, is a writer and woodworker in East Waterboro, Maine. He is the former editor of *Fine Woodworking* magazine.

ROGER HOLMES

Roger trained as a furniture maker in England and has been working wood professionally and for fun for 30 years. Formerly an editor at *Fine Woodworking* magazine, he now lives in Lincoln, Nebraska.

FRANK KLAUSZ

Educated in the Hungarian trade school system, Frank is a master cabinetmaker, author, teacher and owner of Frank's Cabinet Shop in Pluckemin, New Jersey, specializing in fine furniture reproductions and architectural fixtures.

DON MCCONNELL

Don is a planemaker for Clark & Williams in Eureka Springs, Arkansas, and is an avid researcher into the history of the woodworking trade and its tools. Before becoming a toolmaker, Don was a professional woodworker, specializing in ornamental carvings.

RICK PETERS

Rick is a woodworker and publishing professional and resides in Emmaus, Pennsylvania. He is the author of more than a dozen woodworking and home-improvement books, including *Woodworker's Hand Tools: An Essential Guide*.

CHRISTOPHER SCHWARZ

Chris is editor of *Popular Woodworking* magazine, a contributing editor to *The Fine Tool Journal* and teaches traditional woodworking techniques. He has two DVDs produced by Lie-Nielsen Toolworks on nearly forgotten hand tools and on blending hand tools and power tools.

PAUL SELLERS

Paul began his woodworking career 40 years ago as an apprentice in England. An advocate of hand tools in the modern shop, today he builds furniture and teaches in Texas at the School of Woodworking, which he started in 1995.

HARRELSON STANLEY

Harrelson is a teacher and importer of fine Japanese woodworking tools. He is also the host of a number of DVDs, including one discussing his side-sharpening technique in detail and another on setting up and using Japanese planes.

JIM STUARD

Jim is a former editor for *Popular Woodworking* magazine and is currently enjoying his two children and creating fly-fishing videos for the internet.

table of contents

Hand Tool
essentials

REFINE YOUR POWER TOOL PROJECTS
WITH HAND TOOL TECHNIQUES

FROM THE EDITORS OF
POPULAR WOODWORKING MAGAZINE

Read This Important Safety Notice

To prevent accidents, keep safety in mind while you work. Use the safety guards installed on power equipment; they are for your protection. When working on power equipment, keep fingers away from saw blades, wear approved eye protection to prevent injuries from flying wood chips and sawdust, wear approved hearing protection to protect your hearing and consider installing a dust vacuum to reduce the amount of airborne sawdust in your woodshop. Don't wear loose clothing, such as neckties or shirts with loose sleeves, or jewelry, such as rings, necklaces or bracelets, when working on power equipment. Tie back long hair to prevent it from getting caught in your equipment. People who are sensitive to certain chemicals should check the chemical content of any product before using it. The authors and editors who compiled this book have tried to make the contents as accurate and correct as possible. Plans, illustrations, photographs and text have been carefully checked. All instructions, plans and projects should be carefully read, studied and understood before beginning construction. Due to the variability of local conditions, construction materials, skill levels, etc., neither the author nor Popular Woodworking Books assumes any responsibility for any accidents, injuries, damages or other losses incurred resulting from the material presented in this book. Prices listed for supplies and equipment were current at the time of publication and are subject to change.

Metric Conversion Chart

to convert	to	multiply by
Inches	Centimeters	2.54
Centimeters	Inches	0.4
Feet	Centimeters	30.5
Centimeters	Feet	0.03
Yards	Meters	0.9
Meters	Yards	1.1

HAND TOOL ESSENTIALS: REFINE YOUR POWER TOOL PROJECTS WITH HAND TOOL TECHNIQUES. Copyright © 2007 by Popular Woodworking Books. Manufactured in Malaysia. All rights reserved. No part of this book may be reproduced in any form or by any electronic or mechanical means including information storage and retrieval systems without permission in writing from the publisher, except by a reviewer, who may quote brief passages in a review. Published by Popular Woodworking Books, an imprint of F+W Publications, Inc., 4700 East Galbraith Road, Cincinnati, Ohio, 45236. First edition.

Distributed in Canada by Fraser Direct
100 Armstrong Avenue
Georgetown, Ontario L7G 5S4
Canada

Distributed in the U.K. and Europe by David & Charles
Brunel House
Newton Abbot
Devon TQ12 4PU
England
Tel: (+44) 1626 323200
Fax: (+44) 1626 323319
E-mail: postmaster@davidandcharles.co.uk

Distributed in Australia by Capricorn Link
P.O. Box 704
Windsor, NSW 2756
Australia

Visit our Web site at www.popularwoodworking.com for information on more resources for woodworkers.

Other fine Popular Woodworking Books are available from your local bookstore or direct from the publisher.

11   10   09   08   07   5   4   3   2   1

Library of Congress Cataloging-in-Publication Data

Hand tool techniques : combining power and hand techniques / edited by David Thiel. -- 1st ed.
     p. cm.
   ISBN 13: 978-1-55870-815-0 (pbk. : alk. paper)
   ISBN 10: 1-55870-815-4 (pbk. : alk. paper)
   1. Woodworking tools. I. Thiel, David.
   TT186.H35 2007
   684'.08--dc22
                              2006039668

Editor: David Thiel
Designer: Brian Roeth
Photography by: Al Parrish and individual authors
Illustrations by: John Hutchinson
Production coordinator: Jennifer Wagner

fw
F+W PUBLICATIONS, INC.

3
planes

4
saws

7
projects for hand tools

hand tools for power woodworkers

BY CHRISTOPHER SCHWARZ

For me, working wood without hand tools is like trying to write a story without using adjectives.

Power tools and machinery are the nouns and verbs. They do the heavy lifting of reducing rough stock to useful sizes, for roughing out joints, for getting things done. But power tools can take you only so far when it comes to the fine details.

Hand tools are the difference between a flat carcase side and a shimmering, ready-to-finish carcase side. They turn a dovetail into a London-pattern dovetail, with tails that are too close together to accomplish with any router. They turn a mortise-and-tenon joint into a piston-fit joint.

I'm not saying you can't do woodworking without hand tools – lots of people make lots of beautiful objects using electrical tools only. But hand tools are the secret weapon that frees you from the limitations of your machinery.

Have you ever been frustrated by adjusting the fence of your table saw in small increments? Say, less than $1/64$"? Adjusting your stock to thickness, width and length with a handplane allows you to tweak your stock in increments as small as .001". This is child's play for a handplane, not something you have to practice at for years to master.

Do you get frustrated by the endless series of test cuts when setting a miter saw or table saw for a compound

miter? I do. And I used to despair at the amount of decent wood I wasted with these test cuts. Learning to work a backsaw allows you to draw any line at any angle on any piece of wood and cut to exactly that line. It doesn't mater if it's 90° or 23.75°. A handsaw will do both with the same ease.

Do you dislike spending hours building single-use jigs to make a simple cut, such as notching out the corners of the base in a post-and-frame carcase? A saw and chisel will allow you to make any size or shape notch. Even if every notch is a little different, your hand tools don't care. If you can mark it on the wood, they can cut it to that shape.

And do you wish you could add curves to your work without having to invest the time in making lots of router templates or spending money on a spindle sander? A saw and a decent rasp can shape any curve you can think of, and you aren't limited by the depth of a router bit. If you can think it and draw it, a rasp can shape it.

I'm sure that all of this sounds somewhat appealing. Why else would you have picked up this book? But I'm also certain that you have fears and apprehensions about hand work. It seems difficult to master. The tools are foreign. And most woodworker's first experiences with hand tools are frustrating.

I'm not going to lie to you, you need to learn to sharpen before you will have any success with chisels, planes or scrapers. But if you will learn this small skill (there are lots of valid ways to sharpen a tool, and some of our favorite are in this book), the rewards will far exceed the time you spent learning to put a keen edge on a piece of steel.

And, as a bonus, you will find that learning to sharpen a chisel will open up wide vistas of woodworking that might have seemed closed to you before: turning, carving, marquetry. Sharpening is the gateway skill to a wider world of woodworking.

Once you start down this path, I promise you that the distinctions between power tools and hand tools will start to blur. In fact, the adjectives "hand" and "power" will have a lot less meaning for you than the word that they modify: tool.

You will find yourself cutting tenons with a dado stack and adjusting them to perfection with a shoulder plane. You will cut a cabriole leg to shape with a band saw and smooth its sinuous curves with a rasp and file. You will raise a door panel on your router table and fit it with a block plane so it never rattles.

You will work faster without meaning to. The crispness of your work will surprise you. You won't dread sanding because you'll be doing much less of it. You will hunger to get back into the shop more than you ever did before.

Whether you know it or not, we live in a new golden age of woodworking that has never occurred before. Machinery is less expensive in inflation-adjusted dollars than when the Industrial Revolution birthed the industry. Almost any household of any income can afford a table saw, planer and jointer that can turn rough wood into furniture-ready boards.

And hand tools are now of a better quality than at any time since World War II. For almost 50 years, the best hand tools were old hand tools from the late 19th and early 20th century. And to get those old-timers to work you had to learn about tool restoration – removing

Chris' love of hand tools, and planes in particular, led him to create a loving place to store them - built with hand tools. You'll find the plans for this hand plane cabinet in the projects section of this book.

rust, flattening warped cast iron, regrinding hopelessly damaged chisels.

But no more.

Modern manufacturers such as Veritas, Lie-Nielsen, Clifton, Auriou and Ashley Iles now make tools that actually exceed the quality of the old-time tools. These tools take minutes to set up for use, instead of days. They are properly designed and use modern manufacturing and steels to compete against the other premium tools flooding the market. They are, like our machines, a joy to use.

The book you are holding in your hands is the missing link between the world of hand work and machine work. The skills and tools discussed herein are all you need to start incorporating hand tools into your power-tool shop. We've carefully selected each of these chapters to provide this crash course in how to turn your woodworking into fine woodworking. Now let's get to work.

why use hand tools?

BY CHRISTOPHER SCHWARZ

Learning to use hand tools is far easier than acquiring the hand skills to type on a keyboard. I should know – I cannot type worth a dang (despite being a trained journalist) and yet I've picked up the skills to use chisels, planes, rasps, hammers and braces with little effort.

That's because I've found that using hand tools successfully is not really about manual dexterity. It's not about having natural gifts. It's not about years of frustrating training. And it's not about being an apprentice and having an old-world master to guide the way.

Instead, it's about overcoming a barrier that stymies many home wood-

Me at age 8 with my first tool tote. Being limited to only hand tools as a child removed my fear of them in later years.

workers: the fear of taking a gamble and messing up the project you're working on by trying a new process. I see this all the time with woodworkers. After we experience success with a certain operation, we then resist trying a new way to do that operation because it seems risky. And because most of us (though not all) learned the craft with power tools (through shop class, television or magazines), that's what we're comfortable with.

I, however, was lucky. When I was 8 years old or so, my parents embarked on a crackpot adventure. We bought an 84-acre farm in rural Arkansas and decided to build two houses there. There was no electricity on the farm, and so the first house was built using mostly hand tools – a handsaw, brace and hammer. This kindled my interest in woodworking, and I lusted after my father's table saw and radial arm saw, which he kept at our house in town.

For obvious reasons, I was banned from the machinery. But I was allowed to use any of the hand tools, and I had my own small kit in the garage. I built a workbench with the help of my grandfather. I built an embarrassingly wretched tool tote. But it was all with hand tools, and so I knew that these tools could actually work in the hands of a kid.

As a result, when I started to get back into woodworking after college I had little fear as I picked up my first

dovetail saw, plow plane and outcannel gouge. That fearlessness has taken me a long way and it continues to pay dividends as I've begun experimenting with turning and carving.

I can't give you the same experience I had growing up, but I can give you this truth: If an awkward 8-year-old can build a workbench with hand tools, then you can do it, too. Overcoming your fear of failure is the first step. The second step is to understand what the tools are used for – there's not as much information about hand tools out there as there is about power tools. And the third step is to learn basic sharpening. Acquiring this skill is absolutely the Rosetta Stone to all the other hand skills, and that's why we've devoted significant space to the topic in this book.

The Myths of Hand Tools

There are some woodworkers who see little reason to even mess with hand tools. After all, we have all these amazingly fast and precise power tools at our disposal. Why should we "devolve" to an earlier technological state? That's quite against our progressive nature. Well the reason you should incorporate hand tools into your work is because just about everything you hear about hand tools is likely wrong. Let's look at some of the myths.

Myth 1: Hand tools are slow. The truth is that some people are slow. Hand tools have always been built to work as quickly as possible. They just have to be set up and wielded correctly. And you have to pick the right tool for the job. You wouldn't try to reduce a board in thickness with a sanding block, so why would you try to do that operation with a smoothing plane?

All tools are slow when used incorrectly. About seven years ago, one of our editors for our woodworking book line decided to build a cradle for his newborn child. It was a small project, yet he spent three full days planing down all the wood for the project on our Delta 13" cast-iron industrial planer. Why? Because he refused to remove more than $1/64$" in a pass. He was afraid he'd mess up.

The truth is that both hand tools and power tools can be remarkably fast when set up properly and used appropriately. You have to know that a fore plane is used for hogging off $1/16$" of material in a stroke. You have to know that a 7-point hand saw will fly through a board in half the number of strokes you'd make with a 12-point saw. You have to know that a cabinet rasp will shape wood faster than a pattermaker's rasp. Once you know these things, you'll pick up speed.

Myth 2: Hand tools are less precise than power tools. Whenever I hear this one I laugh and ask the person if they can set their table saw to remove .001" from a board's edge. This is virtually impossible to do with a table saw, router, jointer or planer. Yet it is child's play for a hand plane. After an afternoon of practicing with a handplane, you will be able to set any handplane to remove a .001"-thick shaving. Imagine the sort of power that gives you. Fitting and trimming your joints can be effortless when you have that skill. And it's an easy skill to get.

The real truth is that hand tools free you from a lot of these arbitrary measurements anyway. Your door panels

This tool cabinet (quite an improvement over my work 29 years ago) was built using a blend of hand and power tools. The rough lumber was dimensioned with machinery. Hand tools did the rest: truing and refining all the surfaces and all of the joinery in the case and drawers.

Fore planes are rough tools that can hog off $^1/_{16}$" in a pass. The jointer plane's long sole then trues the surface and takes a thinner shaving (about .006" thick). The smoothing plane is then used to remove a thin shaving (about .001" to .002" thick) to prepare the surface for finishing. You need all three planes to surface lumber and you need to use them in the correct order.

don't care if they are .0625" thick or .061". All they care about is if they fit in the rails and stiles. If you cut a panel too thick to fit into its groove on a table saw, you end up engaging in the endless cycle of: cut, go to the bench, check the fit, tweak the setup; cut, go to the bench, check the fit. Then you have to sand the panel for finishing. When you fit a panel with a hand plane you do it all at the bench. Take a few passes, check the fit, take a few passes, check the fit. And here's the real kicker, once it fits you don't have to sand it – the hand plane produces a ready-to-finish surface. So now you're both faster and you're more precise.

Myth 3: Hand tools require great skill. A lot of people are under the assumption that to use hand tools you need years of practice to develop a feel for the tool. While true mastery of any tool (hand or power) is probably unobtainable, most hand tools can be learned after a couple hours (not years) of practice. Go down to the shop and decide to practice on some scrap. Drill it, cut it, plane it, shape it, carve it. When you have some success, then apply those skills to a project.

There's another bit of missing information that helps propagate this myth about hand tools: people think they are

used entirely freehand. This is wrong. There are a number of simple "appliances" or jigs that will help you guide your hand tools. Shooting boards assist you in planing perfect square edges and ends on boards. Bench hooks hold and guide your work while using a backsaw. Sawbenches help make your handsaw fly through the work. Planing stops eliminate complicated workholding apparatuses.

Building a few of these appliances (I'd start with the bench hook on page 140) will immediately unlock the hidden abilities of your hand tools.

Myth 4: Simple hand tools aren't cut out for complex work: We have an amazing array of commercial and shop-made jigs for power tools these days. There are dovetail jigs that cost more than my first pickup truck. Believe me, these modern jigs work. I've used a lot of them. And I think that these jigs sell so well because some woodworkers really like gizmos (nothing wrong with that) and some woodworkers think they need a complex jig to perform a complex operation, such as cutting a mortise-and-tenon joint.

Hand tools largely free you from complex jiggery. Think for a moment how difficult it is to cut a compound miter on a table saw, particularly on a

panel. There is an immense amount of setup and test-cutting involved. Lots of wasted sample pieces. And if you really want to do it well, you should buy an aftermarket miter gauge that is accurate to half a degree.

When I want to cut an unusual angle, I mark it out on my workpiece and simply saw to the line. Then a couple strokes with a plane clean up the cut and get it precisely fit. No test cuts. No wasted material. No jigs. Mark the line; cut the line. It is one of the most liberating feelings you will ever experience. And it's not hard to do. An 8-year-old can handle it.

Or how about fitting a door in a face frame? If your door or face frame is crooked (let's say it's off by $^1/_{32}$"), how are you going to correct that error when using power tools? A tapering sled on the table saw? A few stopped cuts on the jointer? A tapered straightedge guide for your router with a bearing-guided pattern bit? I've used all these methods. Here's what I do now: I mark the taper I need on the door's rail or stile. I plane to that line by using a quick series of stopped passes. When I get to the line, I'm done. As a bonus, the edge of that door is ready for finishing, too.

Myth 5: Hand tools are cheaper than power tools: I bet you weren't expecting me to say that. Good tools cost. Period. End of story. It's true you can buy vintage hand tools or vintage machinery for a lower up-front cost. But getting these tools to work correctly can cost you a lot of time and effort. If you have a lot of free time and enjoy tinkering

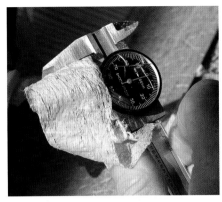

This shaving is .001" thick and you can easily set a hand plane to remove this amount (or more, depending on your needs). Setting power tools to remove such small increments is almost impossible.

with metal things, then this is the route for you.

For those of us for whom time is scarce: Buy the best tool you can. You will end up sharpening it less, fooling with it less and using it more. This has always been the case, even hundreds of years ago. In Joseph Moxon's *Mechanick Exercises* of 1678, he exhorts craftsmen to buy superior steel saws over the less expensive iron ones and even tells them exactly where in London on Foster Street to get them. And virtually every other old text on woodworking I own insists that you should always buy the best you can afford. *Audels Carpenters and Builders Guide* (Audel Co. 1947) puts it thus: "(I)t is important to buy only the best regardless of cost."

As a kid, my first coping saw was a Craftsman. Some tools from Craftsman are good; some are not. This one was decidedly a piece of junk. The blade clamp never worked right. The frame buckled under normal use. The riveted handle was loose. The mechanism that controlled the angle of the blade routinely came loose. Pretty much everything on that saw was a stinker. So it was no wonder I struggled with that tool. I now have a nice Olson Saw Co. coping saw. The day I started using that saw my sawing skills increased ten-fold. Cheap tools are barriers to good work. Good tools make the work as easy as possible.

Where to Begin

If this all sounds good to you, you're probably wondering where you should begin. The first step is to educate yourself about the tools before you start buying them and using them. While there's indeed sound information contained in this issue, you need a few books to help you really get the critical mass of information you need. I have a number of favorite books about hand woodworking. You need at least two: One on sharpening and one about the tools. I'd buy the book on sharpening first.

There are two sharpening books I really like: *The Complete Guide to Sharpening* by Leonard Lee, and *The Complete*

The bench hook guides your back saw and keeps it in place on your bench as you cut. It's a remarkable workshop appliance.

Illustrated Guide to Sharpening by Thomas Lie-Nielsen. Both books are from The Taunton Press and both will guide you in all the basic moves required to sharpen a wide variety of tools.

For an overview of hand tools and their uses, here are some good sources to look for at the bookstore and the library (some of these books are out of print but still available used and at libraries).

• *Hand Tools* by Aldren A. Watson (Norton). Although Watson has a bit of a boatbuilder's perspective, the information and his beautiful hand illustrations are solid gold. This book is inexpensive, readily available and packed with excellent information you'll turn to regularly.

• *Traditional Woodworking Handtools* by Graham Blackburn (Blackburn Books). The first woodworking book I ever owned was written by Blackburn. This book combines many of his columns

Fitting a door with a hand plane is fast and accurate. First mark out how much material you need to remove and draw a line on the door showing what you want to remove (above). Then plane to that line and the door will fit perfectly (right).

for magazines during the years into a very nice reference book on hand work.

• *Tools for Woodwork* by Charles H. Hayward (Drake). Sadly, this fine book is out of print. Hayward explores all the basic tools you need to do woodworking

Good hand tools never wear out (unlike even the best routers or cordless drills). So spending a bit more money on one is a good idea because you'll never have to buy a replacement and you'll never outgrow it.

A good workbench makes the work easier and faster. Buy Scott Landis's book on workbenches to learn everything you need to know before you build or buy one.

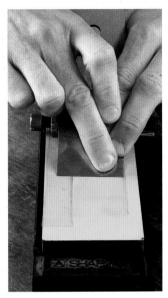

Sharpening your tools is the first skill to master. Once you get past this hurdle, you will find yourself able to master any edge tool.

with clear explanations and perfect illustrations.

• *Restoring, Tuning & Using Classic Woodworking Tools* by Michael Dunbar (Sterling). If you are going to go the route of fixing up vintage tools, you need this book. It can be difficult to find, but it is worth the effort.

• *The Workbench Book* by Scott Landis (Taunton). You need a good workbench for hand work, and Landis's book is the classic. Avoid imitators; this is the best book on benches available.

And then you should get a catalog from Astragal Press, which specializes in publishing and selling books on traditional craft work. You will find many excellent books that will help take you down paths that interest you, such as hand planes or braces or saws. How to contact Astragal: Visit astragalpress.com, call 866-543-3045,

or write to them at: P.O. Box 239, Mendham, NJ 07945.

Not a Rejection of Electricity

There's one final point I'd like to make about hand tools. Using them does not force you to reject power tools or machinery. Many people who visit my shop at home are puzzled by my big 8" Powermatic jointer, Delta Unisaw and Grizzly 15" planer. "I thought you were a hand tool guy," is the inevitable comment that falls from their lips.

Then I point out the obscene number of braces hanging on the wall behind my band saw and the collection of hand planes stored in a cherry cabinet above my grandfather's workbench.

"I like all tools," is my standard reply.

Hand tools and power tools co-exist very peacefully in a modern work-

shop. The two perspectives complement one another in surprising ways and allow you to work faster, more accurately and with less waste and more joy.

You can blend the two perspectives to your heart's desire. I use my powered planer and jointer for prepping all my rough stock, but the hand tools handle all the final truing and make the work ready to finish. I use my table saw for ripping and crosscutting (its true purpose in life) and use my hand tools for most of the fine joinery. The rough work is handled by the power tools in my shop and the fine work is done by the hand tools.

The result of knowing both hand and power tools is that I'm a more fearless woodworker. New tools, techniques and projects are much more doable when you have a lot of different ways of going about any given task. And when I do hesitate or cringe at a task ahead of me, I simply remind myself to act more like an 8-year-old boy.

2

IF YOU'RE A BEGINNER AND MONEY IS TIGHT, YOU CAN **BUY ALL THE HAND TOOLS YOU'LL NEED** TO START WOODWORKING WITH JUST A C-NOTE.

hand tools for $100

BY CHRISTOPHER SCHWARZ

Tool booths can be a little competitive at times. Best advice: go early or go late. Go early for the best selection; go late for the best deals.

Beginning woodworkers have it bad when it comes to buying their first hand tools. First you have to figure out what tools you need to get started. Then you have a hard choice. You can buy the cheapest stuff at discount stores and risk being disappointed with the quality later. Or you can buy the nice stuff from catalogs and specialty woodworking stores that is considerably more expensive. However there's a third option that few beginning woodworkers consider: buy used hand tools.

Flea markets, garage sales and antique malls are usually awash with quality used hand tools at reasonable prices. A #4 Stanley smoothing plane that costs $57.50 new in the box can be had for $15 to $20 used. Wooden handled chisels that average about $10 each new can be bought for $5. There are some downsides to buying used, though. If you're not happy with your purchase, it's unlikely you can get a refund. And some used tools need restoration before use. But if you follow the guidelines in this article, you can minimize the amount of time you'll spend fixing up your old tools and quickly put your new toys to work.

Let me first say that buying used isn't for everyone. It's unlikely you'll be able to go to one flea market on a Saturday morning and equip your entire shop. So you're going to have to shop around. And for many people there's

something inexplicably appealing about owning a brand new tool. But if money is tight and you've got a few weekends free, it's entirely possible to equip your shop with all the basic hand tools for less than $100.

Your Shopping List

First figure out what you need to get started. Even if you're a power tool junkie you're going to have to buy about 20 hand tools (until they invent an electric scratch awl). If you're inclined to do all your work with hand tools, this list is still a great place to start — you'll be able to do a lot of things with these tools. The chart below is a decent shopping list with some average flea market prices that we've seen in the Midwest, South and East. When you go shopping, be sure to take a list of the tools you need, a good-quality steel ruler marked in inches and a pencil.

There are four places to find good used tools: auctions, garage sales, antique malls and flea markets. Auctions are great because you can sometimes pick up an entire box of tools for $20. Because the prices are reasonable, this is where many flea market vendors purchase tools to sell. But auctions are

time consuming. You can sit all day waiting for the tools you're interested in to come up for sale. And even then you might lose to a higher bidder and only end up with a few extra pounds from all those pimento cheese sandwiches you ate.

Garage sales are nice because the person running them might have no idea how to price the tools. I've found good hand planes at yard sales for $5. Problem is you usually have to drive all over town to find a garage sale that may or may not have tools for sale. And most garage sales have just a few tools for sale. Antique malls, on the other

hand, are nice because there are usually lots of tools to choose from. But you have to pay for that convenience. Prices can be higher than those listed here and there's little chance to bargain.

I prefer the flea markets. There are lots of tools to choose from, there's no waiting around and the prices are low, especially if you are willing to haggle.

Chisels

You've gotta have chisels. From squaring up rabbets cut with your router to paring dovetails, chisels are a necessity. Luckily, used chisels are easy to find and inexpensive. The nice thing about used chisels is that the majority of them have wooden handles, which I'm partial to. The downside to used chisels is you're going to have to grind the cutting edge back to square. I've never seen a used chisel that didn't need work.

But don't get too worked up about that. Many new chisels need to be reground right out of the box, too. So when you're looking to buy a used chisel, here's what to keep in mind. First measure the chisel with your steel ruler to make sure it's a size you need. Look for chisels that aren't too rusty, especially on the back. Surface rust is OK, but if there are deep pits on the back of the chisel, you'll have a lot of flattening to do before you can get a decent cutting edge. Rust on the front isn't a big deal, as long as it's not too severe.

How much of the blade is left is also important. Unless the chisel is a butt chisel (which is supposed to have a short blade) you should have at least 3" to 4" of blade remaining. If you've got less, you might not have any tempered steel left in the blade and the chisel won't hold an edge. Pass.

Now check out the handle. Can you pull the handle out of the socket? If you can, you'll need to fix that or turn a new handle. Follow the same rules with mortising chisels, which have consider-

Beginning woodworker Ed O'Connell checks out some of the tool bargains at an antiques market in Kentucky. While you can find used tools at garage sales and antique stores, open-air markets like this seem to be the most fruitful.

Always take a ruler when buying tools. You need only one 3/8" chisel for your toolbox.

Chisels are plentiful, so you can be picky about the quality and price. Here a couple chisels sit among some carving tools—another common item at shows.

ably thicker blades and no bevel on the sides. In addition, make sure these look like they can take a lot more abuse, such as getting whacked by a hammer every day.

Backsaw and Coping Saw

You need a backsaw for cutting dovetails and tenons, and other small work. Backsaws are so named because they have a rigid spine clamped to the back of the blade that stiffens the blade during the cut. Larger backsaws are called tenon saws. Smaller ones are called dovetail saws. And little ones with a round handle are often called gent's saws. You'll find a lot of saws for sale, but they usually need a lot of work, such as fixing missing teeth and resharpening. Let a professional do this for you.

If you're not an old tool purist, I recommend you buy a new Japanese-style backsaw. Lee Valley Tools, for example, sells a great Korean-made Dozuki backsaw for $22.50 (item# 60T55.01 • 800-871-8158). I like Japanese-style saws because they cut on the pull stroke instead of the push stroke, so they're

Shopping list

Tool	Low price	High price	New price ‡
WOODEN-HANDLED CHISELS			$7–$11
1/4" chisel	$4	$7	$7.25–$11
3/8" chisel	$4	$7	$7.50–$11
1/2" chisel	$4	$7	$7.50–$11
5/8" chisel	$4	$7	$8.50–$11
3/4" chisel	$4	$7	$9.50–$11
1" chisel	$4	$7	
WOODEN-HANDLED MORTISING CHISELS			$16
1/4" chisel	$5	$7	$17
3/8" chisel	$5	$7	
Backsaw*	$5	$15	$19–$50
Coping saw	$5	$7	$6–$10
Low-angle block plane	$7	$18	$45
#4 Smoothing plane	$15	$20	$54
Scraper †	$5	$5	$5
Mill bastard file	$1	$2	$6
Burnisher	$3	$5	$10–$20
Screwdrivers	$2	$3	$3 each
Combination square	$5	$25	$20–$65
Scratch awl	$2	$7	$5–10
Marking gauge	$4	$8	$10–$40
Sliding bevel gauge	$5	$8	$16–$20

* I recommend buying a new backsaw. Read why in the story.
† You're unlikely to find a used scraper. Buy a new one.
‡ Prices for "new tools" are for tools comparable in quality to what you'd find used.

A couple of decent block planes. The one on the left was tempting because it was a bargain; however it didn't have an adjustable throat and it was a standard block plane, not the low-angle version. The plane on the right was priced at $18, which is OK for a low-angle block plane with an adjustable throat. The small shiny ring below the front knob of this plane moves the throat forward and back.

easier to control. Plus the kerf is considerably thinner than Western saws.

Coping saws are simple tools that are great for cutting curves and cleaning out waste between dovetails. Make sure a used one is fully adjustable. That is, you can lock the blade at any angle. Buy some new blades that have 15 teeth per inch at the hardware store for about 30 cents each.

Planes

You'll need a low-angle block plane for lots of stuff. For example, when you've glued up two pieces of wood and one edge is slightly proud of the other, a low-angle block plane is great for leveling the joint.

You'll usually find two kinds of block planes for sale: one is your plain old block plane, the other is a low-angle block plane. Block planes have the blade set at about a 20-degree angle to the sole. The blade in the low-angles is set at 12 degrees. Low-angle planes will cut everything that a block plane will, and they work better on planing end grain and highly figured woods. So try to buy a low-angle version if you can.

You also want this tool to have an adjustable throat. The throat is the opening between the blade and plane body. It's important that this is adjustable because the thinner the opening you can create, the less tearout you'll get — especially in figured woods. To see if a block plane has an adjustable

throat, unscrew the front knob on the plane and try to wiggle the piece of metal on the sole in front of the blade. If it moves, your throat is adjustable.

Another issue with used block planes is the blade itself. Look for one that's not too rusty and has some life left in it. New block plane blades are about $4\frac{1}{2}$" long. If yours is considerably smaller, you might be in for trouble. Replacement blades for some block planes can be tricky to find, especially for oddball brands. It's safe to pass on block planes with stubby blades.

Now check the plane bottom for flatness. Hold your straightedge — edge on — against the sole of the plane and up to a light. If you can see some significant gaps

Ed checks the sole of a smoothing plane to see how flat it is. You can flatten plane bottoms using a slab of glass, some kerosene and 90-grit silicon carbide (available in many woodworking catalogs). However, the more light you can see under that ruler, the more work you'll have to do to flatten the sole.

between the ruler and sole, you could be in for a lot of work. Flatter is better.

Another nice feature in block planes is called "lateral adjustment." This allows you to pivot the blade slightly to the left or right to get a perfectly square cut. Lateral adjustments aren't the same on all planes so look for a lever on the back of the plane that moves the blade left or right.

Smoothing planes are useful for heavy-duty planing. If you have a rough-sawn edge on a board, a smoothing plane can dress it. You also can use it for the final smoothing of rough-sawn lumber. Most smoothing planes, especially those made by Stanley, will have a #4 on them. If you can't find a

#4 plane, a #3 or a #5 will also serve you well as a first all-purpose plane.

Many of the same rules for block planes apply to smoothing planes, except smoothing planes do not have adjustable throats. Instead they have adjustable frogs. The frog is the piece of metal that the blade sits on. By moving it forward you can close the throat. Look for a frog screw at the back of the plane. Planes without this screw are still somewhat adjustable, but it's more of a pain to accomplish.

Scrapers

Scrapers are simply a piece of hardened metal that have a special burr on them. These useful tools work like supercharged sandpaper and can flatten tabletops and remove glue squeeze-out. I have yet to see a used one for sale. Buy a new one. You'll also need to buy a mill bastard file and burnisher to sharpen your scraper. Mill bastard files will be marked as such. Burnishers look like a metal magic wand with a wooden handle.

Combination Squares

The combination square is a constant companion of the woodworker. It can lay out joints, draw lines parallel to the edge of a board, draw 45-degree miters and set up all your machinery. So be careful when you buy one. I usually look for a Starrett-brand square. They cost more ($25 used; $57 new), but they're worth every penny. Other squares are serviceable if money is tight. Here's what to look for.

First make sure your square is still square. Put the square against the edge of a piece of wood and mark a line.

Look for a frog adjustment screw when picking out a smoothing plane. This screw moves the frog forward and back, which opens and closes the throat of the plane.

a word about white elephants

There is something magical about finding a mint-condition tool at a flea market that sends all reason into a tailspin. A few months ago I was looking at two #4 smoothing planes in a shop in Florida. Both were Stanleys. One was obviously very old but looked so sparkling new that it could have had robot dust on it. Price $63. The other one was cruddy and used and only $23. Like a crow that's drawn to bright and shiny objects, I was mesmerized by the pretty one, even though it was way too expensive.

Then I came to my senses. I checked the sole of each plane with a straightedge. The old plane was almost perfectly flat. The shiny one was horribly warped, twisted, you name it. It was unusable, except as a paperweight. So if you see a shiny tool at a flea market be careful. There's a reason that tool might never have been used. It could be that it was born a piece of junk.

Now turn the square over and mark a second line very close to the first. If the lines are parallel, your square is square. Otherwise pass.

Make sure you can lock the blade down tightly. If you find one that passes all these tests, don't think about it, buy it. Good squares are hard to find.

Marking Gauge

The marking gauge lays out mortises, tenons and dovetails. A pin on one end of the gauge marks the wood while the head determines where that mark is made.

Look for a marking gauge with a pin that hasn't been ground out of existence. Some gauges have two pins. These are nice for laying out mortises and tenons. If you find one of these, consider it a bonus. Also, make sure you can lock the fence tightly on the beam.

Sliding Bevel Gauge

These handy contraptions are useful for transferring angles from one place to

The rust on this sliding bevel gauge isn't much to worry about. Be more concerned with the gauge's ability to lock down.

another. Say you need to set your table saw's blade to a particular angle that matches a piece on your project. Adjust the bevel gauge to the angle on the project and lock the blade down. Now put the gauge against your table saw's blade and tilt it until it fits perfectly against the bevel gauge.

There are two things to look for. First make sure the blade isn't too rusted or warped. You want it to be as straight as possible. Second, make sure you can lock the blade down tightly so it won't move if you bump it slightly.

Bargaining

Some people love to haggle; others won't do it except when buying cars. I'm indifferent, but I can almost always get a better price one of two ways — without being rude. First, assume they'll come down about 15 to 20 percent on most items, then offer that much. If a plane is $25, offer $20. They'll almost always take it. Second, buy two or more items from the same dealer. Usually the price becomes more flexible. I once bought a $25 plane, a $25 combination square and an $8 bevel gauge for $40 — 31 percent off.

One more thing: prices at flea markets usually go down as it gets closer to quitting time. Sure, the selection isn't as good, but if you're ready with cash, the dealer won't have to pack up the item for his next show. You just might get lucky.

3

PERFECTION DOESN'T EXIST.
BUT YOU CAN COME CLOSE.

the ultimate hand tool shop

BY ADAM CHERUBINI

One of the first things any beginning woodworker must do is set up a workshop. Like so many other things a novice woodworker must do, the preparation of a workshop shapes the capabilities and enjoyment of the craft long after the novice has become an intermediate or advanced woodworker.

Fortunately, many books and articles have been published on the subject. Unfortunately, few – if any – address the unique needs of hand tool usage. All too often, I see benches that are much too short, free standing or shoved into some filthy corner. Provisions for sharpening appear to be haphazard afterthoughts. Tool storage solutions are typically completely inadequate for the unique needs of hand tools and their convenient usage. The general lack of consideration for the unique needs of hand tool usage conspires to limit the potential of any would-be hand tool craftsman.

Unlike modern shops where each new tool purchase requires a corresponding additional allotment of floor space, once a few basic hand tool work areas are established, there's rarely a need for any additional growth. The trick is getting these areas laid out in such a way that they don't prevent your future success.

Space to Plane
A workbench is used for hand planing and a host of joinery operations. When

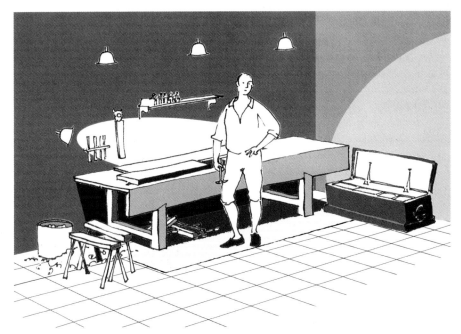

I'm using cartoons to illustrate most of this chapter for two important reasons. Not only does it allow me to show the "ultimate" shop without actually having the ultimate shop, it also helps to reinforce the notion that the "ultimate hand-tool shop" exists only in our imaginations, and is totally devoid of the real-life compromises and practicalities that shape real-world workshops.

I built my 6'-long workbench, I thought carefully about the size of furniture I wanted to make. Nothing on that list was more than 4' long, so I thought a 6' bench would be plenty long enough. But there were two things I missed: First, a 40"-wide by 20"-deep chest of drawers needs approximately 8' of base moulding. You can't make 8'-long passes over stock resting on a 6' bench. Crosscutting the stock before moulding has disadvantages. Second, I find it best to plane my stock before I saw it.

That way, I know where the knots are, where the sapwood or difficult grain is, etc. This helps me avoid those areas when I cut mouldings or saw joints. Consequently, I prefer to plane my stock in the lengths in which I purchase it. Because I buy mostly 8' stock and rarely need more than 8' of moulding, I recommend setting aside space for a roughly 2' × 8' workbench.

Eight feet of shop space isn't enough room for an 8' bench. All planes need "run-off" room. Because the shavings tend to fly off this end of the bench anyway, I find this a convenient location for a trash barrel.

Don't put the end of your bench too close to a wall. Someday you may take my advice and get yourself a 30"-long plane. Make sure you have room to use it. I think it wise to allow a couple feet for run-off room.

Locating your bench with the back against a wall provides it with stability for sawing or other work perpendicular to the long front edge of the bench. A piece of scrap placed between your stock and the wall provides a convenient backstop for material being planed. The wall also prevents tools from being knocked off the back and provides a convenient location for a chisel rack and other tool storage.

An anti-fatigue mat in front of your bench is more than a luxury. Plane shavings can make finished wood or concrete floors quite slippery, even after they've been swept away. Planing long stock requires quite a bit of foot work, so I recommend considering a sweepable non-slip work mat of some sort.

Room to Saw

Learning to saw by hand offers woodworkers the opportunity to explore traditional joinery. Like anything else one attempts to learn, it's easier to saw with good tools and the right space. In Anglo-American shops, ripping is performed on sawhorses using a wide-bladed "western" saw.

The size and shape required for ripping fits well directly adjacent to the bench. I think this resulting 4' × 11' rectangle is the absolute minimum size for the ultimate hand tool shop.

One advantage of working wood with hand tools is that you have the ability to work very wide stock that would be too heavy or unwieldy to muscle across machines. Having space to rip directly in front of your workbench saves you from having to carry some big boards through your shop. That said, if space is tight you can rip almost anywhere. It's quite easy to take your sawhorses outside and rip on the patio or in the garden.

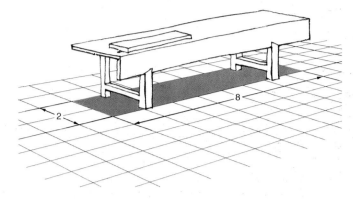

First, place your bench against a wall. A 2' x 8' bench is, in my opinion, the minumum amount of space necessary for the bench.

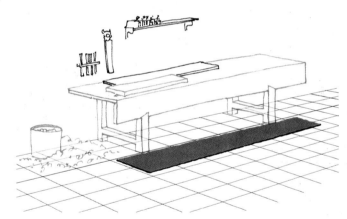

You don't want to strike the wall with your jointer plane. Put the end of your bench 2' from the wall – and it's a good place for a trash can.

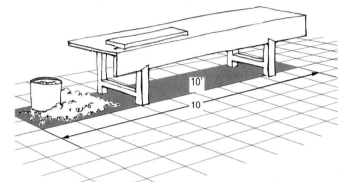

An anti-fatigue mat in front of your bench is an essential part of your shop. It gives you sure footing and is good for your back, too.

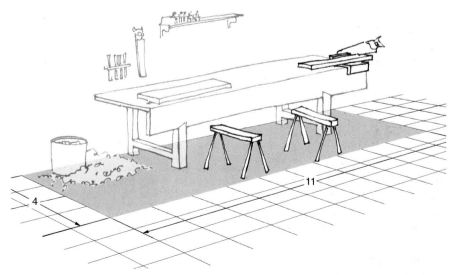

Set aside 2' of space in front of your bench for ripping at the sawhorses. Add 1' to the right of the bench for crosscutting.

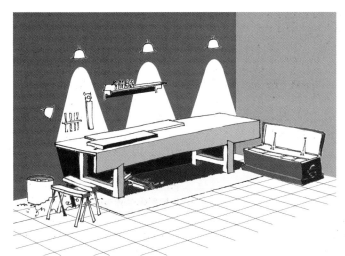

Creating shadows on your bench is important. Shadows allow you to see a profile develop on your work. Create light sources by having lamps you can switch off individually.

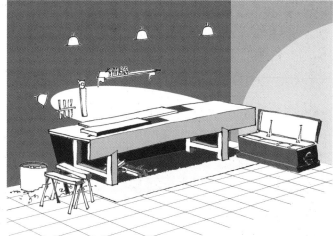

A raking light, as shown above, will quickly point out imperfections in your work, from tear-out to plane tracks.

Many woodworkers enjoy the convenience of a tail vise. Not me. Its limited usefulness is overshadowed by the difficulties it creates for essential crosscut sawing. The right end of the bench is the perfect place for cutting joints and accurate crosscuts. Anglo-American woodworkers got away without tail vises for at least 100 years and so can you. You needn't leave much space to the right of your bench for the offcut. A long offcut is difficult to support here anyway.

Tool Storage Space

Hand tools aren't like hand-held power tools. Dropping them is generally disastrous. Metal tools are sensitive to rust, which can cause pits in polished metal blades. Wooden tools are sensitive to changes in humidity. Finding efficient ways of storing hand tools has been the effort of craftsmen for centuries. Rather than propose a revolutionary solution made from medium-density fiberboard, a quick look back at what has been done might be wise.

Images of pre-industrial shops clearly reveal a two-pronged approach to storing tools. Oft-used tools, generically referred to as "bench tools" because of their ever-present location on the bench, are shown stored on open shelves, or hung from hooks on the walls.

Tool chests, frequently painted a blue green color (perhaps because the copper-based pigment was inexpensive), are shown in several images of pre-industrial shops. For many years I believed these chests were merely a convenient means of transporting a journeyman's tools as he "journeyed" from shop to shop. I was wrong. These chests are deceptively large and insanely heavy. And the term "journeyman" is an English corruption of the French word for "work day" (journée) referring not to the traveling nature of the worker but rather the way in which he is compensated for his work (for a day's work). These chests are a surprisingly efficient way to store hand tools. Tools are easily accessed, safe from the hazards of the workshop, movable (with some difficulty) and the chest is unobtrusive. Made correctly, the chest's tight-fitting lids seem to protect the contents from rust. *Popular Woodworking* has offered a variety of plans for tool chests and wall-hung cabinets. One advantage of a traditional tool chest is that it can be relocated seasonally if necessary.

If we define the "bench tools" properly and narrowly as those tools used almost continuously, rust should not be a problem. But great changes in humidity or temperature require us to reconsider the whole concept of bench tools. A fine tool chest may make an excellent window seat or coffee table. Tool chests from the 18th century are often indistinguishable from blanket chests. So why not put one in your bedroom? Tools required for a day's work could be unpacked and hung on walls or laid on open shelves only to be returned at the end of a day's work with no great loss in efficiency and some significant gain in peace of mind.

Lumber Storage Space

Planing and sawing by hand forces you to read the grain, and feel its movement, variations in density, etc. I'm not one of those people who falls in love with wood or its grain. But a thorough familiarity with the material is inescapable. Before too long, every hand tool user develops preferences for certain lumber species, air-dried stock as opposed to kiln dried or steamed, and even specific cuts of wood such as quartersawn, plainsawn heart wood, flitches, etc. Consequently, and without exception, the hand tool users I know purchase wood that meets their preferences regardless of whether they have an immediate use for it or not. So I think it is wise, if at all possible, to prepare for the long-term storage of a great quantity of lumber for future projects.

However, your lumber rack needn't necessarily share your workspace. You may find your garage, woodshed, or even a shady portion of your lawn or garden a convenient location for your lumber rack.

While a dedicated sharpening station is preferred, if tight space requires that you sharpen on your bench, consider some sort of mat to protect it from oil or water – and to keep the stone from slipping around.

Multiple low-wattage lights such as these offer great flexibility. The diffusers are a great help in reducing glare.

When designing your lumber rack, consider such things as providing sufficient airflow through the racks, accessibility and shading the lumber from sunlight. If children are a part of your life, please take every precaution to make your lumber rack safe for someone who may mistake it for a jungle gym.

Sharpening Space

It has been said that the key to working with hand tools is first learning how to sharpen them. No ultimate hand tool shop is complete without some provisions for sharpening. Although

Jacques-Andre Roubo's 18th-century text clearly shows a dedicated sharpening area, this isn't an absolute necessity. The workbench can be a convenient place to sharpen because it is sturdy and just the right height for such an activity. But there are several reasons why many prefer a dedicated area as Roubo illustrated. Most sharpening equipment requires some sort of lubrication, which can make a mess of your bench and any future projects. Grinders used by many woodworkers spew nasty abrasive particle dust. Let's face it. Sharpening is messy business.

If space is short, consider some sort of mat to protect your bench from oil or water that will fly off the end of your stones. This rubber mat serves double duty. It protects the bench and keeps the stone from slipping around.

For light honing, your bench may indeed suffice, but when more serious work is needed, it's nice to have a dedicated sharpening area. A grinder and a small shop-built table of a convenient height will fit the bill. Now the sharpening station needn't necessarily be in the workshop. This could be in an unheated or otherwise undesirable location. But an inconvenient sharpening area may discourage you from sharpening. Nothing will discourage a woodworker faster or more completely than working with dull tools. In the "ultimate" workshop, there would be some well-equipped sharpening area. The rest of us just need to find a space we can make a mess in.

Lighting Your Workspace

In an article I once wrote about the Anthony Hay cabinetshop in Colonial Williamsburg, master cabinetmaker Mack Headley described some of the benefits of working in "raking" light. The natural

light from a nearby window casts shadows, allowing him to read a surface when planing or carving. I have found knife lines to be all but invisible under the shadow-less flood of light from 4'-fluorescent shop lights. Soon after that visit to Colonial Williamsburg, I removed the 4' shop lights over my bench and began experimenting with different sorts of lights. Here's what I ended up with. Lighting the ends of the bench is important. Although it's counter-intuitive, the ability to turn off lights individually can help you better see what you need to see.

Over my bench I'm using an array of 13-watt, compact fluorescent bulbs in clamp work light fixtures (they have a color temperature of 3,500K). These bulbs shed a nice white light, are inexpensive, and, most important, can be turned off individually or quickly repositioned, giving me shadows when and where I need them. I made sure to position lights over the ends of the bench where the finest work is done. You could substitute standard incandescent bulbs in similar fixtures or choose the much hotter and even brighter halogens, but these would need special fixtures. I found higher-color temperature compact fluorescent (CF) bulbs provided better illumination than lower-color CF bulbs with twice the wattage.

With the raking light switched on and the over-bench lights switched off, I can easily see when I need to sharpen my smooth plane.

I prefer the flexibility of multiple low-wattage lights. I can't think of a better application for this approach than these "raking" lights. A strong light would blind you.

To produce a raking light, I'm using the same 13w, 3,500K CF bulbs attached to the wall behind the left end of my bench. To keep from being blinded, I attached a photographic filter material (Cinegel #3,000) called a "gel" (it looks like tracing paper) to the front of each fixture with binder clips to act as a diffuser (see photo above). This material won't catch fire even in direct contact with the fluorescent bulb and is inexpensive.

the dominy shop

The reconstructed Dominy Shop at Winterthur offers a peek into a rural pre-industrial woodshop. The Dominy family produced a wide variety of items, including furniture and clocks, in their East Hampton, N.Y., home from the 1760s to the 1840s.

Although the "ultimate" hand tool shop I've described in this article was not based on this reconstruction, we can see many of the elements I discussed including the position of the workbenches, tool storage and even the color of the chest in the back corner.

This unique reconstruction, (which was based on 1940s sketches of the original shop and eyewitness accounts) validates our notions of period shops. The Dominy-made furniture and clocks included with the exhibit earn the shop its inclusion in any "ultimate" hand tool shop article.

Winterthur, formerly the estate of H.F. DuPont, is located in Delaware's Brandy-wine Valley. The museum, which includes a celebrated collection of American art and antiques, is open year-round. For more information, call 800-448-3883 or visit winterthur.org.

An Inviting Shop

By far one of the coolest things about an ultimate hand tool shop is that with a few precautions, it can be made safe enough for a baby. Woodworking is such a solitary hobby, but it needn't be so. Without the noise and the dust of machinery, the shop can be a pleasant place to be. My shop has toys for my children (although they prefer tenon cheeks and plane shavings) and a comfortable place to sit down. The warm wood paneling didn't take long to install, but it really took away the harshness of the cinderblock walls. The ultimate shop is a shop you want to be in. The ultimate shop is a shop where a child or grandchild, neighbor or spouse feels welcome. The ultimate shop is a shop in which woodworking can be shared.

Conclusion

I hope I haven't misled you though. There is no actual "ultimate" hand tool shop. Every shop is the result of several, often unfortunate, compromises. Nor should you consider the hand tool shop as necessarily separate from a modern shop. Instead, you can incorporate "ultimate" hand tool shop features in the space created by pushing aside your 12" planer and 6" jointer.

But the one aspect of the ultimate hand tool shop that really earns its title is that it can fit into the end of a garage without moving your car, or just as easily into a spare bedroom, or garden shed, or patio. It's the ultimate workshop because it can allow someone in a big city to make something wonderful in a very small space.

The truly ultimate hand tool shop offers craftsmen not just a different way to work, but an opportunity to work.

4

WE'VE TRIED JUST ABOUT EVERY SHARPENING SYSTEM THERE IS — FROM SANDPAPER TO CERAMICS TO WATERSTONES. HERE'S HOW TO GET THE **BEST POSSIBLE EDGE WITH THE LEAST FUSS.**

sharpening plane irons

BY CHRISTOPHER SCHWARZ

W hen I took my first class in woodworking some years ago, the first thing the instructor showed us was his shop-made waterstone pond.

With a reverence and care usually reserved for religious artifacts and small injured animals, the teacher brought the pond out from its special place in his cabinet. For more than an hour he talked with a furrowed brow about secondary bevels, wire edges and polishing the backs of our edge tools.

All of us in the class did our best to stifle our yawns. I kept looking at the rows of chisels and backsaws and wondered when we were going to get to the important part.

Within a week we all realized that we should have paid more attention to the sharpening lecture. Soon there were only two sharp chisels in the shop for a class of 10 students, and we quarreled over them. Trimming tenons with the equivalent of a butter knife was no fun.

So I made it a point to learn to sharpen well. And I've been fortunate to be able to use a variety of methods, including oilstones, diamond stones, waterstones, ceramic stones, sandpaper, electric grinders and the Tormek system.

Each system has its good and bad points. Some are simple, others don't make a mess, some are less expensive and most systems can put an astoundingly good edge on tool steel.

Learning to sharpen your edge tools will open up a lot of doors in woodworking. Sharpening is half the battle when learning handplanes, turning and carving.

For me, the two most important qualities a sharpening system needs are that it must be fast and it must produce the keenest edge. I'll pay a little more and suffer a little mess to get a good edge in a hurry and get back to the bench.

That's because I'm more interested in woodworking than I am in the act of sharpening. I have no desire to look at my edges under a microscope or fret about tiny imperfections in the metal. I'm not the kind of guy who wants to meditate on my power animal as I proceed up to #500,000 grit. I want to be done with it and get back to the good part.

Familiarity Breeds a Keen Edge

The steps I'm about to describe will work with every sharpening and honing system I know of on the market. That's because no matter what system you use, sharpening is about one thing: Grinding and polishing the two intersecting planes of a cutting edge to as fine a point as possible.

The tools you use to get there are up to you. But here are a few words of advice: Pick a sharpening system and stick with it for a good long time before giving it up. Many woodworkers who I've talked to jump around from system to system, trying to find the best thing (and spending a lot of money).

If you stick with one system, your edges will improve gradually as you get better and better at using your particular set of stones or sandpaper. Skipping around from one system to the next will only stunt your sharpening skills.

Second, please buy a honing guide. It's a big old lie that these things slow you down. In fact, these simple and inexpensive guides are quick to set up and ensure your edge will be perfect every time you sharpen.

However, don't buy a whole rolling army of honing guides. I use a $14 Eclipse-style guide (the gray-colored side-clamp contraption shown in most of the photos) for sharpening my chisels and most plane irons. I also own a Veritas honing guide. It excels at sharp-

ening skew chisels and specialty plane irons that won't fit in the Eclipse guide, such as irons for shoulder planes.

Each honing guide holds the blade a little differently, and few of them are ever perfectly square. That's OK because what you're after with a honing guide is repeatability. Use the same guide over and over, and your edges will come out the same.

Polish Your Backside

There are three sharpening operations that must be performed on all chisels and plane irons that are new to you. First you must polish the flat backside (sometimes called the "cutting face") of the tool. Next you grind the cutting bevel. Finally you hone and polish a small part of that cutting bevel, which most people call the "secondary bevel."

To begin grinding your edge, put the tool in your honing guide and adjust it until the cutting bevel is flat on your stone. Eyeball it at first. After a couple passes on the stone you'll know if you're off or not.

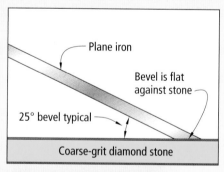

- Plane iron

Bevel is flat against stone

25° bevel typical

Coarse-grit diamond stone

Flat-grinding your cutting bevel should not take long on a coarse diamond stone. If you're having trouble gauging your progress, color the cutting bevel with a permanent marker and you'll get a quick snapshot of where you stand.

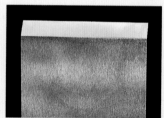

When you're done grinding, this is what your edge should look like.

why i switched to waterstones

There are a lot of sharpening systems out there. And while I haven't tried every one of them, I've tried most. After much experimentation, I settled about seven years ago on a system that used DMT diamond stones and oilstones. My system worked pretty well, but the oilstone part was slow, and my final cutting edge was always "almost" perfect.

A few years ago, I got my hands on a set of Norton's American-made waterstones and it was like a door had been opened for me. These things cut wicked fast. And the edge they produce is darn-near perfect.

They feel different than many Japanese waterstones I've used. The best way to describe the difference is that the Norton stones give you different "feedback" as you sharpen. The #4,000-grit Norton actually feels like it is cutting (it is). The #4,000-grit Japanese stones I've used have a more rubbery feel to them in my opinion. And they didn't seem to cut as fast at that level. The #8,000-grit Norton waterstone also provides great feedback to the user.

The downside to all waterstones is that they need to be flattened regularly. For this job, I use a DMT DuoSharp stone with the coarse grit on one side and the extra-coarse on the other. I also use this same diamond stone for grinding the cutting edge of all my chisels and plane irons.

The most economical way to get started with this system is to buy a Norton combination waterstone that has #1,000 grit on one side and #4,000 grit on the other. Then buy an #8,000-grit Norton waterstone for polishing. Norton also makes a #220-grit waterstone, but if you buy the DMT diamond stone you won't need it.

If you don't polish the backside of your newly acquired chisels and plane irons, your cutting edges will always be jagged and easily dulled. You need to polish just the area up by the cutting edge. This is a process you'll only have to do once.

When honing narrow chisels, this is the best way I've found to keep things steady and square. Put one finger on the cutting edge; put the other behind the jig to move it.

Keep in mind that these three steps are only for tools that you have newly acquired. Once you do these three things, maintaining an edge is much easier. You'll probably only have to polish the backside once. You'll have to regrind an edge mostly when you hit a nail or drop the tool. Most sharpening is just honing and polishing the secondary bevel so you can get back to work.

Begin with the backside of the tool. This is the side that doesn't have a bevel ground into it. It's half of your cutting edge so you need to get it right.

Start sharpening by rubbing the backside back and forth across a medium-grit sharpening stone or sandpaper. You don't need to polish the entire back, just the area up by the cutting edge. I begin this process with

a #1,000-grit waterstone, then do the same operation with the #4,000-grit and then the #8,000-grit stone. The backside should look like a mirror when you're finished.

The Not-So-Daily Grind

The next step is to grind the cutting bevel of the tool. You can do this on an electric grinder that has a tool rest, which will produce a slightly dished cutting bevel called a hollow-ground edge. Or you can do it on a coarse sharpening stone, which will produce a flat-ground edge.

A lot has been written about the advantages and disadvantages of each system. In comparing my hollow-ground edges vs. flat-ground edges, I personally have found little difference between them in terms of edge durability.

I typically grind using a diamond stone for three reasons. First, it will never destroy a tool due to overheating (which can happen with electric grinders). Second, I use the diamond stone to flatten the waterstones. And third, the diamond stone is great for touching up my router bits.

I use DMT's extra-coarse stone for grinding my edges unless I have a lot of metal to remove (800-666-4368 or dmtsharp.com). Put the tool in your honing guide and set it so the cutting bevel is dead flat against the stone. Most tools come ground at a 25° bevel, which is good for most tasks. Mortising chisels should be set for 30°; tools for light paring only can be set for 20°.

Don't get too worked up about angles as you begin sharpening. Somewhere in the 25° neighborhood will be fine for most tools.

I use mineral spirits to lubricate my diamond stone. Most people use water, but a sharpening guru at DMT turned me on to mineral spirits. It evaporates more slowly than water and won't allow rust to build up on the stone easily.

Rub the cutting bevel against the diamond stone and then check your progress. You want to grind the entire cutting bevel of the chisel or plane iron all the way across. If you set the tool properly in the jig, this should be approximately five to ten minutes of work.

As you progress on this coarse stone, you should make a substantial burr on the backside of the tool. This is called a "wire edge," and you'll want to remove it by rubbing the backside on your finest-grit stone a couple times. Never rub the backside on your coarse stone. That will just undo all your polishing work there.

shapton stones: the latest thing in sharpening

If you think white-lab-coat wizardry is reserved for the manufacturers of power tools, think again. Some of the highest-tech science-fiction stuff happens in the knuckle-dragging hand-tool industry: think unbreakable "nodular" cast iron, cryogenically treated tool steel and super-strong "rare earth" magnets that are incorporated into both tools and jigs.

And now the latest innovation is in sharpening. Shapton waterstones from Japan are all the rage among the sharpening gurus, who say the stones cut faster and wear longer than other stones. They also are expensive. There are several grades of the Shapton stones, and a basic setup of three stones can cost more than $200 – plus you'll need some way to flatten them.

We use the stones in our shop now and are impressed. They do cut faster and stay true longer than other waterstones.

Visit shaptonstones.com or call JapaneseTools.com at 877-692-3624 for more information.

honing the edge

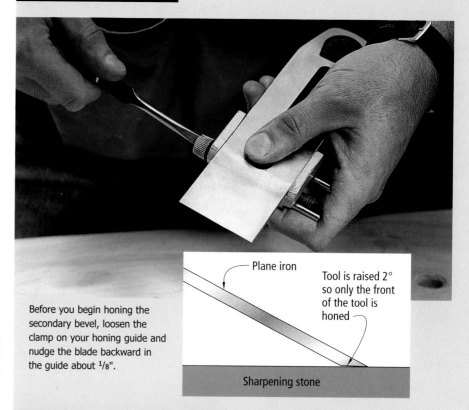

Before you begin honing the secondary bevel, loosen the clamp on your honing guide and nudge the blade backward in the guide about 1/8".

Plane iron
Tool is raised 2° so only the front of the tool is honed
Sharpening stone

Begin with a #1,000-grit stone and rub the tool back and forth across the work. Try to wear the stone evenly by moving the tool in a regular pattern.

After a dozen licks, turn the tool over and remove the burr from the backside by rubbing it a couple times over the #8,000-grit stone.

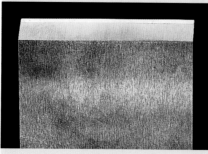

After honing the tool on the #1,000-grit stone, this is what the secondary bevel should look like.

How you hold the jig is important, too. For plane irons and wide chisels, put a finger on each corner of the tool up near the cutting bevel and use your thumbs to push the jig. For narrower chisels, put one finger on the tool by the cutting bevel and push the jig from behind with one finger.

With the cutting bevel ground, it's time to refine the leading edge to a keen sharpness.

Honing: The Fun Part

Honing is quick and painless if your stones are flat and you've done the first two steps correctly. The first thing to do is to reset the tool in your honing guide. Loosen the screw that clamps the tool and slide the tool backwards about 1/8". Retighten the screw of the honing guide.

This will set the tool so only a small part of the cutting bevel will get honed. This speeds your sharpening greatly.

Start honing with a #1,000-grit waterstone, soft Arkansas oilstone or #320-grit sandpaper. I use the #1,000-grit Norton waterstone. Lubricate your stones as recommended by the manufacturer. Rub the tool back and forth on the stone. Turn it over and check your progress. You should see a secondary bevel appear up at the cutting edge. Rub your thumb along the backside; you should feel a small burr all the way

more honing and polishing

Continue honing the edge by switching to a #4,000-grit stone. Remove the burr on the backside with the #8,000-grit stone. Note that some woodworkers skip this intermediate #4,000-grit stage when honing. I have found this trick works best with waterstones and when the secondary bevel is small.

After working the #4,000-grit stone, here's what the secondary bevel should look like. It got a little bigger and it is more polished.

Repeat the same process on the #8,000-grit stone. You are almost finished. Tip: You can move the tool back 1/32" in the jig and hone a third bevel, another trick used by some sharpeners. If your entire bevel isn't getting polished after a few strokes, your stone likely needs to be trued.

Polish the secondary bevel on the #8,000-grit stone until it is a mirror.

Here's how to test your edge without flaying your finger open. Pull your thumbnail across the edge at about a 90° angle. If the edge catches and digs in immediately, you're sharp. If it skids across your thumbnail, you have more work to do.

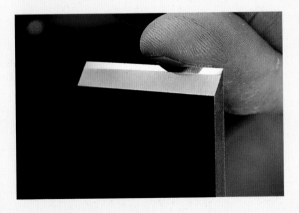

sharpening jigs for almost every job

There are a lot of honing guides on the market these days. After trying most of them, I'm convinced that two will handle most edge tools.

The gray side-clamp jig you see at woodworking shows is the work-horse in my kit. You can find this tool for about $12 to $14. None of these gray jigs I've inspected grinds a perfectly square edge, but they're close. Be sure to tighten the jig's clamp with a screwdriver when you fix a tool in the guide.

Veritas (Lee Valley Tools, 800-871-8158 or leevalley.com) has two guides. The original guide (below) handles many oddball tools, including skew chisels, shoulder-plane blades and irons that are tapered in width. The Veritas Mk. II jig does all this and comes with a special registration guide that allows you to set your honing angle with amazing precision. Plus, you can even hone back-bevels on your tools. It's fantastic for sharpening any tool with a straight cutting edge. For sharpening curved edges, you'll need something else.

The original Veritas jig will help you hone tools that would normally have to be sharpened freehand. It's a good investment.

Supplies

Woodcraft
800-225-1153 or woodcraft.com
- Side-clamp honing guide #03A21, $11.99
- DuoSharp 10" coarse/x-coarse #817201, $124.99
- Norton 1,000/4,000 waterstone #818263, $54.99
- Norton 8,000 waterstone #822462, $89.99
- Veritas honing jig #03B41, $32.99

Lie-Nielsen Toolworks
800-327-2520 or lie-nielsen.com
- Lie-Nielsen sells the Norton stones. The 1,000/4,000 stone is $45; the 8,000 stone is $75. There also is a 1,000/8,000 stone available for $65.
Prices correct at time of publication.

across the cutting edge. If there's no burr, then you're not sharpening up at the edge; so continue honing until you feel that burr.

Once you have that burr, remove it by rubbing the backside across your #8,000-grit stone. Go back to your #1,000-grit stone and refine the secondary bevel some more until all the scratches on your secondary bevel look consistent. Use less and less pressure as you progress on this stone and remove the wire edge on the backside as you go.

Put the #1,000-grit stone away and get out a #4,000-grit waterstone, a hard black Arkansas oilstone or #600-grit sandpaper. Go through the same process you did with the #1,000-grit stone.

Remove the wire edge on the backside with your #8,000-grit stone. At this stage, the bevel should look a bit polished in places.

Finally, you want to polish the secondary bevel with your finest-grit stone or #1,500-grit sandpaper. I use an #8,000-grit Norton waterstone. There are Japanese water-stones at this grit level, too. However there are no comparable oilstones. A translucent oilstone is somewhat close.

Polishing is a little different. You're not likely going to feel a wire edge on the backside of the tool after polishing the bevel. Work both the secondary bevel and the backside of the tool on the #8,000-grit stone and watch the scratches disappear. And when they're gone, you're done.

Test the edge using your fingernail – see the photo on the previous page for details. Some people finish up by stropping their edges at this point with a piece of hard leather that has been charged with honing compound. I don't find it necessary. In fact, if you're not careful, you will round over your cutting edge while stropping.

Remove the tool from your honing guide, wipe it down with a little oil to prevent rusting and go to work on some end grain.

The tool should slice through the wood with little effort. And if that doesn't convince you of the value of sharpening, I don't know what will.

5

sharpen a chisel

BY CHRISTOPHER SCHWARZ

There are two things you must learn to get your chisels sharp enough for woodworking. The first is easy. Your cutting edge is the intersection of two planes: the bevel and the face of the tool. As the metal is abraded, the point where those two planes intersect becomes finer, sharper and more durable. The ultimate goal of sharpening is to make that point of intersection as small as possible. The smaller that point of intersection, the sharper your edge will be.

The second thing isn't as obvious. Good sharpening is more about learning to observe your progress than it is about rubbing a tool on a sharpening stone. Ultimately, a good sharpener spends little time rubbing the tool and more time making every stroke count.

If this sounds odd, think for a minute about how you viewed furniture before you started woodworking. Most non-woodworkers can see a piece of furniture as a whole form. But it takes training to see the individual details (such as recognizing inset doors that have perfect reveals all around) and to know what they mean (which is good craftsmanship). As your woodworking skills develop, your eye becomes more discriminating. At that point, creating fine furniture has more to do with seeing the details than with ripping lumber on a table saw.

With sharpening, you must develop your eye to know what a good edge looks and feels like. Once you know what sharp is and how to get there, your edges will get better every time you sharpen. And you'll spend less time at the stones. Ultimately, it should take you only five minutes to bring a dull edge back to perfection.

The Right Sharpening Kit

Buying the right equipment is important. Some systems are slow (oilstones), some need more maintenance (waterstones) and some have peculiarities (such as the tendency of sandpaper to round over an edge). I have used every system, and after years of experimenting and sharpening hundreds of edges, I've settled on a hybrid system that consists primarily of the following:

• A DMT diamond stone for removing metal quickly and truing my other sharpening stones (dmtsharp.com or 800-666-4368).

• A coarse waterstone (#800- or #1,000-grit) for shaping the tool's secondary bevel.

• A fine waterstone (#6,000- or #8,000-grit) for polishing the secondary bevel and face.

• An inexpensive side-clamp honing guide.

This list is a bit unusual because of what I've included and what some may say is missing. The honing guide is a bit controversial, but it's the key to early success. Many excellent craftsmen dispense with these "training wheels" and insist beginners sharpen without it. However, without hands-on instruction, most beginners will struggle needlessly learning freehand technique. Producing your first keen edge will take far more practice. And your progress will be slower. The honing guide allows you to succeed on your first or second try. And once you know what sharp is, you can then choose to use the guide or not.

The second reason the above list is radical is because there is no medium-grit stone between coarse and fine. British craftsman and teacher David Charlesworth recently convinced me that the medium-grit stone was unnecessary. After sharpening about 100 edges his way, observing them with a 30× jeweler's loupe and putting them to work, I'm convinced he's correct. A fine-grit waterstone cuts fast enough to polish your edge and remove the scratches left by the coarse-grit stone.

In addition to the above equipment, I recommend a plastic container to store your stones (a $6 expense), a spray bottle to mist water on your stones, a plastic non-skid mat from the housewares

STAGE 1: flattening the face

More work needed here

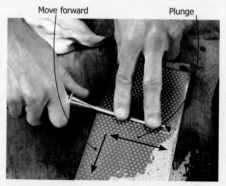
Move forward   Plunge

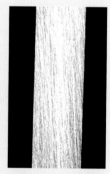

Flattening begins on the diamond stone. I use DMT's extra-coarse stone for this, which is #220-grit. I use mineral spirits as a lubricant. The first type of stroke is used for 1/2" chisels and wider. Rub the face against the stone as shown, keeping the face flat against the stone. Start with 20 strokes and check your work.

The scratches should run left to right on the face of the chisel after this stroke. This chisel is getting there, but it needs more work.

The second stroke (used with all chisels) is to plunge the chisel back and forth on the stone. After each plunge, move the chisel forward a little bit on the stone. Note that with narrow chisels (1/8"-3/8") this is the only stroke possible when flattening the face. (The first type of stroke will round over the edges of the face.)

After 20 strokes of the plunging motion, the scratches should look vertical. Repeat these strokes until the first 3" of the chisel's face shows a consistent scratch pattern. Then repeat these strokes on the coarse #325-grit diamond stone, then the coarse and fine waterstones.

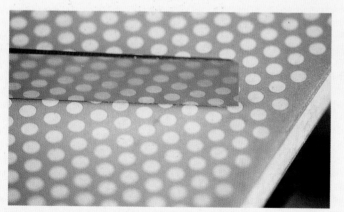

Here is a picture of the polished face of the tool reflecting the surface of the diamond sharpening stone. Ultimately, this is what your face should look like: a mirror along most of the face of the tool. There will be some small scratches from polishing, but these are OK.

department to contain your mess, some oil, a small square and some rags.

Know Your Chisel

Before you can sharpen a chisel, you must know your goal. Chisels are somewhat Zen-like tools. Though they are the simplest woodworking devices, properly setting them up is tricky.

The first thing to understand is the function of the face of the chisel. The face is the flat, unbeveled side of the blade. For a chisel to work correctly, this surface must be flat. If you polish only near the cutting edge (a tempting time-saver) the chisel won't cut true. When you guide your chisel on one surface to pare a mating surface, the tool will wander up or down, depending on whether the face is convex or concave. When you attempt to clean up a routed corner or remove waste between dovetails, you will have difficulty steering the tool straight for the same reason.

You should also remember that the face of the tool is half of your cutting edge. If left unpolished, your edge will be less durable. Why? Pretend that your hand is a chisel and the spaces between your fingers are scratches in the metal left by grinding on a coarse stone. If you jabbed someone with your fingers stretched out and spread apart (similar to an edge with deep scratches), you'd probably break your hand. But if you brought your fingers together into a fist (similar to an edge with smaller and shallower scratches), your hand would endure the punch pretty well.

The second important thing to know is that the cutting edge must be 90° to the sides of the tool. A skewed edge will tend to wander in a cut.

Third, the bevel of the tool must be evenly polished at the cutting edge. The best way to determine if you are truly sharpening at the cutting edge is the emergence of a "burr" on the face of the tool during sharpening. The importance of this burr cannot be overstated. Your edge might look nice and shiny, but unless you created a burr on the face of the chisel on your coarsest stone, your edge isn't sharp. The photos below discuss how and where to look for this burr.

STAGE 2: grinding the primary bevel

Shaping the primary bevel is done on the coarse diamond stone. The angle of the bevel will affect the toughness of the edge (higher angles such as 30° are more durable) and the ease of cutting (lower angles such as 20° cut more easily). Most chisels come from the factory with the bevel ground at 25°. Here's my recommendation after years of experimenting: Grind the primary bevel of your 1/8", 1/4" and 3/8" chisels at 30° – these tools are used mostly for light chopping and need the edge durability. Keep your 1/2" chisel at 25° – it's an all-around do-anything size. And grind your 3/4" and 1" chisel at 20° because the wider tools are used mostly for paring.

Set the chisel in the honing guide. The angle of the bevel is determined by how far out the tool projects from the honing guide. I mark these measurements on my bench to speed sharpening (they work for all the side-clamp guides I'm aware of). For a 30° bevel, set the chisel so 1¼" projects from the guide. For a 25° bevel, set the chisel so 1⁵/₈" projects from the guide. For a 20° bevel, set the chisel so 2¹/₈" projects.

Unlike honing, grinding involves lots of strokes. Keep even pressure on the tool and move it forward and back on the diamond stone. Check your work after every 20 or 30 strokes. If you're not sure where the sharpening is occurring on the edge, paint it with a permanent marker and take a stroke or two. That will point out where the chisel is contacting the stone. Also, check your work with a small square to ensure you are grinding a square edge.

After a couple of cycles of grinding, the primary bevel should look scratched and you should feel a burr on the face, which is what my index finger is feeling for here. Keep working until you feel the burr. Once you feel the burr, you can move on to honing.

This is a chisel ready for honing. You can see the bevel created on the diamond stone.

STAGE 3: honing the secondary bevel

To hone the secondary bevel, you want to sharpen only at the cutting edge – sharpening the entire bevel is a waste of time. So you need to shift your tool in the guide a bit so only the leading edge contacts the stone. I usually shift the tool back ¼" in the guide; this adds a 2° or 3° secondary bevel. This works with all makes and models of the side-clamping guide that I'm aware of.

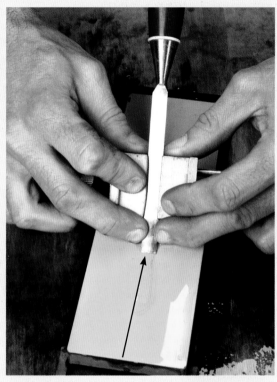

First loosen the screw on the guide and shift the tool backwards. I mark this second setting on my bench, which speeds my sharpening. Retighten the guide's screw.

Second, place the guide on your coarse waterstone at the far end. Place even pressure on the chisel and pull the guide toward you in a smooth motion. Roll the guide forward using almost no pressure. Repeat this motion five more times and then examine your edge.

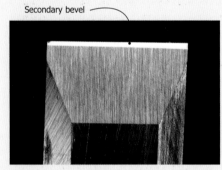

Secondary bevel

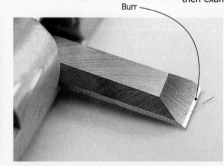

Burr

Your secondary bevel should appear as a series of fine scratches in a narrow band at the cutting edge. Feel for the burr. If you can't feel it, repeat the six strokes on the coarse waterstone. When you can feel the burr and the scratches appear consistent on the secondary bevel, move to the next step.

The burr is almost impossible to photograph because it is so small, but we got lucky here. The small wire lying across the bevel of the tool is indeed the burr, which detached from the face when I pushed my thumb against it. Now you know how small the burr is.

You must remove the burr before proceeding to polishing. Use your polishing waterstone. When removing the sizable burr left by the coarse waterstone, you want to take care because the burr can score the stone. Press the face lightly against the polishing stone and push forward. Repeat this a couple of times and increase the pressure slightly. When the burr is gone, you can move to polishing.

STAGE 4: polishing the secondary bevel

The motions are the same for polishing as they are for honing. Keep the tool in the same position in the guide and place it on the waterstone. Some polishing stones require you to first build up a slurry with a second little stone, called a Nagura. Add a little water and rub the Nagura on the polishing stone until a thin film of slurry appears over the entire surface of the waterstone. Now you are ready to polish.

Place the guide on the far end of the stone and roll it toward you. Repeat this motion five more times and examine your edge.

The edge should look like a mirror all the way across. You should not be able to feel a burr on the face of the chisel, but it's there.

Remove the burr from the face of the chisel. Remove the chisel from the guide, place it facedown on the polishing stone and push it forward once. Rubbing back and forth will scratch the face needlessly.

The Act: Brief but Bountiful

As you follow the photos that illustrate the steps to sharpening, keep these things in mind:

Honing the chisel does not require a lot of strokes on the stone. In fact, the more back-and-forth motions you make, the more likely you are to put pressure in the wrong place or dish your waterstone unnecessarily.

Here is another trick I learned from Charlesworth: When honing on the waterstones, start with about six strokes. Then observe the edge carefully by eye and rub your finger up to the edge of the face to feel for the burr. If you don't feel the burr but it looks like you're sharpening the bevel, switch to a coarser stone and try again until you can definitely feel the burr.

When you can feel the burr and the scratch pattern is consistent, move to the next finer grit.

One mistake beginners make is that they use too much pressure when honing the bevel. Excessive pressure wears the stone unevenly and can result in the edge being sharpened more in one place than in others. Just use enough pressure to keep the chisel and honing guide under control. Let the stone do the work.

Another big mistake beginners make is not truing their waterstones regularly. If your sharpening session isn't proceeding as planned or your results don't look like they're supposed to, the culprit is almost always the stones. Waterstones cut fast but wear fast – usually by "dishing out" in the middle of the stone. You need to flatten them regularly. I flatten mine with the diamond stone after honing three tools. It takes just a few minutes and pays big rewards.

I flatten my stones in the sink under a slow but steady stream of water. Place the diamond stone in the bottom of the sink. Place the waterstone on the diamond stone and rub the waterstone forward and back. Cock the waterstone left 30° and rub it back and forth. Then cock the waterstone right 30° and do the same. Repeat these three motions over and over. If you are not sure if your stone is flat after a minute or so, try scrawling a pencil line on the waterstone and rubbing it on the diamond stone. If you can still see pencil lines, you have more flattening to do.

Sharpen Regularly

Here's the real brain teaser about sharpening to consider: The more you sharpen your tools, the less time you'll spend sharpening.

This is true because of the way an edge tool degenerates. A freshly sharpened tool starts out with an extremely keen edge. After just a little bit of work, the edge quickly degenerates to what I like to call a state of "working dull." The edge isn't as sharp as it can be, but it's sharp enough for the task. Then the edge degenerates slowly, if it's not abused. The last stage of an edge is what I call "edge failure" – this is where the edge gives up and becomes chipped and ragged.

The best time to sharpen a tool is before edge failure occurs. A chipped and ragged edge takes considerable time to renew, but an edge that is still at the working-dull stage can be honed very quickly. So if you sharpen your edges before they're destroyed, you'll have more sharpening sessions, but they'll be brief.

If all this makes your brain hurt, you're not alone. Sharpening challenges even the best woodworkers. My advice is to sharpen regularly and your tool's edges will improve over time. I find this true even after 15 years of sharpening.

Recently I dug out of my toolbox a 2"-wide slick (a very large chisel) that I use infrequently. When I'd put the tool away a few years ago it was sharp. But when I examined the edge recently I saw that the tool needed honing. The edge hadn't changed a bit in three years, but my definition of what is sharp sure had.

So I sharpened up the slick, put the tool to use and put the sharp tool back in the toolbox. And I bet the next time I get the tool out I'll hone it first again. Good sharpening, like good woodworking, is a continuously moving target.

6

side sharpening

BY HARRELSON STANLEY

grit progression

As you work through the multiple grit stones you remove the scratches left from the prior stone. The photos below show the scratch progression as the back is flattened and eventually polished.

#1,000 grit

#2,000 grit

#4,000 grit

#8,000 grit

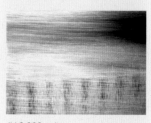

#16,000 grit

(Blades shown at 200x magnification.)

I like to equate sharpening to a golf swing. Through practice, you memorize the motion that will improve your game. You can always get better, and there's always something new to learn.

For me, sharpening is just as much fun as planing – or hitting a bucket of balls. I don't find it to be drudgery at all, because I have a system that responds to my needs as a woodworker. An important part of that system is something I call "side sharpening." Trying to balance the blade on its narrow bevel while sharpening is asking for trouble. It's much easier to sharpen using the width of the blade to support the bevel.

Along with side sharpening, keeping your stones flat as you sharpen, properly removing the burr and another step that I call "jointing" the edge, all combine to make a simple and efficient system for sharpening plane blades.

Flat Backs Make Sharp Edges

The first time you sharpen a blade it's important to flatten the back of the blade correctly. This is a one-time step. If you get it right the first time, you won't have to do it again for a very long time.

But before you put steel to stone, it's important to make sure each grit stone is flat. I use a diamond lapping stone for this step. Just a dozen or so passes with the diamond stone on each stone

prior to use ensures that you'll be working with a flat surface.

To flatten the back, start with the #1,000-grit stone. Start with the edge of the back (I feel it's only necessary to flatten the first $5/8$" of the blade), rubbing back and forth along the edge of the stone. Keep your left elbow down low, perpendicular to the stone so that the rubbing motion is a smooth back-and-forth motion rather than swinging up and down. This keeps a constant, even pressure on the blade. If you're left handed, feel free to switch hands; it's an ambidextrous method.

This process is repeated through the multiple grits until you've achieved a clean, flat and polished surface. For the best results, I recommend working through all seven grits (#1,000 to #16,000).

While a necessary step when first preparing a plane blade, flattening the back face only has to happen the first time and rarely thereafter. Start with the #1,000-grit stone, flattening the first $5/8$" or so of the blade.

Before moving to the bevel, it's time to "joint" the edge. Simply set the blade perpendicular to the #16,000 stone, with just the edge touching the stone. While applying moderate pressure on the edge, run the blade lengthwise along the stone a few times. This jointing step removes any fatigued or ridged steel from the blade's edge and leaves a clean starting point for sharpening the bevel.

Sharpen the Bevel

Now you're ready to sharpen the bevel. To get it right you need to perfect some body mechanics – just like perfecting your golf swing. Once perfected, you'll be able to use the side-sharpening technique to master freehand sharpening without years of practice.

First, I hold the blade in my right hand in a loose grip at the tips of my fingers, with the tips spread around the blade – as if I'm imitating a spider. My left hand is laid flat on the back of the plane blade, parallel to the edge. I position my body to the left of parallel with the stone, with my head positioned directly over the blade.

I'm using my left hand in a pushing motion across the stone almost like using a hand saw, swinging my arm, not my body. I keep my left arm rigid from the tips of my fingers all the way up to my elbow. My right hand is used only to support the blade; the left arm is doing all the work.

An important part of the side-sharpening process is to grip the blade correctly. The blade is grasped loosely in the right hand, held by just the fingertips.

The right forefinger is held in position at the right front corner of the blade to steady the blade and provide balance.

The left hand provides pressure on the bevel. The hand is spread across the iron's width, parallel to the blade edge. The left arm is held rigid from finger tip to elbow.

Body position is important. Standing with my head positioned directly over the blade puts my line of sight directly in line with the blade tip and where I'm sharpening. This "line-of-sight" position is the same whether flattening the back or sharpening the bevel.

As you prepare to sharpen the bevel, the right hand is again loosely holding the blade, providing light support with the bevel flat against the stone. Seat the bevel on the stone. Your right hand is only supporting and balancing the iron; the index finger applies light pressure to hold the bevel flat on the stone.

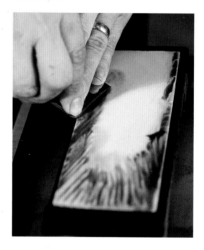

While ceramic stones cut quickly, they also wear slightly faster. Because of this, it's important to work to keep the stone's surface as flat as possible. By working around the perimeter of the stone and actually pushing off the stone, you'll use more of the stone, and not dish the center of it.

Here is the circular pattern that I recommend. I tend to work in a clockwise pattern, but if counter-clockwise feels more comfortable, that will work as well.

This is the point where the term "side sharpening" comes in. Rather than sharpen the bevel by pushing the blade in the direction you would when making a cut with the blade (and thus contacting the stone with only a small amount of metal), side-to-side sharpening allows you to use the more substantial width of the blade to more fully support the bevel as you sharpen.

Seat the bevel flat on the stone and then start making short side pushes along the perimeter of the stone, allowing the corner of the blade to come off the edge of the stone. By working only on the perimeter, you avoid dishing the stone in the center, which can cause the blade to be rounded over on the bevel side. Keeping the stones flat makes the entire sharpening process easier.

After working through the first (and every) grit, you want to check for the burr that is formed as the steel is rolled over the edge. This is fatigued metal and needs to be removed. I use my #16,000-grit stone and make a few passes on the flat back of the blade along the length of the stone. That's enough to shear off the burr.

One other step that I add between grits is a what I call a "jointing" pass. Even with the burr removed, there are microscopic teeth left on the edge of the blade. By making two light passes over my #16,000-grit stone with the blade held perpendicular, the teeth are

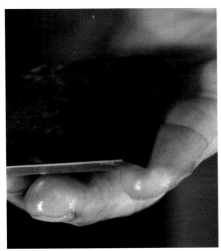

After sharpening the bevel with each grit stone, you will develop a wire-edge burr on the back side of the blade. I check the burr by running the blade over my fingers (carefully) along the length of the edge, never across the edge. This burr is fragile and if you run your fingers across the burr you stand a good chance of breaking the burr off leaving a very "toothy" edge that is more difficult to sharpen effectively. It's best to shear the burr off, leaving a clean, even edge.

To remove the burr, run the back of the blade flat along the polishing stone (#16,000 grit) lengthwise a few times. By running the blade lengthwise, the burr is sheared from the blade, rather than broken free.

Even after removing the burr after sharpening with your finest grit stone, you can feel a slight "tooth" to the edge. A step I've added to address that is one I call "jointing the blade," which removes that tooth by running the blade on edge, lightly along the length of the stone. You'll feel the difference instantly.

effectively removed, much like a jointer removes the rough parts of a board.

As you move to the polishing stone to remove the burr, remember to first wipe the blade to remove the coarser grit slurry that remains on the blade from coming in contact with your polishing stone. Otherwise you'll scratch the polishing stone and undo much of the polishing work you've accomplished (not to mention potentially damaging the polishing stone).

Now I'm ready to move to the next grit and repeat the procedure. As you finish with the last grit, make one final short and light jointing pass on the edge of the blade, barely kissing the stone, to remove the last bit of tooth.

Once you've flattened your blade (once), and become comfortable with the side sharpening process, it should take you no more than three to five minutes to put a new sharp edge on your plane blade. So little time – yet you'll get your plane cutting thin wispy shavings every time!

new shapton stones are more affordable

The only complaint you ever hear about Shapton stones is that they are pricey. And it's true that they are more expensive than the Norton waterstones, though the Shaptons also wear more slowly in my experience.

Now there is a more affordable line of Shapton stones that are very close in price to the Nortons. These new Shaptons are thinner (5mm compared to 15mm) and are fused to glass for rigidity. According to our price comparisons at press time, the new Shaptons will be just a few dollars more than the Nortons, and available in a wider variety of grits (#220, #1,000, #2,000, #4,000, #6,000, #8,000, #16,000 and #30,000). I've been using the new stones for several months and am quite impressed. They wear very slowly and cut quickly – just like the thicker Shapton stones. Most home woodworkers

The glass backing strengthens the thin layer of sharpening medium.

will be hard pressed to wear out one of these 5mm stones in their lifetime. I think these new Shaptons really narrow the gap between the two brands – though who knows how prices will fluctuate as market forces kick in. In any case, take a hard look at the new Shaptons. It's high quality stuff and now at a more reasonable price.

The three stones I used the most were the #1,000 grit ($42.95), the #4,000 ($55.95) and the #8,000 ($79.95). For more information, visit shaptonstones.com or call 877-692-3624.

In the more affordable line of Shapton stones, stones are available in eight different grits. One nice perk of the new stones is the grit of each stone is clearly visible through the glass on the back.

very scary sharp

BY NICK ENGLER

Some years ago, Steve Lamantia of Seattle posted a long, rambling letter to the Internet news group rec.woodworking (better known as "Wreck Wood") titled "The D&S Scary Sharp™ System." Once you waded through Lamantia's superlatives, exclamations and stream of consciousness, his message boiled down to this: You can put a very fine cutting edge on hand tools with sandpaper. That's right – sandpaper. (To read Lamantia's original message, check out http://www.shavings.net/scary.htm#original)

Visitors to "Wreck Wood" spotted Lamantia's post, tried his methods and posted their own raves. The news spread, sandpaper stock soared and the term "scary sharp" became part of the woodworking lexicon. All of which amused those of us who remember woodworking before there was so much virtual sawdust flying about.

About 40 years ago, I participated in a rite of manhood known as the Boy Scouts of America. There, in the old *Handbook for Boys*, wedged between square knots and Morse code, is this advice: Sharpen your pocket knife with sandpaper.

It was good advice then and it is better advice now. That's because continuing developments in abrasives make sandpaper an excellent sharpening material. In many ways, it's easier to use, less expensive to get started with and more versatile than traditional sharpening stones.

Not Just for Sanding Anymore

The most common abrasives in sandpaper are aluminum oxide and silicon carbide, both of which were originally intended to abrade steel. Their application to woodworking was an afterthought. Point of fact – these are the very same abrasives in India stones, grinding wheels, ceramic stones and even Japanese waterstones. You see, sandpaper is just another form of the abrasive you may already use for sharpening.

The difference is that sandpaper comes in a much wider range of grits than stones and grinding wheels. Grits between #50 and #2,000 are readily available, and if you look around you can find sandpaper as coarse as #36 and as fine as #12,000. It's this range that gives sandpaper the edge (pun intended) over other sharpening materials. Traditional stones start between #100 and #200. The finest Arkansas stone is roughly equivalent to #900, the finest ceramic and diamond stones are about #1,200, and the finest waterstone, #8,000 in the Japanese grit system, is close to #2,000 in the American system.

Why is range so important? Because proper sharpening technique requires that you hone with progressively finer grits, much like sanding a wooden surface. You can't put a super-keen,

scary-sharp edge on a tool with just one stone. You must start with coarse abrasives to quickly condition the edge and repair any nicks. This leaves deep scratches in the steel and makes the edge jagged. The chisel is sharper than it was, but not sharp enough for woodworking. You must continue sharpening with progressively finer abrasives. As you work your way up through the grits, the scratches grow smaller and the edge becomes keener.

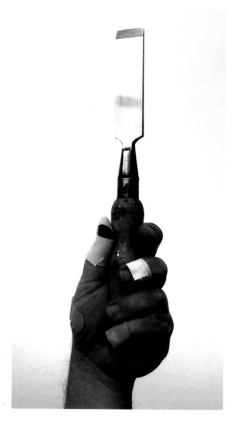

Sandpaper not only extends the range from coarse to fine – it gives you more steps in between. If you've ever tried to jump from #80-grit to #150-grit when sanding wood, you know how long it can take to work out the scratches left by the coarser grit. It takes less time and you get better results if you work your way up in increments. It is the same with sharpening.

The Secret Formula

Stones have it all over sandpaper in one respect – they are rigid. To use sandpaper for sharpening, you must mount it to a flat, rigid surface. Lamantia and those who came after him recommended 1/4"-thick plate glass, but this isn't rigid enough. It will flex slightly if your workbench isn't dead flat or if there is a bit of sawdust under one corner.

Instead, I use a marble slab to back up the sandpaper. (Talk about rigid!) You can purchase a precision-milled granite block known as a reference plate from a machinist's supplier, or you can take your straightedge to a cooking supply store and find a reasonably flat marble pastry stone (for rolling out pie dough) for a quarter of the cost. I have a 20"-square pastry stone that mounts eight different sandpaper grits – four on each side.

You can use ordinary sandpaper and stick it to the marble with a spray adhesive – this yields good results. But I prefer self-adhesive 8"-diameter sanding discs. Because these are made for machine sanding, they have an "open coat" – 40 percent less abrasive on the surface. They cut a little slower, but they last much longer. The open coat prevents the metal filings (the swarf) from becoming impacted between the grits and "loading" the paper. I also look for stearate-impregnated paper; this, too, reduces loading.

For most sharpening tasks, I work my way through four grits – #120, #320, #600 and #1,500. I keep these all on one side of the pastry stone. On the other side, I have #50, #100, #220 and #2,400. The two coarse grits are to recondition badly damaged edges. The #220 provides an intermediate step between #120 and #300 when I'm flattening the backs of large chisels and plane irons. And the super-fine #2,400 is the last step when I'm flattening a tool.

As you sharpen, you should brush away the swarf frequently. I use the stiff bristles on the back of a file card. This keeps the abrasive clean and helps prevent loading.

The last step in my sharpening process is stropping. This is the secret ingredient in every successful sharpening formula, no matter what abrasive material you use. Stropping removes tiny burrs and refines the cutting edge, making it as keen as it can possibly get.

For this step, I mounted a piece of leather to a hard maple board and "charged" it with chromium oxide, a polishing compound. (You might also use jeweler's rouge or tripoli.) Why not mount the leather to the pastry stone? Leather is considerably thicker than the sandpaper. Because of the type of honing guide I use to maintain the sharpening angle, it's important that the stropping surface be at the same level as the other abrasives. I've planed the wood to adjust for the thickness of the leather strop.

For more details, see illustrations on page 43.

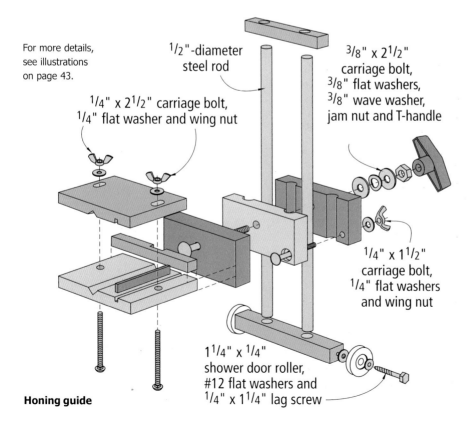

1/2"-diameter steel rod

3/8" x 2 1/2" carriage bolt, 3/8" flat washers, 3/8" wave washer, jam nut and T-handle

1/4" x 2 1/2" carriage bolt, 1/4" flat washer and wing nut

1/4" x 1 1/2" carriage bolt, 1/4" flat washers and wing nut

1 1/4" x 1/4" shower door roller, #12 flat washers and 1/4" x 1 1/4" lag screw

Honing guide

The basic Scary Sharp system consists of a selection of sandpapers and a rigid backing plate. I add a stiff brush and a honing guide.

After honing, strop your tools on a piece of leather charged with a super-fine abrasive polishing compound.

The Secret Weapon – The Very Scary Honing Guide

Yes, I use a honing guide. I know that some experienced sharpeners look down on these jigs as "training wheels," but I don't. If the first secret to successful sharpening is to hone with progressively finer grits, the second secret is to maintain a precise cutting angle as you do so. You can be much more precise with a guide. After all, if our hands were that good at maintaining an angle, we wouldn't need planes to hold plane irons.

One of the reasons some folks don't like honing guides is that the current commercial crop is difficult to adjust and not especially versatile. The home-made jig I developed holds a chisel by its handle, rather than by the blade. Because the jig makes a large triangle with the abrasive surface and the tool, it's easier to adjust and maintain the sharpening angle.

The tool holder conforms to every chisel handle I've been able to find, and it's wide enough to accommodate everything up to the really wide iron from a jointer plane.

Additionally, the holder pivots, and it can be locked in place or adjusted to roll around an axis. This feature makes it possible to sharpen not only chisels and plane irons but also gouges, skews and parting tools. This is a big plus.

The tool holder mounts to two grooved brackets that slide along steel rods. To adjust the angle at which the guide holds the tool, slide the brackets up or down on the rods and tighten the wing nuts that lock them in place. To secure the holder, rotate it to the desired angle and tighten the T-handle. To adjust the holder so it will roll as you sharpen a gouge, insert a jam nut between the T-handle and the washers. Tighten the jam nut until it just begins to compress the wave washer. Hold the jam nut from turning and tighten the T-handle against it.

As shown, this honing guide will accommodate hand tools up to 18" long. For longer tools, extend the steel rods.

Supplies

For stearate-impregnated, open coat, adhesive-backed sanding discs, check your local auto-body supply stores. Or:

Museum of Woodworking Tools
800-426-4613 or toolsforworkingwood.com

1 • 3M Micro Abrasive Film for Scary Sharpening – PSA Sample Pack (2 sheets each of 400-, 1,200-, 5,000-, 8,000- and 12,000-grit)
#ST-MAF.XX, $15.31

Prices as of publication date.

To adjust the holder on the honing guide to rotate, snug the jam nut against the washers, but don't collapse the wave washer. Hold the jam nut from turning with an open-end wrench and tighten the T-handle against it.

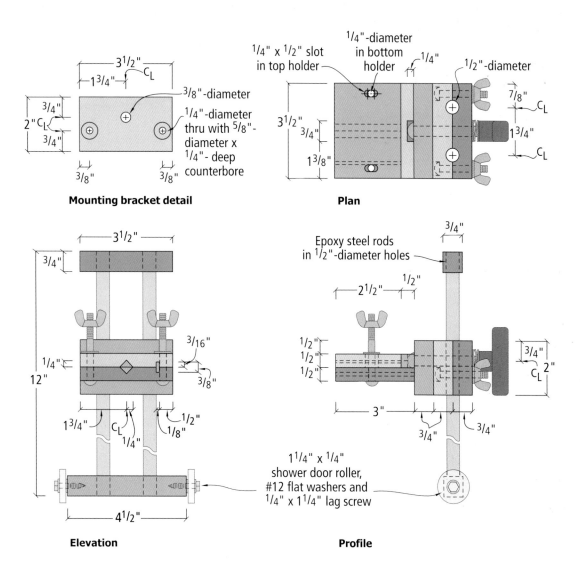

Mounting bracket detail

Plan

Elevation

Profile

Epoxy steel rods in $^1/_2$"-diameter holes

$1^1/_4$" x $^1/_4$" shower door roller, #12 flat washers and $^1/_4$" x $1^1/_4$" lag screw

a very scary shootout

One of the most frequently asked questions about sandpaper sharpening is how it compares to traditional methods. To find out, *Popular Woodworking's* former Associate Editor Jim Stuard and I held a little contest. Stuard's a whiz with Arkansas stones, and we pitted his method against mine.

We each sharpened a $^1/_2$" medium-quality chisel straight out of the box, then passed them around the shop for the staff to try. The winner? It was a dead heat. Both seemed to be equally sharp.

This was no surprise to either of us – we both finished up by stropping our chisels with a polishing compound. Presuming that our sharpening skills are

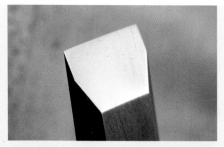

On the right is the chisel I sharpened with sandpaper. At left is the one Stuard honed on his Arkansas set. Both cut the same, but I score points because mine's shinier, don't you think?

relatively equal, the sharpness of each chisel is determined by the grit of the last abrasive used. We used different polishing compounds perhaps, but they were close enough in grit that the end results were indistinguishable. Had Stuard stopped at black Arkansas (about #900-grit) and I at

#1,200-grit sandpaper, my chisel should have been a little sharper.

The conclusion? Strop your cutting tools. No matter what sharpening material you use, stropping gives you the best possible edge on your cutting tool.

8

RADICALLY REDUCE THE TIME IT TAKES TO PREPARE AND SHARPEN A PLANE IRON WITH THE HELP OF A $5 STEEL RULER.

the ruler trick

BY DAVID CHARLESWORTH

I have been teaching furniture making for more than 27 years and am convinced that most amateurs are not getting the best from their hand tools. Bench-plane blades are a good example. I can resharpen a blade in less than four minutes, which includes washing my hands and putting the stones away. This short break from the work at hand should be welcomed as it gives us an opportunity for planning the next stage and the pleasure of working with a razor-sharp tool when we resume. Struggling on with a blunt tool is both tiring and counterproductive.

The methods I have developed to ensure that my students start with razor-sharp tools from day one are unusual (it involves a trick with a ruler). However, they are well-tested and guaranteed to produce the result we want. The techniques have been developed as practical solutions to issues that gave us trouble when we used a more traditional approach.

One of the main problems occurs as the surface of a sharpening stone wears hollow in use. The flat side of our plane blade develops a bump in its length. (See the illustration at right.) One day we flatten the stone and have a disastrous situation where the critical edge area no longer touches the stone at all. This makes it impossible to polish away the wire edge, which is a vital part of the sharpening process.

A Word About Waterstones

I've used Japanese waterstones for many years because they cost less and they remove metal faster than any other system. This fast cutting action is a result of the rapid wear of the surface. Fresh sharp particles of aluminium oxide grit are constantly being exposed as the friable surface breaks down. This is great for rapid removal of metal but it does dictate that we use a disciplined approach to keeping them flat. I probably do a little flattening about every four minutes of use.

The stones are easy to flatten. I do this using

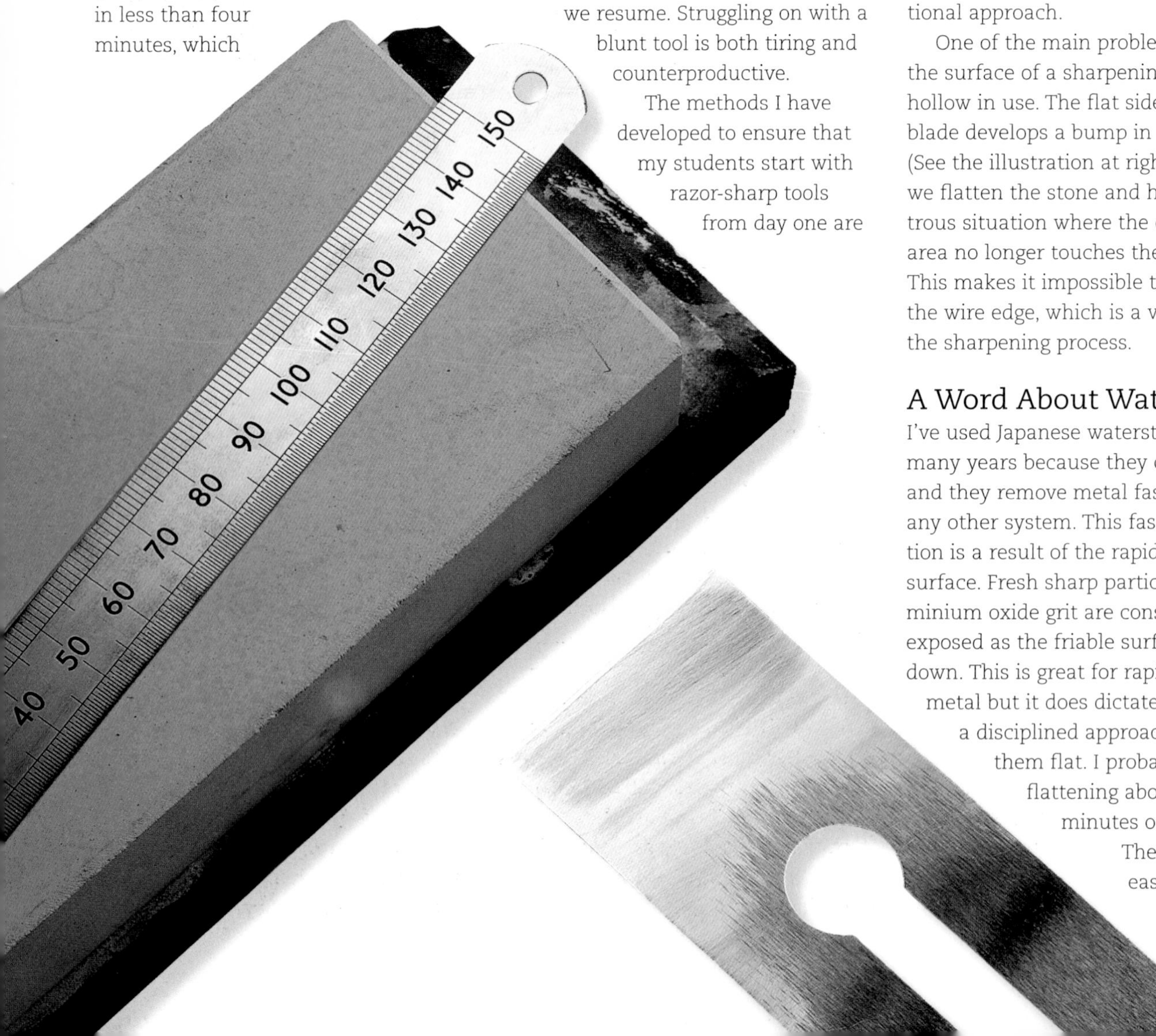

wet and dry sandpaper fixed on a piece of ½"-thick "float glass." Float glass is manufactured on a bed of molten tin. It's readily obtainable from glass specialists and is much flatter than toughened, laminated or plate glass. I fix the wet and dry sandpaper to the glass with a light spray of water from a plant mister. The surface tension of the water is sufficient to keep the paper from sliding about. The waterstones are simply rubbed to and fro until they are flat. I find #180 or #240 grit is suitable for an #800-grit waterstone and #320 grit may be used for fine stones like the #6,000 or #8,000 grit.

If you draw a pencil grid on the surface of the stone before starting it will give you valuable feedback about your progress. The pencil lines will be removed from the high spots first and the stone will be flat when the final traces of pencil disappear.

A coarse diamond stone such as a DMT or EZE LAP brand will also do a good job of flattening waterstones. Some people recommend rubbing two waterstones together, but this does not necessarily produce a flat surface. It is possible for the two surfaces to be spherical and still fit perfectly. To be certain with this method, one needs three surfaces to agree with each other.

There is endless discussion about the merits of different types of stones, but I am sure that the differences between brands are minimal. We use a King #800-grit stone for coarse work and either a King #6,000-grit or King #8,000-grit stone for super-fine polishing (King-brand stones are available from many suppliers.) These are the only stones required to produce a superb edge.

I have been testing the new Norton waterstones for some years and they are very good, wearing slightly slower than King stones. You will only need the #1,000-grit and #8,000-grit stone for plane-blade sharpening.

Arkansas oilstones cut rather slowly and diamond stones do not yet have grit sizes as small as the super-fine waterstones. In other words, the quality of polish is not so fine. Shapton stones are

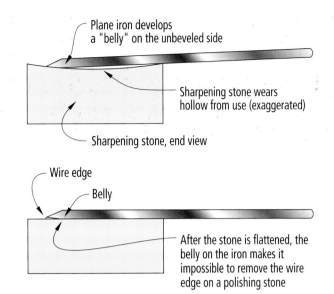

Plane iron develops a "belly" on the unbeveled side

Sharpening stone wears hollow from use (exaggerated)

Sharpening stone, end view

Wire edge

Belly

After the stone is flattened, the belly on the iron makes it impossible to remove the wire edge on a polishing stone

MOVEMENT 1: Begin flattening the back of the plane blade with the cutting edge off the surface of the stone as shown. As you move the blade to and fro, allow the cutting edge to drift onto the stone.

obviously liked by users but the price is significantly higher than King's.

I will assume that you are starting with a new plane blade, as old blades, which have been sharpened on hollow stones, can be almost impossible to deal with. I would also advise anyone still using standard blades to consider changing to an A2 cryogenically treated replacement blade from Ron Hock (Hock Tools 888-282-5233 or hocktools.com) or Thomas Lie-Nielsen (Lie-Nielsen Toolworks 800-327-2520 or lie-nielsen.com). These are about .095" thick and will enable you to work about four times longer than with a carbon steel blade.

Flattening the Back

The first task is to flatten the back side (sometimes referred to as the flat side or face side) of the blade and remove the coarse scratches left by the manufacturer's surface grinding. I use a King #800-grit stone for fast metal removal, but a #1,000-grit Norton stone will also do. A flat back is important as the front edge of the plane's chipbreaker has to make a perfect fit here. I find it helpful to stick a small wooden or plastic handle to the blade with double-sided tape. This gives a better grip with less chance of grinding away your fingertips on the stone. The handle is fixed crosswise, just behind the top of the bevel.

45

The grip of the tape is considerable if you clamp the handle for half a minute. We use two types of movement.

Movement 1: Lengthwise Strokes

I start by laying the blade across the stone, so that the edge of the blade is hanging about $1/2$" off the edge of the stone. Using considerable downward pressure on the handle, I move the blade steadily up and down the length of the stone. I call this the long stroke.

While making the long strokes I allow the edge of the blade to drift onto the stone and move just one third of the way across the width. This might take 10 to-and-fro long strokes. During the next 10 strokes, the edge of the blade is allowed to drift back to the starting position, $1/2$" off the edge of the stone. The cutting edge of the tool spends half the honing time off the edge of the stone.

After about 50 strokes the surface of the stone will no longer be flat. The stone can be rotated 180° so that the other edge can be used for another 50 strokes.

It's now time to flatten the stone and notice the wear that has taken place. By drawing a pencil grid on the surface of the stone and rubbing it a few strokes on the diamond stone, you can see that

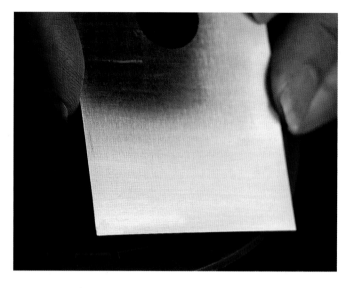

After 100 strokes or so using movement one, the back of a premium blade should be covered in scratches across its width.

the long edges of the stone have become hollow and that the width has developed a bump. This bump is infinitely preferable to the usual hollow created on waterstones. A bump promotes a slight hollowing in the length of the flat side of the tool. By keeping the edge of the tool off the edge of the stone for 50 percent of the working time, a hollow stone can be avoided.

However, the slight hollowing of the length of the stone could be causing a slight belly or bump in the width of the plane blade. To check for and eliminate this problem, I change to a second movement on the freshly flattened stone.

Movement 2: Crosswise Strokes

The blade is laid across the stone at one end, with the edge of the blade about $1/2$" off the edge of the stone. The stroke is crosswise, bringing the edge of the tool one-third of the way across the stone before returning to the start position. Considerable pressure is exerted on the center of the handle. During about 40 to-and-fro strokes the blade is allowed to drift up the length of the stone, and then back down to the starting position.

The stone is then rotated 180° as before, so that the other edge of the stone may be used. The stone should

Handle affixed with tape

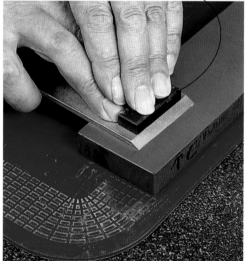

MOVEMENT 2: With this second movement the blade is rubbed across the width of the waterstone.

As you move the blade, allow it to drift up and down the length of the stone. Note the pencil line I've drawn on the stone that helps guide the process.

After this second movement, the scratches across the blade's width will be replaced with lengthwise scratches.

now be flattened again before doing any more work.

Observe the scratch patterns on the back of the blade. The scratches from movement one will lie across the width of the blade. You will have done enough of movement two when all those crosswise scratches have been replaced by lengthwise scratches. If a slight bump has been formed after movement one, you will see lengthwise scratches in the center of the blade only. This would be a signal to do more of movement two on a freshly flattened stone.

The objective is to remove all trace of the deep manufacturer's grinding scratches just behind the cutting edge of the blade. The two types of movement may have to be repeated several times. I don't worry about getting a band of lengthwise scratches more than about a 1/4" wide behind the cutting edge. With A2 blades and careful sharpening technique this will last a long time, and you can do more back flattening in the future when necessary.

That's it for now. And thanks to the ruler trick, a few seconds work later on will be all that is needed to complete work on the back side – none of the mirror polishing of the whole surface, which is so time consuming.

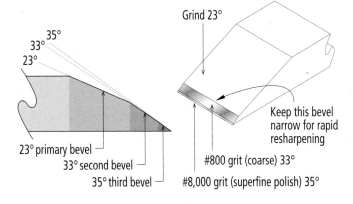

Grind 23°
35°
33°
23°
23° primary bevel
33° second bevel
35° third bevel
Keep this bevel narrow for rapid resharpening
#800 grit (coarse) 33°
#8,000 grit (superfine polish) 35°

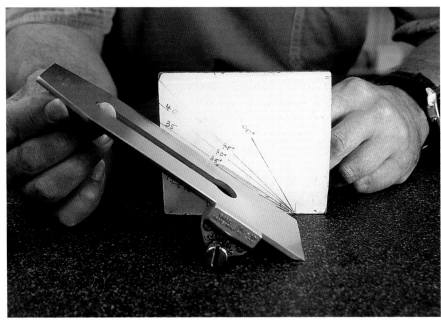

I've drawn common sharpening angles onto cardboard. Once I've set the blade to the proper angle I'll measure its projection from the front of the guide and scribe that measurement directly on the blade for future reference.

With the blade set in the guide, I'll hone the bevel using two or three firm pull strokes on the #800-grit stone. Then I feel the back for the wire edge.

With traditional waterstones, you need to create a light slurry on the polishing stone to aid cutting. Rubbing the Nagura stone on the polishing stone creates this slurry.

Prepare the Cutting Bevel

For speed of resharpening I like to use three bevels. I first grind the blade at about 23°. I then create a wire edge on the #800-grit stone at 33°. Final bevel polishing is done on the #8,000-grit stone at 35°. This is my recipe for bench planes used on hardwoods. By honing at 35° the clearance angle under the polished bevel has been reduced to 10° (down from 15°), but I have found no problems with this arrangement. The 35° final polish seems to make blades last slightly longer between sharpenings. By keeping the grinding angle significantly lower than the honing angles, I can resharpen at least seven times between grindings. If you have a new blade ground at 25° there is no need to change to 23° yet. I am lucky to have a water-cooled grinder, so there is no danger of overheating the blade when grinding.

Honing a Straight Blade

I have a strong preference for the Eclipse-type honing guide with the narrow roller. It only takes a few seconds to clamp to the blade in the guide and ensures accuracy, repeatability and speed.

I determine my honing angles by squinting against a simple card, which has lines drawn with the aid of a child's math protractor. After setting the blade at the proper angle, I measure how far it projects from the jig. I then scribe these measurements on the top of the flat side of the blade. This prevents me from having to work the angles out every time I sharpen.

With the blade at 33°, I freshen up the surface of the #800-grit waterstone (for faster cutting) by rubbing it with a similar grade stone. If worn wet-and-dry sandpaper were used, it could glaze the surface of a stone so that it will not cut fast after the first few minutes.

It should take only two or three firm pull strokes to raise a wire edge on the flat side of the blade. I have a bench light set up so that I can see light reflected from the finest of wire edges. You can feel for a wire edge by gliding a fingertip off the flat side surface. It feels like a tiny hook.

Place the steel ruler on one long edge of the stone – friction from the water will hold it in place. Place the blade on the stone with the cutting edge off the stone. With light pressure bring the blade about ⁵⁄₈" onto the stone. This short stroke removes the wire edge and polishes the back of the blade.

A picture of success: The front of your cutting edge is polished and ready to go to work.

The blade projection is then reset in the guide, i.e. shortened a little, to give us 35°. Now clean the wheel of the guide and the edge of the blade to avoid contaminating the superfine #8,000-grit waterstone. That surface is prepared by spraying with a plant mister, and then rubbing a Nagura over the stone to create a little slurry on its surface. A Nagura is a smaller stone that creates a mud on a polishing stone that speeds polishing and cleans the surface of the stone. Three or four pull strokes with gentle finger pressure on the blade are all we need to polish the front end of the narrow bevel created on the #800-grit stone. The #8,000-grit stone is a polishing stone and I caress its surface with the blade.

The Ruler Trick

This is the radical part! I freshen the slurry on the #8,000-grit stone with the Nagura. It's important that the slurry

The ruler trick greatly speeds the time it takes me to prepare a new blade.

Supplies

Lie-Nielsen Toolworks
800-327-2520 or lie-nielsen.com

1 • Hand Tool Techniques
Part 1: Plane Sharpening with
David Charlesworth video, $25

1 • Hand Tool Techniques
Part 2: Hand Planing with
David Charlesworth video, $25

isn't too sloppy and wet. If it is wet, I sweep the water away with a finger. I then stick a 6" inexpensive steel ruler, (about 0.5 mm thick) to the stone by sliding it to and fro a few times down one long edge of the stone.

The blade is placed in position on the stone for movement two with its edge off the stone. The middle of the blade is resting on the steel ruler. Using four fingertips, placed just behind the top of the bevel, I draw the blade's cutting edge onto the stone. You may feel a slight catch as the wire edge meets the edge of the stone. The blade edge is only allowed to come about $5/8$" onto the stone before going back off the edge of the stone. This short stroke is repeated about 25 times for a new blade and about 12 times when re-sharpening.

Because the flat side of the blade has been raised up by a degree or so on the ruler, you will see a narrow band of mirror polish across the tip. This need be no wider than $1/16$", and will not get much wider with subsequent resharpenings. If examined closely, you should see that the mirror polish has replaced the #800-grit scratches at the edge.

I wipe the blade on a sponge cloth, dry it and apply a thin coat of Camellia oil. The job should be complete and the wire edge should have floated off on the stone, or sometimes on the sponge cloth. It should shave hairs from your hand without difficulty.

9

A CAMBERED CUTTING EDGE IS ESSENTIAL FOR FINE FINISHING
CUTS WITH A HAND PLANE – AND IT HAS MANY OTHER SURPRISING USES.

learning curves: plane irons

BY DAVID CHARLESWORTH

Plane blades that are sharpened straight and square are essential in all shoulder and rabbet planes, and they have other applications such as when shooting an edge with a bench plane. However, I have a very strong preference for using cambered edges in most of my bench planes, most of the time.

There are two powerful arguments for using a slightly curved blade. The first has to do with perfecting the square edges of your work. Let us suppose that you are preparing the edge joints for a tabletop and your powered jointer's fence was a few degrees off square and that you wish to correct the errors of squareness in the edge of your timber.

I have no magic built-in spirit level, which would allow me to plane a perfectly square edge with a straight blade in my plane, and I have no idea how this could be done. The curved blade is a sophisticated device, which allows us to take three different kinds of shavings without having to adjust the lateral-adjustment lever at all.

1. If the plane is centered over the edge of the wood, then an even-thickness shaving will be removed and no change will be made to the angle of the edge.

2. If the center of the plane is moved so that it is over the left-hand side of the edge, a tapered shaving will be removed and the left-hand side of the edge then will be lowered.

To accurately plane a board's edge, position your thumb and fingers as shown.

Use your fingernails as a fence to help maintain the plane body square to the edge of the board.

3. If the center of the plane is moved so that it is over the right-hand side of the edge, a tapered shaving will be removed and the right-hand side of the edge then will be lowered.

In all these positions the plane is kept completely flat against the edge by firm pressure from the ball of the thumb on the plane body casting. I do not use the front knob at all. The thumb is always positioned over the center of the edge, regardless of where the center of the plane is. I use the surface of my fingernails as a fence to keep the plane from wandering about during the length of the stroke. The grip on the back handle is gentle, so that I do not twist the plane sole out of contact with the edge. (Editor's note: You can find more details of this technique in Charlesworth's second book and second DVD; see the Supplies box for details.)

Finally, by carefully allowing the plane to drift from side to side towards the high points during the cut you can

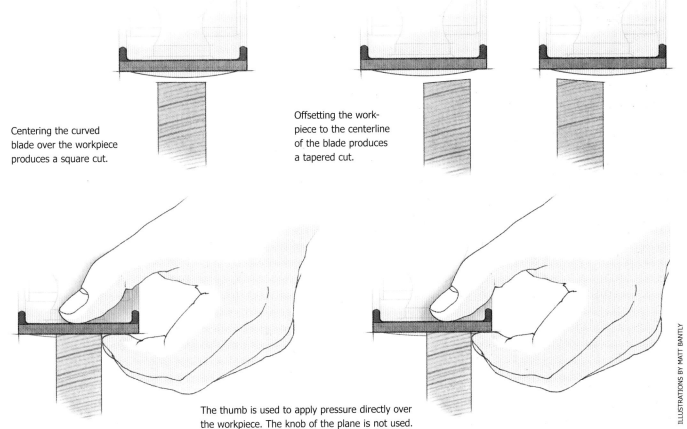

Centering the curved blade over the workpiece produces a square cut.

Offsetting the workpiece to the centerline of the blade produces a tapered cut.

The thumb is used to apply pressure directly over the workpiece. The knob of the plane is not used.

ILLUSTRATIONS BY MATT BANTLY

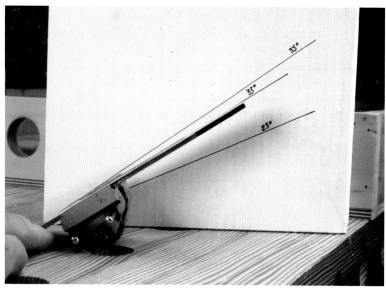

The Eclipse-type side-clamp honing guide (left) has a narrow roller that allows you to more readily rock the guide when forming a curved edge.

Scribe the angles you use most often on a white piece of cardboard, which is most useful for setting a blade in your honing guide.

also correct a twisted edge. This surely has to be the most cunning plan of all time. Of course the curved blade needs to be well centered in the plane for all of these techniques and I will be describing my method later in this chapter.

The second powerful argument for a curved blade is that you will not leave whiskery tracks (sometimes called "steps") from the corner of the blade when you plane across a wide surface. The surfaces you leave will be minutely scalloped in their width, but the depth of these depressions is small indeed and they can be removed easily by sanding if desired.

Blade Angles

I like to grind my bench plane blades at 23°, which is a little lower than tradition suggests. All sharpening and shaping is then done at 33° on a coarse waterstone, such as an #800- or #1,000-grit stone. This is 3° steeper than usual. I then polish the extreme tip of the narrow bevel on an #8,000-grit waterstone at 35°.

Because there is a significant difference between the grinding angle and the angle formed on the #800-grit stone, very little metal needs to be removed for either sharpening or shaping a blade. Shaping a curve does require

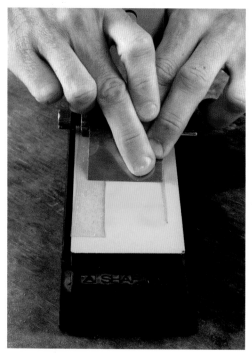

Place a thin sheet of plastic on your sharpening stone and apply finger pressure on the opposite corner. This helps form the curve on your edge.

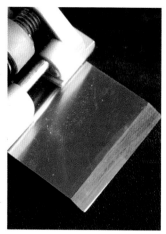

Here is what the corner of your iron will look like after about a dozen strokes. The shiny narrow triangle is where metal has been removed.

To smooth out the curved edge, remove the plastic from the stone and hone using finger-point pressure at five stations on the iron.

more metal removal than normal sharpening, but much less than if a single bevel were used.

Forming a Curve

I take a freshly ground blade and set it at 33° in an Eclipse-type side-clamping honing guide (see the Supplies box for information on purchasing one). The information for blade projection cast on the side of the guide will not mention 33° so you will have to experiment to find the necessary distance. I draw the angles I want on white card or melamine-faced scrap. The angle is checked by sighting across the blade with the card propped behind. Once I have found the correct projection for a blade I measure the distance the cutting edge projects from the honing guide and scribe this measurement directly onto the top of the blade so that it's always available. This saves time in the future. It is also worth noting that different thicknesses of blades will require slightly different projections to achieve the same honing angle.

I prefer the Eclipse-type guide because it has a narrow roller. Jigs with wide rollers tend to dictate to the user. We need some lateral tilting to form a curve, and the narrow roller is easier to tilt than a wide one. I have an old honing guide with a barrel shaped roller, indicating that creating curved blades is not a new idea.

Expert sharpeners produce a curve on a flat stone by subtly applying more pressure to the outer corners of the

Note: Depth of scallop is exaggerated.

Regularly spaced passes over a board produce a gently scalloped surface. The high points can be easily sanded flat, if desired.

Cambered iron cuts a shaving that is thickest in its center, tapering to nothing at its edges.

blade while honing to and fro. I have broken this process down into simpler stages so that the beginner can succeed from the start. I noticed that many students were struggling to start a curve with my old method, which depended on point pressure only. The new technique was developed during a short course a couple of years ago.

The idea is that a $^5/_8$"-wide strip of thin plastic is laid along one long edge of the #800-grit stone. This tilts the blade slightly; and as pull strokes are made, metal will be removed from the opposite corner of the blade. Finger pressure is placed over the area of blade that is touching the stone. Some woodworkers have told me that the plastic sleeve that comes with a cheap 6" ruler is ideal for this job. I use strips of plastic from the covers of cheap ring files; we originally used cardboard, but it did not last long. I think precise thickness is not important, but something around .012" to .015" will do.

If you coat the grinding bevel with a permanent marker before starting, you will see that an elongated triangle of metal has been removed. It is difficult to specify how many pull strokes will be needed. I press fairly hard on coarse stones and would expect to achieve a result after about a dozen strokes.

The plastic is then placed on the opposite long edge of the stone and the process is repeated on the opposite corner of the blade. Try to produce a symmetrical result. We now have a blade with three straight facets, whose shape is an approximation of a curve.

To judge the shape, I offer the edge up to a piece of flat plastic. I would expect to see gaps of about .012" at either outer edge. This is approximately the thickness of a quality business card.

I now use point pressure about halfway from the center to the corner of the blade by stacking my forefingers on top of each other. The two positions for this pressure are indicated as positions

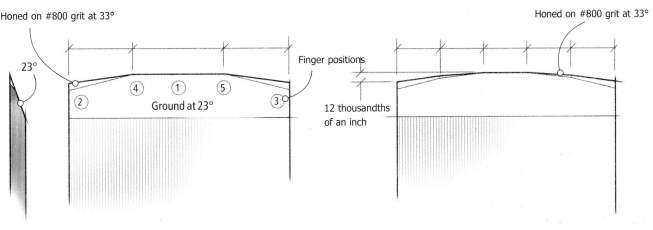

Honed on #800 grit at 33°

23°

④ ① ⑤

②

Ground at 23°

③

Finger positions

12 thousandths of an inch

Start with 3 facets.

Honed on #800 grit at 33°

Blend 5 flats to form a curve.

To polish the unbeveled side of my plane iron, I use an inexpensive metal ruler as shown. The ruler allows you to remove only a small amount of metal quickly and repeatably.

I like to set my chipbreaker close to the cutting edge for fine planing. Here it is shown 1/64" from the edge of the iron.

smooth those five facets into an even smoother curve. It is not necessary, but a good exercise in controlling finger pressure. (It seems to go better when accompanied by a sound effect, such as a rising or diminishing hum!)

The wire edge created on the unbeveled face of the blade is then polished off in the usual way, using the ruler trick on the #8,000-grit stone. (For more on this procedure, see "The Ruler Trick" on page 44.) I always dry the blade and coat it with a thin smear of camellia oil, as this protects against rust. The whole process is much quicker to do than it is to describe.

"4" and "5" on the diagram on the previous page. This operation is done without the plastic strip. It's important that weight is kept off the jig itself and only applied to the blade, near the edge. The idea is to create new, smaller flats at the meeting points of the three previous flats. Fewer strokes will be required at these points, possibly six. A certain amount of balance and judgment will be required here. However we do get good feedback from the surface of the stones, and it is usually possible to see a track on the surface where the blade is touching.

The blade edge and shape can now be examined again against the flat plastic. If you have succeeded it will appear as a gentle symmetrical curve. If it is not, just take more strokes, with the finger pressure in the appropriate position. You will see that I have indicated five possible finger positions for a $2^{3/8}$" plane blade.

When satisfied, clean the blade and the roller of the guide to avoid contaminating the superfine #8,000 grit stone, which is used next. This stone is prepared by spraying the surface with a little water from a plant mister. A Nagura is then rubbed over the surface to produce a little muddy slurry or paste. The blade projection is shortened slightly in the jig, to raise the blade angle to 35°. Four gentle strokes are then made with the finger pressure in each of the five positions shown in the illustration. This polishes the tip of the coarse stone

bevel, and is all that is required for a razor edge.

Sometimes, mostly for fun, I take a couple of extra strokes on the polishing stone. During a pull stroke, I start with finger pressure on the right, and try to transfer it steadily to the left. My forefingers are on the two outer edges of the blade. If done well, this will draw an elongated X on the surface of the stone. This is just a fun way of trying to

Different Curves for Different Work

When planing relatively narrow edges, say about $1/2$" to $5/8$" thick, I find I need a pronounced curve on the blade.

When planing a wide surface such as a tabletop, I use less curve. The gaps seen at the edges of the blade, when it is offered up to a flat surface might be around .006", roughly half as much as you would employ for edge planing. If

When reinstalling the iron, I recommend holding the plane so the frog is level with the floor. This prevents the freshly sharpened iron from slipping down the frog and striking the plane's body, perhaps ruining your edge.

When setting a balanced shaving, the protruding curved blade is centered relative to plane body.

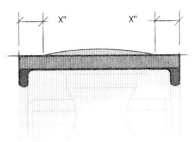

This setting is balanced, i.e. centered.

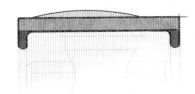

This setting is unbalanced, i.e. off center.

This is the view we get when sighting against illuminated paper.

you have a very shallow curve in your blade, the plane would need moving a very long way to the right or left, to have any squaring effect at all. When the plane is moved this far off center, it can be quite difficult to keep it balanced flat on the narrow edge.

Resharpening a Curved Blade

When the blade dulls, it is likely to be worst in the center. I set it in the jig at 33° and go to the #800-grit stone. Using point finger pressure in the center, I find how many strokes it takes to produce a minute wire edge. The small wire edge is a signal that enough metal has been removed to get past the wear on the blade. The same number of pull strokes are then performed with the stacked finger pressure in all the remaining four positions i.e. halfway to each edge, and just inside each edge of the blade. This will maintain the existing curved shape. If you wish to change the shape, more strokes are used in the appropriate positions.

After cleaning the tool and roller of the honing guide, adjust the projection to give 35°, and do four gentle polishing strokes on the superfine stone in all the finger positions. Polish the wire edge off using the ruler trick.

With each sharpening, it will take more strokes to produce a wire edge. This is because the #800-grit bevel gets wider with each sharpening, and you

are honing a larger area of steel. After about seven sharpenings, I regrind the blade and start the cycle again.

When grinding, I never go right to the edge of the blade. A small sliver of the #800-grit bevel is left at the tip, as this contains the shape that we have worked so hard to produce. Grinding right to the edge shortens the life of a plane blade, and it's not necessary unless you have a large chip in the cutting

edge. Sharpening a recently ground blade takes me about four minutes.

Setting Up the Plane

I use a No. 5½ bench plane for the majority of my work because I like the weight and the length. It is tuned up as a super smoother, with the sole lapped flat and the mouth set very fine, about .004" wide. (I recommend ¹⁄₃₂" for beginners.) This plane is used to perfect the accuracy and finish of the surfaces that come from my machine planer. I do not take heavy shavings, so the chipbreaker is set very close to the edge of the blade. I prepare the front edge of my chipbreaker with a slight camber as well, which allows me to set it as close as ¹⁄₆₄" to the blade edge. The connecting screw needs to be tightened very firmly.

When placing the blade and chipbreaker assembly into the plane, I hold the plane in my left hand with the frog's surface horizontal, having brushed away any loose shavings or

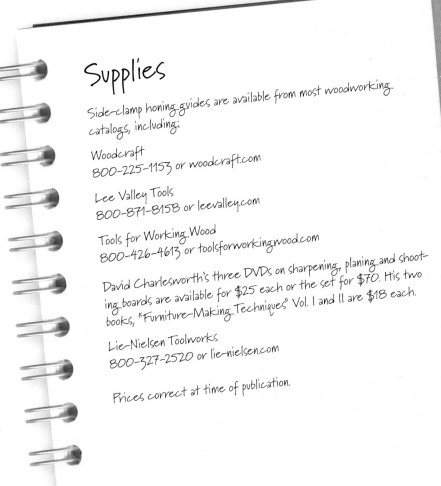

Supplies

Side-clamp honing guides are available from most woodworking catalogs, including:

Woodcraft
800-225-1153 or woodcraft.com

Lee Valley Tools
800-871-8158 or leevalley.com

Tools for Working Wood
800-426-4613 or toolsforworkingwood.com

David Charlesworth's three DVDs on sharpening, planing and shooting boards are available for $25 each or the set for $70. His two books, "Furniture-Making Techniques" Vol. I and II are $18 each.

Lie-Nielsen Toolworks
800-327-2520 or lie-nielsen.com

Prices correct at time of publication.

new diamond stones designed for creating a curved cutting edge quickly

Achieving a perfectly curved and polished cutting edge on your plane irons is an essential skill that many new hand plane users struggle with. Getting the right amount of curvature in the right place on the iron takes a fair amount of practice, patience and an observant eye.

Eventually, it is a skill that becomes second nature. And David Charlesworth's methods outlined in this chapter will give you a tremendous leg up in acquiring this skill. As with everything in woodworking, of course, there are several ways to get the same result. A new type of diamond stone is just now becoming available that sharpens a perfectly curved edge the first time you use it. I've sharpened about 25 plane irons with the product and am quite impressed with the results it gives.

The Odate Crowning Plate was developed by woodworker and author Toshio

Odate, and David Powell, the founder of Diamond Machining Technology Inc. (DMT). In essence, the stone is a 3^1/$_4$" x 7^1/$_4$" piece of cast iron that has been machined so it has a slight and consistent concavity across its width. Then it is plated with diamond particles – it is available with #60, #45, #30 and #9 micron grits. The amount of concavity corresponds to a slight 37^1/$_2$' radius. In more technical terms, the chord to arc height on a 3" width is .0025".

In practical terms, I've found the stones produce an edge that's just slightly more curved than what I achieve using finger pressure on a flat stone. This actually makes setting the curve in the center of the plane's mouth easier, though it reduces the width of shaving you will make.

Powell says you can reduce the curvature of the iron on the plate by skewing the iron slightly as you sharpen. I've also

found you can increase the curvature by using finger pressure on the corners as you sharpen the iron on the plates.

Also note that even the finest version of this stone (#9 micron) isn't fine enough to polish a plane iron's edge – you'll still need to finish up the edge on your polishing stone. There are two ways to go about this. You can use finger-point pressure as described in this article, which works very well in my experience. Or you can dress your polishing stone so it also has the same concavity as the diamond stones. Powell is making a convex diamond stone that will dress conventional sharpening stones expressly for this purpose. This dressing stone was not available at press time so we were unable to use it in our trials.

The bottom line is this: Veteran sharpeners probably won't need these stones (though I find they help me achieve consistency even when I'm having a bad day). But if you struggle with achieving a curved iron, the Odate Crowning Plate will fix your problem immediately and perfectly.

The stones are about $100 each. If you wish to purchase only one, I recommend the #30-micron stone, which shapes the edge quickly and takes you to the point where you can refine the edge with a #1,000-grit stone and then your polishing stone.

The stones are available from Powell Manufacturing Co., 396 Washington St. #114, Wellesley, Mass. 02481 or 781-237-4876.

The Odate Crowning Plate allows you to achieve a curved edge on your plane iron with about a dozen strokes without varying your finger-point pressure.

dust. This prevents the blade from sliding down the frog and colliding with the front of the throat. This would blunt the blade before we even get started. It is not a bad idea to retract the blade adjuster wheel by a couple of turns, too.

It is easy to see that when the blade-adjustment dog is engaging the slot in the chipbreaker, but care is needed to ensure that the lateral adjusting disc is engaged in the plane's blade slot. I wiggle the lateral lever a few times to see that it is so, and try to set the lever in approximately the right position. The lever cap is now installed, and everything held firm with my left-hand thumb, while the lever cam is closed. I now advance the blade with the wheel, watching from the top, to see that the blade edge is not crooked enough to bang into the front edge of the throat.

Setting the Plane for a Fine Finishing Shaving

The plane heel is now placed on a sheet of well-lit white paper on the bench. Lighting the blade is not helpful. I hold the front knob with my left hand and sight down the sole. The right hand is available to advance the blade and adjust the lateral lever. Start with enough blade projection so that you can see it clearly, and adjust the lateral lever for a "balanced shaving." The projecting blade will appear as a black shape against the white background. I now retract the blade, just until nothing shows.

A Setting Trick

The setting can be confirmed with a small piece of thin wood. I use a close-grained hardwood, about $1/16$" thick, by 1" wide, by $1^{1}/_{2}$" long. The long edge is held firmly down to the front sole and moved backwards over the throat, as if trying to take a shaving off its whole length.

I now advance the blade, very slowly, until the shim is just shaved by the center of the curved blade. You will encounter a phenomenon called backlash when you change from retracting the blade to advancing it. The wheel will turn freely for a while before you feel resistance. The blade will not ad-

A sheet of paper below your plane allows you to easily sight the blade as you position it laterally in the mouth of the plane.

vance at all while this happens. Once resistance is felt, the blade will begin to move. This "dead spot" is caused by play in the adjustment mechanism. It can be as much as two whole turns on an old worn plane. Less backlash signifies a high quality mechanism. All mechanical systems have some, and as long as you always set the blade while advancing the blade's projection, it will not trouble you. Conversely, if you set the proper projection while retracting the blade, you are likely to lose all blade projection as the blade works its way back into the body.

When winding the blade out, I turn the wheel as little as "three minutes on the clock," – that's an old-fashioned analog clock! – at a time. We only want a few thousandths of an inch projection for fine work, and it is easy to go too far, and then you have to start the whole process again.

This is where the setting shim is so useful. You can judge shaving thickness

This small block of wood is invaluable for determining if the iron is positioned in the center of the mouth of the plane.

by feel. You can also confirm that the blade projection is well balanced.

To do this, rub the long edge of the shim to and fro, as if taking full-length shavings from its edge. Start at the outer edge of the throat and progress towards the center of the plane, and you will be able to hear, feel and see exactly where the curved blade edge first protrudes. With luck a small shaving will stay wrapped round the blade. Now repeat from the other edge of the throat. This will confirm whether the curved blade is well centered in the plane. Some woodworkers perfect the final lateral adjustments by tapping the top of the blade with a small hammer. This may be easier than trying to make minuscule adjustments to the lateral lever.

I don't worry if the balancing is not perfect, as long as I know where the blade is! My final move is to take test shavings off the edge of a practice board. These can be measured with dial calipers to assess their thickness.

Suitable Shaving Thickness

For final finishing of difficult hardwood I take a .001"-thick shaving. For general cleaning of a machined board, I take a .002" shaving. In hardwood it is difficult to push a plane that is cutting much more than .004" to .006".

I do hope that this chapter helps you to get the most out of your bench planes. They are one of the most wonderful, versatile and accurate tools in your kit.

THE CABINET SCRAPER IS AN EFFECTIVE WEAPON
IN THE WAR AGAINST TEAR-OUT.

10

the useful cabinet scraper

BY DON MCCONNELL

In trained hands, a cabinet scraper can prepare a surface for final finishing and remove localized areas of tear-out left behind by a hand plane or machinery.

The cabinet scraper (also known as a card scraper) holds a remarkable place among the traditional woodworking tools that are used to deal with especially dense timbers and difficult grain.

When woodworkers discuss hand planes that are able to deal with such woods, the talk invariably turns to earnest consideration of tiny mouth apertures, secure iron bedding, carefully considered angles, flat soles and a fine depth of cut.

The cabinet scraper gets included in such discussions, even though the tool – essentially a piece of thin steel usually cut into a rectangular shape – doesn't exhibit any of these traits. Its inclusion is based on the fact that it's capable of taking fine shavings while hardly ever tearing out the wood fibers. Further, the denser and harder the timber, the better the tool seems to perform.

The cabinet scraper is capable of this performance because, despite the fact that it's called a scraper, it actually is a self-limiting cutting tool when it's properly prepared, sharpened and manipulated. Let's take a closer look:

Scraper Actually Slices

Without getting into a tedious analysis, this self-limiting cutting action is determined by the geometry and scale of the tool's burr, or wire edge, which enables it to perform as if it were a very finely set, high-angle smoothing plane with an extremely short sole. This, however, has consequences that place some limits on its usefulness, which we'll touch on in a moment. But first, a little about its traditional role in furniture making.

I was introduced to the cabinet scraper during my apprenticeship in traditional cabinetmaking, as part of a general approach to preparing surfaces for finishing. This approach consisted of truing up a surface with a try plane, addressing any localized areas of tear-out and tool marks with a smooth (or smoothing) plane, then following that up with the cabinet scraper only if there were areas of tear-out that the smooth plane could not address. The idea was to eliminate any surface defects with cutting tools because they remove material efficiently.

Any noticeable differences in surface texture or minor marks left from the cutting tools were removed (some might say obscured) by subsequent hand sanding. The argument was that sanding was less tedious (more efficient) for removing the very small amounts of material necessary to produce a uniform surface texture for finishing.

Many hand-tool woodworkers today are drawn to finishing right after cutting – avoiding sanding altogether. But for them, the cabinet scraper may actually complicate things.

For one thing, if the surface texture from the scraper is different than that of their smooth plane, they may not be able to use it on a small area of tear-out without having to scrape the entire surface. Also, because the tool performs as if it has an extremely short sole, it can be difficult to use over an entire surface without leaving obvious marks. This is particularly true at the ends of pieces (starting and stopping cuts) and in curly grain where it's possible to wind up with a "washboard" surface.

With enough skill and care, it may be possible to produce a scraped surface with nearly the same qualities you get with a finely tuned smooth plane, but it's going to be more tedious. In this instance, it may be more productive to lavish the same care and attention on a smooth plane to make it capable of handling the difficult woods – getting the mouth tight and learning to sharpen back bevels.

Qualities of a Good Tool

So, what should you look for in a cabinet scraper? The choice of sizes and thickness depends to a large extent on each person's preferences and the type of work intended.

I think a good place to start is with a 3" × 5" scraper with a thickness between $3/64$" and $1/16$". It needs to be good quality steel so it will take a decent edge. It must be hardened and subsequently tempered so it's soft enough to be filed. And it must be ductile enough to allow you to form the burr with a burnisher, also called a ticketer. This hardness (about 53 to 55 on the Rockwell "C" scale) is in the same range that you find in good hand saws. In fact, many cabinet scrapers have been made from damaged saws.

Sharpening the Scraper

When new, the scraper may need to have at least a narrow strip at each edge of its faces honed and polished prior to any sharpening. Some commercial scrapers have been honed and may require only a bit of polishing on a fine stone. Others come straight from the final grinding used in producing the steel plate and will require more work.

First, file each of the long edges with a single-cut file to remove blemishes and produce a straight, square edge. This can be done by drawfiling freehand, or with a file held in a commercial or shopmade saw jointer. I've been successful with both methods, but I have come to appreciate the speed and predictability of using a file in a special jig, as shown in the illustration above.

Next is to hone and polish these filed edges on a sharpening stone. While a number of methods have been devised to hold the scraper square while honing (including resting it on the stone's box while honing on the stone's side and using a square block of wood as a guide on the surface of the stone), I've had good results by bowing the scraper slightly to widen the edge so it will register square on the stone. By skewing the bowed scraper in this fashion, I have found that I can hone all my cabinet scrapers on waterstones

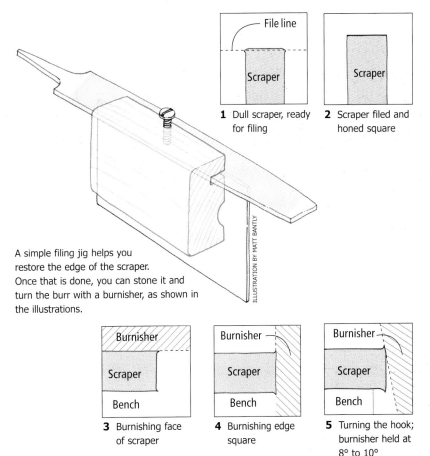

1 Dull scraper, ready for filing

2 Scraper filed and honed square

A simple filing jig helps you restore the edge of the scraper. Once that is done, you can stone it and turn the burr with a burnisher, as shown in the illustrations.

ILLUSTRATION BY MATT BANTLY

3 Burnishing face of scraper

4 Burnishing edge square

5 Turning the hook; burnisher held at 8° to 10°

and avoid the localized wear that would otherwise occur.

After the edges are polished, it is customary to hone the adjacent faces on a stone, as shown in the photos on page 60. You want to arrive at four crisp, clean arrises at the juncture of two polished right-angle surfaces, as shown above. This largely determines the quality of your wire edge.

Burnishing Turns the Burr

The last steps in forming the cutting/wire edge involve the use of a burnisher. The burnisher needs to be polished and harder than the scraper. New ones are relatively inexpensive, but my favorites are a couple of older ones I've found at flea markets.

The burnisher is used to deform, on a very small scale, the square arises into a "burr," or wire edge. The standard approach is to first lay the scraper flat on your bench surface and run the burnisher along both faces near each edge, keeping the burnisher flat on the face with moderate pressure near the edge of the scraper.

Scrapers come in a variety of sizes and shapes to allow you to clean up mouldings and other curved work.

Then, the burnisher is passed along the edge of the scraper to turn the wire edge. One way to do this is to hang an edge of the scraper off the edge of the bench and burnish in two steps as shown in the photos below. The first

59

stroke is kept perpendicular to the face to consolidate any small burr already in existence. Then, the burnisher is held at about 8° to 10° from vertical to form the burr – your cutting edge.

The amount of pressure you should use during burnishing is a matter of debate, and a real sense of this can be developed only through experience. I think the tendency of many beginners is to use too much pressure. After all, you are using a curved burnisher on a very narrow portion of the edge, so the pressure is very localized. I think it's better to start with a lighter touch and slowly increase pressure until you are satisfied with the results you're seeing. Too much pressure may prevent you from being able to renew your edge with just burnishing.

It would be logical to ask whether it is absolutely necessary to file the edge of the cabinet scraper at the beginning of each resharpening session. While theoretically it would be possible to remove burnished metal from the previous sharpening on a bench stone, it is simply easier and faster to do it with a file.

There are any number of methods to sharpen cabinet scrapers, including special commercial devices for burnishing the edges. I suggest that you explore the various options before settling on one because you should develop an approach you find both comfortable and predictable. Otherwise, the tendency is to wait too long to resharpen your scraper, resulting in a loss of efficiency (producing "dust" rather than shavings) and a poor surface quality on your work.

On the other hand, it is indeed possible to renew the cutting edge of the tool a couple of times by going back through the burnishing process before you get ready to begin the entire resharpening regimen. It's your call.

Using the Scraper

Using a cabinet scraper takes a little practice. Each species of wood can require a slightly different angle of attack. When you're just starting out, you will want to flex the scraper a bit with your thumbs and hold the tool at about 60° to your work. Make minor adjustments in the angle and curvature until you produce fine shavings. After some practice, your hands will naturally fall into the correct position.

When dealing with some of the more difficult grains, particularly in hardwoods, the cabinet scraper can be invaluable to a woodworker who has taken the time to learn how to sharpen and to use it correctly. It even can be useful for removing powered-planer marks in these difficult woods, without risking tear-out from a hand plane or needing to resort to some of the more heavy-handed power sanding techniques.

1 To drawfile a scraper edge, hold the file at an angle as shown and push it across the tool's edge. Cut only on the push stroke.

2 If you stone the edge freehand, bow the tool slightly to keep it flat on the sharpening stone.

3 After the edges are polished, you can hone the faces of the scraper, as shown.

4 The first step in burnishing is to consolidate the edge by running the burnisher flat on the face.

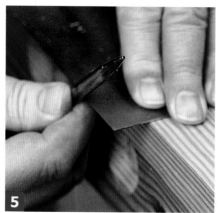

5 Next, hold the burnisher square – perpendicular to the face – and rub the edge.

6 Finally, to turn the hook, tilt the burnisher 8° to 10° and rub the edge with light pressure.

IGNORE THE NAYSAYERS. THIS JIG PRODUCES SQUARE, SHARP EDGES EVERY SINGLE TIME.

side-clamping honing guide

BY CHRISTOPHER SCHWARZ

Many of my fellow hand-tool users give me grief about my side-clamp honing guide – a fixture on my workbench since 1993.

"Isn't it time you learned to sharpen properly?" they ask. And then they rattle off a list of the advantages of sharpening freehand:

• Freehand is faster because you don't have to set up a jig every time.

• You remove less metal with freehand sharpening so your hand tools will last longer before they're used up.

• Freehand sharpening produces edges just as sharp as with a jig.

• The side-clamp jig won't work for odd-shaped or very short tools.

• Sharpening with a jig is just for beginners. Real hand-tool users can sharpen without this little one-wheeled crutch, they say.

To most of those criticisms I roll my eyes. I can sharpen freehand, and I'm pretty good at it. After all, some tools must be sharpened freehand because they won't fit in the jig properly (such as gouges and skew chisels), which is one of the few valid criticisms of the jig.

But most furniture makers spend more time sharpening bench chisels and plane irons than they do odd-shaped specialty tools. And when it comes to sharpening these basic and common tools, nothing beats this jig.

Here are the facts: Sharpening with the side-clamp honing guide is as fast

or faster than sharpening freehand. Using a few well-placed marks on my bench, I can set a chisel or plane iron at the perfect sharpening angle in just a couple of seconds. Freehand sharpeners sometimes forget that it takes time to adjust the tool in their hands so its cutting edge contacts the stone at the right angle. And they have to make this adjustment every time they lift the tool from the stone.

As to the complaint that sharpening with a jig removes more metal and shortens the lifespan of the tool, I say "So what?" Few home woodworkers ever use up a chisel or plane iron in their lifetimes. If the jig does shorten the usable life of the tool, it won't be a problem until our grandchildren use it decades in the future.

When it comes to producing a quality edge every time, sharpening with a jig is unbeatable. Beginners who have a jig can produce edges as good (sometimes better) than people who have been sharpening freehand their entire adult lives. This is because the jig takes all the guesswork out of the angle the tool must be held at during sharpening, and produces perfect and repeatable edges every time. Freehand sharpening is more prone to error. Even experienced sharpeners will occasionally round over an edge.

As I stated earlier, one of the criticisms of the jig is indeed valid: You

can't sharpen everything with it, but it does take care of 90 percent of my sharpening needs.

And as to the claim that the jig is a crutch for beginners, I disagree. This side-clamp honing guide is for anyone who wants square edges every time they sharpen so they can get back to woodworking. As a bonus it offers results that are easily repeated – that's good no matter how skilled you are.

Sharpening shouldn't take years to master the muscle memory. This jig creates good edges the first day you use it, and that's reason enough to own one.

Supplies

Side-clamp Honing Guide
Street price: $12 – $14
For more information: The jig is available through Woodcraft, Rockler, Lie-Nielsen and Lee Valley.

Prices correct at time of publication.

THE BIGGEST OBSTACLE TO MASTERING THIS TRADITIONAL TOOL IS GETTING IT RAZOR SHARP.

sharpen a drawknife

BY SCOTT GIBSON

If you visit a crafts school that specializes in traditional woodworking, you'd almost certainly run across at least one student seated at a shaving horse, drawknife in hand, coaxing a chair leg out of a length of green hardwood. Chairmakers are among the first to sing the praises of this uncomplicated but versatile hand tool, but it's only one of many trades that has put it to good use.

Once available with blades in many different lengths and in a variety of straight and curved patterns, drawknives have been used to make everything from ship masts and barrel staves to gunstocks, wheel spokes and wooden shovels. Some patterns disappeared long ago, along with the trades that used them. For example, you won't find a crumming knife (a cooper's tool for shaping staves) at your local hardware store. But drawknives are still available from mail-order suppliers and having one around is an advantage even if it's used only for fitting an occasional hammer handle or sculpting the edge of a tabletop. They are also fairly safe to use, making them a good choice for children who are just learning how to use hand tools.

Like any edge tool, a drawknife works best when it's razor sharp. There are many approaches to sharpening them, depending on whether the blade is straight or curved and exactly what kind of equipment you have on hand.

Large-diameter grinding wheels, like the one on the water-cooled Tormek, or a 1" belt sander with an adjustable tool rest are both well adapted for sharpening drawknives, but most of us will turn to the sharpening stones or sandpaper that we already use to sharpen plane blades, chisels and other common edge tools.

First, Get the Back of the Blade Flat

A drawknife has a flat back and a single bevel on the opposite side of the blade. But sharpening both parts of the tool can be complicated because of the handles bent at right angles to the blade. They tend to get in the way when you try to sharpen the edge on

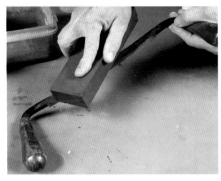

Just as if you were sharpening a chisel or plane blade, start with the back of the drawknife. This #220-grit water stone will remove material quickly.

Follow the coarse stone with a succession of finer stones to remove scratches and create a smooth, uniform surface.

When you're finished, the back of the knife should be almost flat. Hone a very gentle crown in the blade so you can start a cut when working with the bevel side up. A perfectly flat back will allow only very light cuts.

a bench-mounted stone or a grinding wheel. Instead, you can make a jig that allows the handles to straddle a stone, or sharpen the blade by clamping it to a workbench or simply prop the drawknife up at a convenient angle with one hand and guide the stone with the other.

Start by flattening the back. Like a plane blade, it should be free of pits and other imperfections that would degrade the quality of the honed edge. Experts like Thomas Lie-Nielsen, the Maine planemaker who wrote *The Complete Illustrated Guide to Sharpening* (Taunton), suggests starting with a circular axe stone made from silicon carbide. A fairly coarse sharpening stone, such as a #220-grit Japanese waterstone, also works well. Follow that up with successively finer grits. I used #1,200- and #4,000-grit stones on the back of my drawknife until the surface looked flat and uniform.

There is such a thing as too flat. Kentucky chairmaker Brian Boggs says a drawknife with a perfectly flat back will be hard to use with the bevel up for anything other than very light cuts. A blade must be turned slightly as it starts a cut, and a very gently crowned back makes this possible. But because most of us won't succeed in flattening the back to a machinist's tolerances, Boggs says the best approach is to try to make the back as flat as you can. Chances are it will have the right amount of crown when you're done. (A DVD from Lie-Nielsen Toolworks explains in detail how Boggs uses and sharpens these tools.)

Although you can use a belt sander to flatten the back of a drawknife, you may end up removing more material than you want. Moreover, Boggs says the technique often results in a back that's rounded or crowned too much.

Lie-Nielsen recommends grinding a slight hollow in the back of the blade with the large-diameter wheel on a Tormek – if you own one. The hollow created by the wheel's radius makes it easier to sharpen the back because you only have to remove material near the front and back edge of the tool's backside, not all the way across (the same idea behind the design of a Japanese chisel). But if you have only a 8" or 6" grinder, skip this step because the hollow would be too pronounced.

Sharpening the Bevel On a Straight Blade

Bevel angles vary, but they generally range between 30° and 40°. You may want to experiment with the bevel to find the optimum angle for the kind of work you do and the wood you're working with. Whatever angle you choose, it will be difficult to form the bevel on a standard bench grinder because the tool's handles are likely to get in the way. Instead, you can use a bench stone and hold the drawknife with one handle propped up on the bench, clamp the tool to a bench or cradle one end against your shoulder. Or use a belt sander secured in a vise. If you do use a belt sander, be careful to orient the blade so the edge can't dig into the belt and make sure to wear safety gear.

Some woodworkers advocate grinding a slight hollow in the back of the knife with a large-diameter grinding wheel, like the one on this water-cooled Tormek.

If you'd rather work the tool over a stationary bench stone, a simple jig will help. It consists of a block of wood that holds the stone and an attached leg that can be clamped in a bench vise. You can make the jig from scrap lumber by tracing the outline of a bench stone on a short length of board, nailing on strips of wood to hold the stone, and then attaching the leg with a couple of wood screws. Alternately, you could trace the outline of the stone on a board and use a router or laminate trimmer to carve a shallow depression for the stone. The hollow doesn't have to be very deep to hold the stone in place. However you do it, the jig will give you more control in keeping a consistent bevel angle because you can use both hands to guide the tool. (See "Making a Sharpening Stone Jig" on page 65.)

A belt sander clamped upside down on the bench quickly forms a new bevel. Use very light pressure so you don't remove too much material, and be sure to orient the blade so the edge can't dig into the belt.

A bevel reshaped with this #150-grit belt will need work on several stones to remove the deep scratches.

One way of securing the knife while working on the bevel is to clamp the tool to a workbench. Face the cutting edge away from you.

Another approach is to hold the drawknife with one hand against the bench, and to hold the sharpening stone in the other as you work the bevel.

You can also hold the knife with one handle pressed against your shoulder, as if you were playing a fiddle. Keep the sharp edge up and watch your fingers.

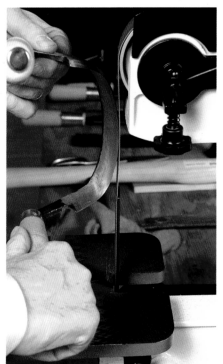

A 1" belt sander with an adjustable tool rest makes short work of regrinding a bevel on a drawknife. The tool's handles won't get in the way.

If the edge is in relatively good condition, you can start with a #1,200-grit stone and work up from there, finishing off with a #4,000-grit or higher stone. As a wire edge develops, flip the stone to the back and hone the wire edge away. Whichever method you use, keep the sharp edge of the blade facing away from you as you hone it. If the blade faces you, a slip or miscalculation could lead to a nasty cut.

Drawknives are not usually given a secondary bevel, but some people think a small back bevel makes a drawknife a little easier to use. If you want to try one use a fine stone to hone one on the back.

Sharpening Curved Blades

Drawknives intended to scoop out hollows have curved blades. One surface of the blade is flat; the other has a bevel. Some drawknife patterns have mild curves, but others, such as inshaves and scorps, have a pronounced bend that can't readily be sharpened on a flat stone.

A 1" belt sander does a good job of grinding the outside of a sharply

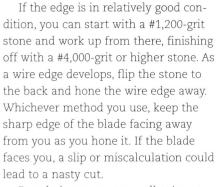

To work the outside of a sharply curved draw-knife-like tool, such as a scorp or an inshave, glue a piece of sandpaper to a length of wood with spray adhesive.

curved blade. It can be followed up with stones to remove the scratches left by the belt. If you don't own a belt sander, the blade can be stoned by hand or flattened with sandpaper that's been glued to a flat board with spray adhesive. Start with a grit that's appropriate for the condition of the blade – #60- or #80-grit paper for blades that need a lot of work, finer paper for blades in good condition.

After using the sandpaper, hone the outside of the blade with sharpening stones.

For final polishing, Lie-Nielsen uses diamond paste and a small block of wood.

To sharpen a bevel on the inside of the blade, use a curved slipstone or a piece of plastic pipe on which you've glued silicon carbide sandpaper with spray adhesive. If there is a lot of material to remove, you can also use a sanding drum mounted in an electric drill and finish up with finer grits of paper mounted on a section of pipe or with a slipstone.

You can finish the outside of an inshave with diamond paste and a piece of softwood for a very polished surface and a keen edge, as Thomas Lie-Nielsen does here.

A sanding drum mounted in an electric drill is an effective first step for dressing the unbeveled face of a curve.

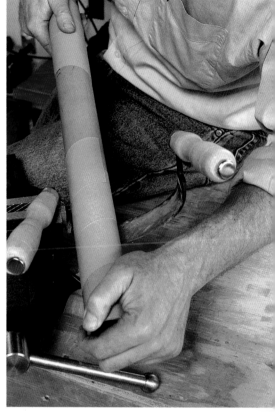

Sandpaper glued to a length of PVC pipe makes a good tool for working the inside of a curved drawknife, inshave or scorp.

making a sharpening stone jig

1

To make a jig for a sharpening stone, first lay the stone on a scrap of wood and mark the ends.

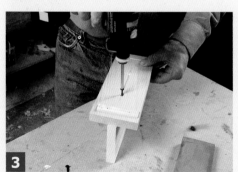

3

Another piece of scrap forms a leg that can be slipped into a bench vise or clamped to a workbench.

2

Scraps of wood nailed to the board with brads will serve as stops and hold the stone in place.

4

Now the full length of the knife can be worked on a stone without interference from the handles. Using both hands also allows more control and a more consistent bevel angle.

USING BENCH PLANES WITH YOUR MACHINERY WILL SPEED YOUR WORK. BUT FIRST YOU MUST UNDERSTAND **HOW THE BENCH PLANE SYSTEM WORKS.**

13

coarse, medium & fine

BY CHRISTOPHER SCHWARZ

Too often we hear that hand tools are slow and power tools are fast. Even people who love hand tools talk about how they enjoy handwork because it forces them to slow their work on a project, to ponder the details, to enjoy the smell of the freshly cut lumber and to labor in quiet harmony with the wood.

That's all very bucolic – but it's also a bit ill-informed.

To my mind, people who think hand tools are slow are either using the wrong tool for a task, or they are people who will work slowly no matter what tool is in their hand. I have found that to become truly efficient at woodworking is to first ignore whether or not the tool in your hand has a power cord or a finely honed blade. Instead, you should make sure that you know whether that tool is a coarse tool for hogging off material, a medium tool for refining and truing the work or a fine tool that's the last to touch your work.

This classification system – coarse, medium and fine – works for many of the tools of the craft, from sandpaper to hand planes. And putting each tool into its place is the first step toward knowing its true use at the bench.

Once you know what each tool is used for, you'll also be able to figure out which tools (if any) should be used before it and which tools (if any) should be used after it. Plus you'll know – in

general terms – how long you should be using that tool before you switch to a finer one.

The net result of this is you will become much faster because you'll always have the right tool in your hand.

To show how this approach works, let's look at surfacing lumber. This coarse, medium and fine system will first help you understand what bench planes are for and then show you how bench planes can be blended seamlessly with powered jointers and planers and other surfacing tools.

First Understand the Bench Plane System

Bench planes are the mainstay of a shop that uses hand tools or blends hand and power tools. Bench planes were designed to make lumber smooth and true before any joinery operations (and before applying a finish).

To surface wood with bench planes, you need three planes: a fore plane, a jointer plane and a smoothing plane. It sounds simple, but the problem is that over the years, hand-plane manufacturers have designed bench planes in

Like a powered planer, the fore plane produces thick curls so it can rapidly reduce a board in thickness. Shown is my crusty-but-trusty Stanley No. 5 (some people call this a jack plane) and my sweet Scioto Works 16" wooden-stock fore plane.

many lengths and widths (too many, really), and they have given them misleading numbers. Stanley, for example, numbers its bench planes from the diminutive No. 1 up to the massive No. 8. And there are more than just eight planes in that numbering system (there are Nos. 4½, 5¼ and 5½, too). Do you need all 11 planes? No. Do you need to start working with the No. 1 then progress to a No. 8? Absolutely not. So which planes do you need? Good question. Let's hit the books.

Ignore Some Numbers

What's more important than the model number that's cast into a plane's bed is the overall length of the tool – that's the key to unlocking its function.

And once you understand the plane's intended function, then you'll know how to incorporate it into your shop, no matter what set of tools or machines you own.

In a nutshell, the fore plane is the tool for coarse work, and it does a job similar to a powered jointer and power planer. The jointer plane is the medium tool, and it works like a random-orbit sander, drum sander or belt sander (in the right hands). And the smoothing plane is the fine tool; it does the detail work performed by powered pad sanders, hand scrapers and sanding blocks. So let's first take a close look at these three planes.

Fore Planes: Rough & Ready

Fore planes are between 14" and 20" long and are so named because they are the planes that are used "before" the other hand planes. They are the "coarse" tool – the roughest of the bunch. They require more strength and stamina to use than any other hand tool, and I use mine as little as possible now that I own a powered jointer and planer.

In the Stanley numbering system, the No. 5 (14" long and commonly called a jack plane) and the No. 6 (18" long) planes qualify as fore planes.

The fore plane is used to rapidly take a bowed or cupped board to a state where it's reasonably flat. Fore planes

Working diagonally is the key to using the fore plane. The diagonal motion reduces tear-out and assists in truing the face.

Fore planes need a wide-open mouth to pass the thick shavings they produce. A tight mouth will clog and slow you down.

A silhouette of the shape of my fore plane's cambered iron. It's an 8" radius, which allows me to take an almost ¹/₁₆"-thick shaving in softwood.

Cambering the iron on a fore plane is a task best handled on a bench grinder.

don't take a fine shaving. They take coarse curls of lumber so the work gets done quickly. Their middling length is an advantage. They are long enough so that the sole touches a lot of the surface of the board. This helps you true the face of the board more easily and prevents you from overshooting your mark – turning high spots into deep valleys by accident. (Why are scrub planes so short, then? I think these 10"-long tools were used more for hogging wood off edges or for localized work – but that's another story.)

If the length of the fore plane is an asset, why not make them really long?

Working with fore planes is strenuous, so having them shorter and lighter makes them easier to handle than a longer plane. Whenever I use my fore plane, I marvel at its perfection of design. It's exactly long enough – but no more.

Once you know that the fore plane is for roughing, this also tells you how to set up the tool for use. The flatness of the sole isn't a concern for rough work. If the sole looks flat and the tool won't rock when the tool is flat on your bench, you're in good shape.

I wouldn't recommend you spend hours flattening the sole of your fore plane so you can take .001" shavings.

Winding sticks (I like aluminum angle) exaggerate any warp or high spots on the board's face. View the winding sticks so they are in line with one another.

There are lots of ways to get the proper camber on the iron for a jointer plane. Shown is the Odate crowning plate from Powell Manufacturing – essentially, it's a diamond sharpening stone that's concave in the middle.

A jointer plane's major asset is the length of its sole. The longer the sole, the flatter your board will become. Shown is a Lie-Nielsen No. 7 plane (left) and the Veritas bevel-up jointer. The jointer I covet (not shown) is the Clark & Williams jointer, which can be as long as 30".

The mouth of the jointer plane is a fine balance. You want it open enough to pass a fairly thick shaving, yet tight enough to limit tear-out as much as possible.

Save that drudgery for another plane (or avoid the drudgery – more on that later).

My metal fore plane is a sorry old Stanley No. 5 with a handmade tote that looks like it was fashioned by a blind beaver. The tool is rusty in spots. The sole's flatness is questionable – but it works like a dream.

Back to set-up. Because you want to remove thick shavings, open up the mouth of the tool and make the tool easy to push by cambering the tool's cutting edge. A fore plane with a blade sharpened straight across (like you would with a chisel or block plane) can be quickly immobilized by a tough

A silhouette of the shape of my jointer plane's cambered iron. I placed a feeler gauge on the end to see how far back the corners were swept: it's .005".

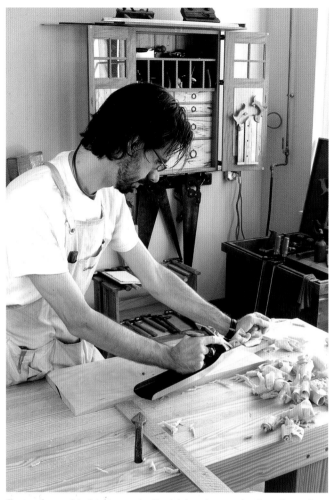

On narrower cabinet components, the jointer plane works along the grain. Skewing the tool slightly during the cut makes it easier to push and does assist in flattening. One wider panels – say 14" and wider – I'll begin with a few diagonal passes before switching to long-grain ones.

Smoothing planes are the elite (and most demanding) planes in your shop. Shown are a Lie-Nielsen No. 4, a Veritas bevel-up smoother, a wooden-bodied Clark & Williams smoother and my most guilty pleasure: a custom-made plane by Wayne Anderson (bottom right). Yes, it's a smoothing plane, too.

Smoothing planes remove wispy shavings and prepare a surface for finishing.

The mouth of a smoothing plane should be as tight as possible. This requires tweaking and experimentation. Once you get the mouth set, however, you shouldn't have to change that setting.

patch of wood. And the cambered iron (I like an 8" radius) helps reduce tearout because there are no corners digging into the wood. If your plane has a chipbreaker, set it so it's back at least $1/16$" from the corners.

Fore planes are pushed diagonally across a board's face. Work diagonally one way across the face, then diagonally the other. Check your progress with winding sticks. Working diagonally will generally get you where you need to be, but if there's a persistent high spot, work at it selectively with the fore plane. The goal is to get the board flat and almost to your finished thickness – as close as you dare.

A silhouette of a smoothing plane iron. The camber is slight: .002" or maybe a little more.

Jointer Planes:
Join the Flat-World Society

When the work is nearly flat and nearly to finished thickness, fetch your jointer plane – sometimes also called a try plane. Jointer planes are tools with soles 22" long or longer. Longer is better in the world of jointer planes. In the Stanley system, the No. 7 (22" long) and the No. 8 (24" long) are the jointers. Wooden-bodied jointer planes can be much longer.

The jointer plane is the "medium" tool. It brings the surface of the board to a state where joinery can be performed. Jointer planes take a finer shaving than the fore plane, but nothing that would be called gossamer. I

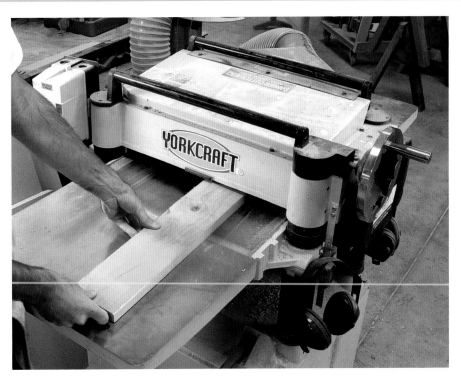

The powered jointer (above) and planer (right) are faster than a fore plane (though they won't burn as many calories during use).

generally go for a shaving that's about .006" thick. That's about the thickness of two or three sheets of typing paper. The length of the jointer plane is its greatest asset. When you can push a jointer plane across the entire surface of the board and remove a full-width, full-length shaving from every point, the board is quite flat (flatter than most machinery can get it, I've found). The plane's sole rides over the valleys of a board and flattens the hills. When the hills are the same level as the valleys, you're done.

If this tool is so accurate, why not begin work with a jointer plane and skip the fore plane? Though a .006"-thick shaving sounds like a lot, it's not. With rough-sawn wood, you could work one face all day with a jointer plane – a fore plane can remove much more wood in a hurry. And the jointer planes are more unwieldy. I'd much rather push my fore plane, which weighs less than 5 lbs., for a lot longer than my No. 8, which weighs 10 lbs.

Because the jointer plane is a precision instrument, it requires more attention than its coarser, shorter cousin. The sole should be reasonably flat. There's been a lot written about this topic, but the bottom line is that the tool must work – that's its true test. Can you flatten the sole of an old metal jointer plane yourself? Perhaps, but I can't. Though I've flattened the soles of many planes, I end up making jointer planes worse. There is too much cast iron to work with there.

And that's why I recommend you spend a little money when buying a jointer plane. In fact, if I had to buy only one precision plane, it would be a toss-up between the jointer plane and the smoothing plane. There's a good argument for buying a premium metal jointer plane and a vintage wooden-soled fore plane and smoothing plane. Then you could use the metal jointer to true the soles of the two wooden planes.

No matter which jointer plane you acquire, the setup is similar. Some historical texts recommend an iron sharpened straight across, but I prefer a slight camber to the cutting edge, which is also historically correct – it depends on who you read. The camber should be much slighter than the curve on your fore plane. I like a curve that allows a .006"-thick shaving that's almost the entire width of the iron. Practice will get you where you need to be.

The mouth needs to be fairly open to pass this shaving, but there's no need for a gaping maw. Keeping the mouth fairly tight can reduce tear-out. And though the jointer plane isn't generally a finishing plane (that's the job of the smoothing plane), reducing tear-out will make less work for the smoothing plane. The chipbreaker needs to be

somewhere between $\frac{1}{16}$" and $\frac{1}{8}$" from the cutting edge in my experience.

When I work a board's face with a jointer plane, I tend to work in the direction of the grain – not diagonally like with the fore plane. However, when I'm flattening a big tabletop, a largish panel or my benchtop, I'll begin with diagonal strokes. This helps keep a larger surface in true.

As you start to work, the first pass or two should produce irregular shavings as you remove the high spots left by the fore plane. After a few passes, long and wide shavings should emerge from the mouth. When this happens all the way across a board's width, you are ready to work the other face of the board.

If you're surfacing the board entirely by hand, use a marking gauge to scribe the finished thickness on all four edges of the boards and work that rough face with the fore plane almost to the scribe line. Then true the second face with your jointer plane.

This is the point at which I'll typically perform joinery on the piece (with some exceptions). If you proceed to the smoothing plane before you cut your joints, you can make more work for yourself in the end.

That's because joinery can be hard on a board. You'll mark it up with the typical shop bruises from cutting and clamping. When the joinery is complete, I'll generally assemble the project and then smooth the exterior – if possible. Sometimes you have to go to the smoothing plane before assembly. Experience will be your guide.

Smoothing Planes: An Addiction for Some

The smoothing plane is the tool that usually hooks woodworkers into hand tools. It is the "fine" tool in the troika of hand planes and it produces gossamer shavings and leaves shimmering surfaces. I like my smoothing planes, but if I've done a good job with my other planes, the smoothing plane should see only a little use.

This is a good thing because it saves you on sharpening and setup. Fore planes are the easiest tool to set up and sharpen (they don't have to be surgically sharp), jointers take a little more work in both departments and smoothing planes are the trickiest tool.

Smoothing planes require a cutter with a gently curved super-sharp cutting edge, a fine mouth, perfect alignment of the cutter in the center of the mouth and a lot of other fine tweaks that demand fussing, fussing, fussing. So if you're using your smoothing plane as little as possible, then you're also spending less time tweaking and more time woodworking.

There are a lot of sizes of smoothing planes, but in general they are 7" to

Hand scrapers and sanding blocks are an accepted and historically accurate way to prepare a piece of wood for finishing.

10" in length. The Stanley No. 4 is the most common size at 9" long with a 2"-wide cutter. The bigger planes, such as the No. 4½, are suited for larger-scale work, such as dining tables. The smaller planes, such as the No. 3, are suited for smaller work, such as narrow door stiles and rails.

The smoothing plane needs to take a fine shaving, anywhere from .002" thick down to stuff that cannot be measured. So you need the sole to be as flat as possible to consistently take this shaving. You can try to tune the sole of your smoothing plane, or you can do what I do – let someone who knows what they are doing handle this job with a surface grinder. If you purchase a nice hand plane from Veritas, Lie-Nielsen or Clifton and the sole is out of whack, then send it back. You shouldn't have to flatten the sole if you pay more than $175 for a plane.

Other considerations: The mouth needs to be as tight as you can get

without it clogging with shavings. The chipbreaker needs to be set near the cutting edge. I like less than $1/16$" – as close as I can get without clogging. And the iron needs to have the slightest camber, just a couple thousandths at the corners. I achieve this by applying selective finger pressure at the iron's corners while sharpening. I also find that smoothing planes are the place to lavish your sharpening skills. To get the edge as perfect as you can, polish it up to the highest grit you have available. In my experience, sharper edges reduce tear-out as much as a tight mouth or the pitch of the blade (higher pitches reduce tear-out but make the tool harder to push).

When working with a smoothing plane, make passes parallel to the grain of the board, making sure that your strokes overlap slightly. Work from the edge of the board near you across to the far edge. Your first strokes will remove the high spots left by the jointer

A drum sander (left) can level and true a panel much like a jointer plane. A random-orbit sander (above) is ideal for removing machining marks in a power-tool workshop.

plane and your shavings could look inconsistent. Once you make a couple passes across the face, you should be able to get full-length shavings that are as wide as your blade allows. When this occurs and the board looks good, put down the plane. Clean up any localized tear-out with a hand scraper.

If necessary, I'll make a few strokes with #220-grit sandpaper to blend the planed surfaces with the scraped ones. This should take only a few strokes.

What This Means: Blending Hand and Power

Armed with this understanding of hand planes, you can now unlock an important secret. Almost all of our power tools can be classified as coarse, medium or fine tools – just like the hand planes used for surfacing wood.

Think about your powered jointer and planer as coarse tools, like the fore plane. Their job is to remove lots of stock in a hurry. But the surface they leave needs to be refined before finishing (unless you build only chicken coops).

What are the medium tools? I classify large random-orbit sanders, belt sanders and drum sanders as medium tools. They remove the marks left by the coarse machining process and can indeed true a board when wielded by a skilled user. Some people are satisfied to stop at this phase – and truth be told, I'll sometimes stop after using my jointer plane when building something intended for the shop or for pure utility.

But most power-tool woodworkers go a step further. They scrape and hand sand to remove the scratches left by random-orbit sanders and pad sanders – the so-called pigtails you see on so many furniture-store pieces. In the power-tool world, these hand tools are the "fine" tools.

Once you classify your power tools, you can use them in conjunction with your hand tools. Let's say that the only bench plane you own is a smoothing plane. When should you use it? First joint and plane your stock (a coarse operation). Get it as true and flat as possible with your drum sander or belt sander (that's medium). And then finish

The concept of coarse, medium and fine works with other operations as well. For cutting curves, think of your band saw as the coarse tool, your rasp as the medium tool and your spokeshave as the fine tool.

things up with the smoothing plane, scrapers and sandpaper (fine).

This information can also be used to guide your tool purchases. What plane should you buy at the flea market if you don't own a powered jointer or planer? (A fore plane.)

Here's how I personally blend power and hand tools in my shop. My coarse tools are my powered 8" jointer and 15" planer. Though I own two fore planes, I use them only when a board is too wide for my powered equipment.

Once the coarse stuff is over, I use my jointer plane to true my stock before cutting my joinery. This medium tool removes snipe and machine marks, and makes the boards flatter than my power equipment can. Finally, my smoothing plane is my primary fine tool, although I scrape and hand sand, too.

It's important to use the tools in the right order (start with coarse; end with fine) and don't skip any steps between. Skipping wastes time. It's frustrating to use a fine tool right after a coarse tool. Try using a smoothing plane on a larger board that's fresh from your powered planer. Then use a smoothing plane on a board that you first dressed with your jointer plane. You'll notice a significant difference.

The other important idea is to work as long as you can with the coarse tool. You wouldn't remove $1/16$" of a

board's thickness with a random-orbit sander. So don't use your jointer or smoothing planes to do that, either. This is a common error and is one way hand tools get a reputation as slow.

One last thing: I don't use hand tools because of a romantic obsession with the past. Once I adopted this system of coarse, medium and fine, I became faster, my joinery became tighter (because my boards were perfectly true) and my finished results looked better.

And once you understand how coarse, medium and fine works with surfacing lumber, you can apply the idea to other workshop processes. Here's a hint at the possibilities: When cutting curves, the coarse tool is the band saw, the medium tool is the rasp and the fine tool is the spokeshave. And there's more. A lot more.

Sources

Anderson Planes
763-241-0138 or andersonplanes.com

Clark & Williams
479-253-7416 or planemaker.com

Lie-Nielsen Toolworks
800-327-2520 or lie-nielsen.com

Powell Manufacturing
781-237-4876

Veritas (Lee Valley Tools)
800-871-8158 or leevalley.com

14

the names of planes

BY ADAM CHERUBINI

Learning the true names of your planes will allow you to figure out the appropriate use of each one – leveling your stock, fitting joinery or adding ornamentation.

Ever-increasing numbers of woodworkers are using hand planes in their shops. Their demand for fine planes has given rise to boutique plane makers such as Clark & Williams, Lie-Nielsen Toolworks, Veritas and Shepherd Tool Co. to name a few.

These users' interest has given rise to another industry, no less substantial than the plane manufacturers: The opinionated and self-righteous wood plane experts! These dreaded, self-proclaimed experts offer their opinions in magazine articles, DVDs and yes – you guessed it – books. They offer gems in dribs and drabs, promising that (with their help, of course) you can magically turn any rough-sawn surface into wood as smooth as gold.

Naturally, each expert's opinion is as individual as the woodworker offering it, leaving you no alternative but to buy all of the woodworking magazines, videos and – you guessed it – books available on the subject. Worse still, each new plane acquisition requires a new set of books and videos because the experts never attempt to impart a greater understanding of the larger context that would allow you to answer your own questions. No. You must come to me, the wood plane expert. The only way you can break your dependence on me and my fellow magicians is to learn my name. OK, the plane's name actually.

In the children's story of Rumplestiltskin, the princess gained the upper hand by learning the magician's real name. The proper names for wood planes are no less elusive or powerful. Learning them is absolutely the key to gaining an important advantage in selecting, tuning and using wood planes in your work.

In this chapter on working wood quickly and efficiently with hand tools, we'll begin to explore the mysterious and sometimes contentious world of hand planes. I'll attempt to provide a simple framework that will serve as a reasonable starting place from which

you can venture, and to which I suspect you will inevitably return.

"Who Told You That?"

If learning the name of each plane is the secret to unlocking its power, then plane manufacturers and we plane "experts" have done everything we can do to keep you in the dark. Stanley listed its 14"-long No. 5 plane as a jack plane and called the 18"-long No. 6 a fore plane. Wooden jacks were typically 16".

Joseph Moxon, a 17th century chronicler of woodworking tools and methods, tells us the fore plane and jack plane are two names for the same tool:

a roughing plane. According to Moxon, "jack" was the term used by carpenters, while "fore" (ostensibly describing the order in which the plane was to be used) was used by joiners to describe their roughing planes.

To add to our confusion, 18th-century estate inventories listed both jack and fore planes in the same shop indicating, at least by then, there was a perceptible difference.

The difference between a try plane and a jointer plane has been long debated. Though the planes may appear identical, their appearance is their only similarity.

The confusion about the differences between dados and grooves, or fillisters and rabbets, is forgivable for the uninitiated. But when manufacturers call fenced rabbet planes (such as the Stanley No. 78) a "duplex fillister," somebody ought to call a good lawyer. The first time you try to cut a fillister with a plow plane or a dado with a rabbet plane, you realize either that you've been had, or that hand tools are hard to use and not worth the trouble.

Sorting Things Out

Archeologist, historian and tool collector Henry Chapman Mercer (1856-1930) organized the wood planes he collected into three unique categories according to their purpose. Mercer could have organized his planes as others have since then: by the original users' trade, or the tools' outward appearance. But Mercer was far more than just a wealthy collector with a penchant for odd things:

"Who has ever fully described this ancient tool, in its 18th century varieties? Owing to the confusing and

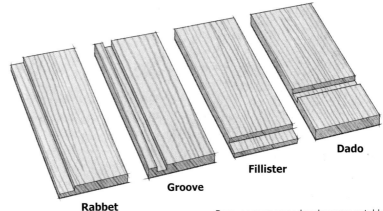

Rabbet   **Groove**   **Fillister**   **Dado**

non-descriptive names given to it, it is hard to understand until we overlook the endless variations in its make and shape and grasp the three purposes of its construction." – Henry Mercer, *Ancient Carpenter's Tools*.

It is a shame Mercer's categories have not received greater acceptance from woodworkers. As it turns out, Mercer's system is both helpful and robust. It's an excellent starting place for any would-be planer.

Leveling Planes

The leveling planes, often generically called bench planes because they're needed for every job and therefore never leave the bench, are the jack or fore plane, the try plane and the smoothing plane. All leveling planes benefit from having curved irons for the reason Moxon explained in his *Mechanick Exercises*.

"Should the iron of the plane be ground to a straight edge and be set ever so little ranker on one end of the edge than the other, the ranker end would (bearing as then upon a point) in working, dig Gutters on the Surface of the Stuff."

Because many woodworkers use a table saw with a dado blade to cut the joints above, their proper names have fallen out of use. When things were made by hand, every workman knew these names and the different tools required for each.

The lengths of leveling planes vary in accordance with each tool's specific use. Smoothers are shortest. Their principal duty is to leave a smooth surface regardless of its flatness. Try planes are the longest of the group. Their length leaves a flat surface. Fore planes are the roughing planes. The fore plane's traditional 16" length is a convenient size for rough use.

Which one is the jointer again? Obviously the longest plane has the advantage when straightening an edge, but of the three, the widest may be the best choice, for it has advantages when edge planing thick stock.

Stanley named the #78 (left) a duplex fillister (whatever that means). It has many of the features of the wooden fillister at right except the one feature that makes it effective for creating fillisters. Can you tell what that is? Stanley's #78 is really a fenced rabbet.

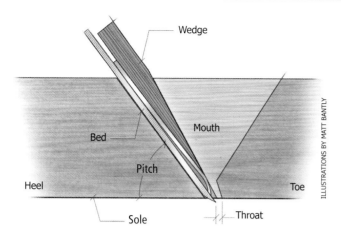

Wedge

Bed

Mouth

Pitch

Heel

Toe

Sole

Throat

ILLUSTRATIONS BY MATT BANTLY

Anatomy of a wooden plane

The degree of blade curvature varies: smoothers (left) have the least, fore planes (center) the most. As a side benefit, the curved blades eliminate the necessity for lateral-adjustment mechanisms. At right is a try plane.

Smoothers' mouths must be tight; as tight as possible to leave a truly smooth surface. Similarly, smoothers benefit from higher blade pitches. Fore planes may have wide-open mouths. Tear-out is limited by working at some angle across the grain. Try planes need a moderately tight mouth to work with the grain when needed. If a try plane's mouth was as tight as a smoother's it would work much too slowly.

Fitting Planes

The fitting planes are specifically designed to prepare square features for joints. The fitting plane category includes the dado, rabbet, "match" planes (which make tongue-and-groove joints), fillister, plow, router and the "glewing" jointer, which is often mistakenly placed with the leveling planes.

One needn't have all of these planes initially, though such a set would have been fairly typical in a professional cabinetshop in the 18th century. A com-

mon wide skew rabbet can be used with a batten or applied fence to produce both rabbets and fillets of different sizes. Only buy a jointer if you need to glue up panels, otherwise a try plane can work your edges straight. Plows, dados and match planes work quickly and efficiently, and should be on the top of your tool wish list. Once sharpened and tuned correctly, you'll find little use for your electric router.

The blades of all fitting planes are always ground to form a perfectly straight edge. The "gutters" Moxon spoke of are not a problem with these tools because fitting planes are never called upon to work a surface broader than the width of their blades. In every case, except the jointer, a fitting plane benefits from a wide mouth. This allows the user to waste away wood fast. A flawless surface finish is never important because, by definition, the surface created is a joint that will be covered up. The "glewing" jointer is

an exception to this last rule. Its fine mouth facilitates the creation of lightly sprung match joints and very straight edges. Also, an edge with tear-out may blemish the face after the joint is glued.

Fitting planes designed to work perpendicular to the grain typically have skewed blades. This is a distinct advantage for this type of work. When working with the grain, the skewed blade pushes the plane sideways. This can be advantageous when guiding the plane along a batten, or banking the tool against a pre-established fillet. But it's a distinct disadvantage when establishing a feature freehand.

Ornamentation Planes

Ornamentation planes produce mouldings. A seemingly infinite variety of ornamentation planes exist.

Simple moulders are often called hollows and rounds, each named for the shape of the plane's sole, not the moulding it produces.

When making a moulding, one often needs to remove a great deal of material from a long length of stock. Naturally we prefer to do this quickly, and

Shown from left are a set of four dado planes, three skew rabbets, a pair of side rabbets, two pairs of match planes for different size stock, moving fillister, specialty drawer bottom plow, wedged arm plow, old widow's tooth router (uses plow plane irons) and a 30" jointer plane behind them all.

A skew rabbet plane (top) can work across the grain or with it. The square rabbet plane (bottom) is easier to freehand.

Complex moulders produce shapes with complex curves or multiple features; simple moulders produce a single, fillet-less, convex or concave arc.

Here is a half set of round planes.

Here is a half set of hollow planes.

Technically, beads and sash planes (as shown here) are complex moulding planes, but they are rarely categorized as such.

that means a sharp iron and an open mouth. But the decorative nature of the moulding requires a tight mouth for a smooth finished surface. So should a moulding plane have an open mouth for fast work, or a tight mouth for a smooth finish? We can't have both. Unfortunately, I don't know the answer.

In Michael Dunbar's excellent book, *Restoring, Tuning, and Using Classic Woodworking Tools* he recommends purchasing hollow and round planes in matched pairs. I've never come across a technical reason for this practice. It suggests some functional requirement (like making a joint) that should theoretically never exist within the category of ornamentation planes. Maybe Dunbar was thinking of using hollows and rounds for rule joints? Until we figure this out, I recommend sticking with Mercer and buying or making any

shape you think will be helpful and forgetting about looking only for matching sets. It's also a lesson to beware of arbitrary requirements.

Back Where We Began

Mercer's categories are the starting place I promised. Mercer saw the arts and mysteries in the commonality of design and function. That enabled him to solve the problems he faced in identifying unusual planes.

But it helps us precisely the same way: One needn't consult an expert to learn how to tune or use an unfamiliar plane. Use the design (including length and other physical characteristics) to help you place the plane into its proper functional category and name. Once properly identified, you will instantly know how the iron should be sharpened and how tight the mouth should be.

Likewise, by determining what function you require, (such as surface leveling, making rabbets, dados, grooves, mouldings etc.) you can select the design of the plane you need, regardless of what the manufacturer calls it. This way, you can determine if a skewed iron or tight mouth really is a benefit for your work. Unfortunately, you can't trust the manufacturer to always know such things.

Mercer's categories are a starting place, but also an inevitable destination. See, there's much more to Mercer's categories than just cataloging the tools in a collection, or tuning and using planes. Implied but never discussed is the notion that each plane fits into only a single category and has but a single name. So naming each plane correctly is an important first step. Recognizing that a plane can only have one true name is the next.

restoring a handplane

BY RICK PETERS

A diamond in the rough. That's how I view every old tool I pick up at an auction or a yard sale. And the old, rusty Stanley No. 5$^{1}/_{2}$ that I bought recently for $4 is no exception. Before the auction, I examined the plane just like a diamond merchant would when buying a rough stone — I looked for flaws. I made sure all the parts were there, that castings were intact, and rust was only surface deep.

With my new treasure in hand, I headed for the shop to restore it. Why bother you might ask? Why not purchase a new plane? Three reasons. First, you can't buy a quality hand plane for four bucks. Second, the old adage "they don't make 'em like they used to" is true; it's virtually impossible to find castings as nice —and of such high quality as these old planes. And third, I really enjoy restoring one of these old beauties. There's tremendous satisfaction gained from giving a fine, old tool a new life.

There are three main tasks involved with restoring a hand plane: disassembly and cleaning, reshaping parts for optimum performance and re-assembly and adjustment.

Disassembly and Cleaning

The first thing to do to your old plane is disassemble it. Take the time to familiarize yourself with the parts and learn their correct names (see the illustration for the parts to most planes). Start by lifting the thumb lever and sliding off the lever cap. Remove the plane iron and chip breaker, unscrew the frog, and remove the front knob and handle.

Now give all the parts a mineral spirits bath and a good scrubbing with an old toothbrush. In many cases, this removes the surface rust along with caked-on dirt and grime. Set the parts on a clean rag to dry overnight.

With your squeaky-clean plane parts in hand, the next step is to remove any remaining rust on the parts. If the rust is light, you can rub it off with steel wool or a rust-erasing abrasive product called Wonderbar™. If the rust is stubborn, consider using the miracle of electrolysis. (See the story on p.80.)

Reshaping Parts

Although it has a funny name, the frog is one of the most important parts of the plane. It holds the plane iron firmly at the proper angle, while at the same time allowing you to adjust the depth of cut and the position of the iron. It's a shame the frog is often overlooked when restoring a plane; a poorly tuned frog is the leading cause of blade chatter.

For a frog to do its job well, it's imperative that its mating surfaces—the bottom where it contacts the sole, and the sloped face that holds the plane iron—be absolutely flat and square. For the sloped face, I use a diamond hone or a small stone and gently rub it on the surface. Check for flatness often with a straightedge. Because the bottom surface usually requires more work, I use a fine file. Here again, go slowly and check often.

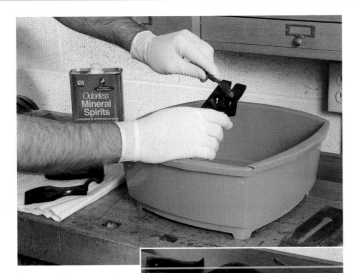

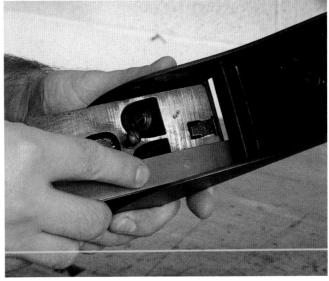

Remove old grease and grime by scrubbing all the plane parts with an old toothbrush and mineral spirits (top). Steel wool, abrasive pads or a Wonderbar (shown here) all work well to strip off surface rust.

To ensure solid contact between the frog and the blade, use a diamond hone (shown) or a small file to flatten the top surface.

With both surfaces flat and square, reattach the frog to the body with the screws you removed earlier. (Don't worry about positioning now, we'll fine tune this later in final adjustments.)

I can't tell you how many times I've seen a woodworker spin a depth adjustment knob, first one way, and then the other when trying to fine-tune the depth of cut. It doesn't have to be that way. All you need to do is remove the slack in the Y-shaped yoke that accepts the depth adjustment knob. The only thing to be careful about here is applying too much pressure as you remove slack. The yoke is cast, so it'll only bend so far without breaking. I've found steady pressure from a clamp or bench vise works best. Don't strike the arms of the yoke with a mallet unless you've got a replacement handy.

There's not much to do on the lateral adjustment lever; check for burrs on the cam and smooth any you find with a fine file or piece of emery cloth.

The sole of the plane, on the other hand, usually requires quite a bit of work—and it's worth it. Next to a solid frog and a sharp iron, the flatness of the sole will have a great impact on how well your plane performs. The

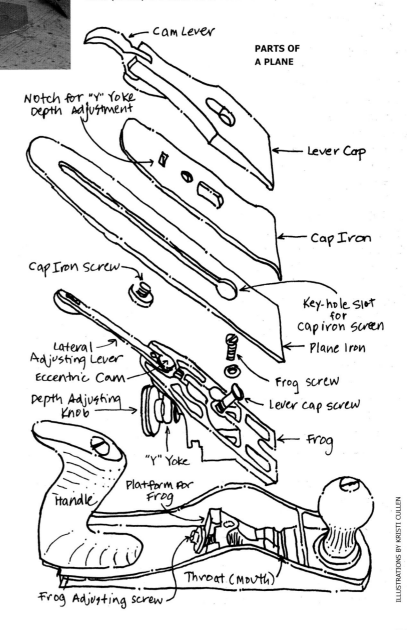

PARTS OF A PLANE

Cam Lever

Notch for "Y" Yoke Depth Adjustment

Lever Cap

Cap Iron

Cap Iron Screw

Key-hole Slot for Cap iron screw

Plane Iron

Lateral Adjusting Lever

Eccentric Cam

Frog screw

Lever cap screw

Depth Adjusting Knob

Frog

"Y" Yoke

Platform for Frog

Handle

Throat (Mouth)

Frog Adjusting screw

ILLUSTRATIONS BY KRISTI CULLEN

easiest way to check a sole for flatness is with a straightedge. I've found that holding the plane up against a bright light will show any dips or high spots the best. It's also important to check the sole for twist. For this, I use winding sticks and sight down the length of the plane.

To flatten a sole, I affix a couple sheets of silicone carbide sandpaper to a flat surface with spray adhesive. For years I used the bed of my jointer. But a while back I picked up a piece of replacement glass for a jalousie window at the local hardware store—it's 4" wide, 30" long and $1/4$" thick. What's really nice about jalousie glass is the edges are rounded over for safety. I usually start with 80-grit and work my way up to 220-grit.

Before you begin, however, it's paramount that you re-install the iron, chip breaker and lever cap. Why? An installed blade puts tension on the sole. If you flatten it without this tension, and then install the iron, it won't be flat. Just make sure to back off the iron $1/8$" or so before rubbing the sole on the silicon carbide paper. Use firm, steady strokes and flip the plane end-for-end occasion-ally to ensure even pressure over the entire length and width of the sole.

Check the sole often for progress. Although purists will flatten the entire sole, the only parts where it's critical that it be flat are the toe, heel and front of throat.

A side effect of flattening the sole is it often changes the shape of the throat opening. Take the time to check to make sure the throat is straight and square to the sides of the plane. A small engineer's square works great for this. If necessary, use a small file to square things up.

Just like the lateral adjustment, the lever cap doesn't require much attention. Check for smooth operation and a positive lock. Remove any burrs with emery cloth and lubricate the hinge with a drop of light machine oil.

I mentioned earlier that an un-tuned frog is one of the main causes of blade chatter. Another culprit of this pesky problem is a sloppy cap iron. The job of the cap iron is twofold. First, it adds rigidity to the plane and prevents it

removing rust with electrolysis

I was surfin' the web recently and came across a great way to remove rust—using electrolysis. In a nutshell, electrolysis passes a small electrical current from a battery charger through a rusty tool that's submerged in an electrolyte solution. An exchange of ions takes place resulting in rust removal. Magic? I think not—just simple science. Here's how easy it is to do.

First, mix up an electrolyte solution (one tablespoon of baking soda per gallon of water) in a non-conductive, plastic container. Then, remove anything that's not metal from the tool. Next, clean the tool in warm sudsy water to remove any oil or grease. Now clamp the positive (red) lead of a 2-amp battery charger to the anode—this is just any large, flat piece of steel (like a kitchen pan lid)—stainless steel works best as it erodes slowly. And connect the negative (black) lead to the rusty tool.

At this point you're ready to fire up your science experiment. Set the rusty tool and anode in the electrolyte solution so they're a couple inches apart. Make sure the tool is completely submerged and that the red clip that's attached to the anode is above the solution (this will prevent it from corroding). Turn on the battery charger and check that it's not drawing more current than it's rated for (this is where a built-in ammeter is indispensable). If it is drawing too much, or not enough current, simply move the tool father away or closer to the anode. (Safety note: make all adjustments with the charger unplugged!) You can tell it's working when you start to see bubbles forming on the surface of the tool.

The average tool will de-rust in about two hours, resulting in some fairly nasty-looking electrolyte. Turn off the charger, slip on some rubber gloves to remove the tool, and unfasten the clips. You'll notice a lot of black crud on the tool. The quickest and easiest way to remove this is with a non-metallic abrasive pad. Just scrub the surface with a pad dipped in warm, soapy water. If the rust is gone, you're done. If not, repeat the process until it is. A note of caution here. Prolonged electrolysis can remove the japanning (the black paint) on a tool—check the tool often and stop as soon as the rust is removed.

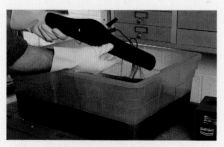
A battery charger, some baking soda electrolyte and a scrap metal anode are all it takes to remove heavy rust with the power of science.

For a more in-depth discussion of removing rust with electrolysis, key in this URL on your computer: http://www.galootcentral.com/modules.php?name=Web_Links&l_op=viewlink&cid=48.

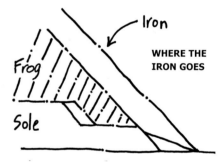
WHERE THE IRON GOES

A small metal file works well to clean up the area where the frog meets the sole.

Don't put up with a sloppy yoke—remove the slack by applying gentle pressure to the yoke with a C-clamp.

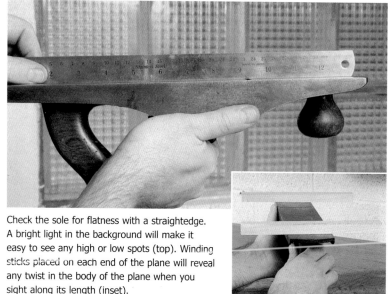

Check the sole for flatness with a straightedge. A bright light in the background will make it easy to see any high or low spots (top). Winding sticks placed on each end of the plane will reveal any twist in the body of the plane when you sight along its length (inset).

The toe, heel and front of the throat (shown) are the critical areas where the sole of the plane must be flat (near right).

To support the blade and prevent chips from jamming between the cap iron and blade, hone a bevel on the front edge of the cap iron (far right).

from flexing during use. Second, the slight hump at its business end serves as a tiny wedge to break chips as the iron cuts into the wood. Neither of these jobs can be done properly if the cap iron doesn't come in full contact with the entire edge of the plane iron. To ensure this contact, flatten the front edge on a stone as shown. I also like to polish the chip breaker portion of the cap iron so chips will slide smoothly on and off of it.

Finally, you can turn your attention to the handle. If the screw bottoms out before the handle is tight, grind 1/8" off the screw. For stripped screws, re-tap at the next larger size. On handles that are cracked, you can fix them with epoxy, or make a new one. To make a new handle, use the old handle as a template. It's best to drill the hole for the handle screw before shaping the handle. Then cut out the shape, then

smooth and sand the handle to fit your hand.

Even if there's nothing wrong with the handle (or front knob), I always suggest shaping them to fit your hand. The factory-made handle is designed to fit the masses, not your hand. You'd be surprised how much nicer a custom-fit handle feels.

Re-assembly and Adjustments

Now that we've tuned all the individual parts, it's time to tune them all together much like a symphony orchestra does before a performance.

Before you attach the cap iron to the iron, the iron needs to be sharpened. I start by hollow grinding the iron. Then flatten the back and hone a bevel on a waterstone.

Position the cap iron on the sharpened iron square to the front edge

and set back about 1/16". Slip this assembly onto the frog, and lock it in place with the lever cap. Adjust the depth of cut and the lateral adjustment lever as necessary.

Although you re-attached the frog before flattening the sole, it still needs to be fine-tuned to fully support the blade. Start by loosening the frog screws so they're friction-tight. Then use the frog adjustment screw to slide the frog into perfect alignment with the sole at the throat opening, see the illustration on the previous page. (You'll most likely need to remove the handle to get to this screw.)

Now for the test. Secure a scrap of wood in your bench vise and take a few passes with the plane. Ahh... the joy of rescuing a fine old tool. And the sweet sound it makes as it glides over the wood, shearing off paper-thin, crisp shavings.

16

**HARDLY OBSOLETE, THESE TOOLS ARE
CAPABLE OF YOUR FINEST WORK.**

traditional wooden planes

BY DON MCCONNELL

Wooden planes once were made for a dizzying array of woodworking operations, from dimensioning rough stock to cutting intricate joinery. Though there are only a few contemporary makers of wooden planes these days, vintage planes are still widely (and usually inexpensively) available at flea markets, garage sales and antique stores.

My heart sank as my master pointed to a 22"-long wooden try plane he suggested I use until I filled out my personal kit of tools. I was training as an apprentice at The Ohio Village, a "living history" site where visitors experience life in a typical 1860s Ohio town. Though I was intrigued by the wooden stock planes, the metal Bailey/Stanley-style planes were in regular use in the shop, and I felt I was going to be at a disadvantage using the more primitive wooden ones.

Deciding to make the best of it, and with my master's guidance, I ground and sharpened the iron (checking its fit to the bed, the cap iron and the wedge), and I jointed the sole. The mouth opening was pretty tight, so we decided to use it for a while before making a decision on re-mouthing it.

After some instruction on how to adjust and set the iron, as well as learning where to put my hands for face- and edge-planing, I took my first shavings with it.

To my relief and surprise it worked quite well. Further, I found that I liked the feel of the wood-on-wood action, the unique sound and the authority with which it took shavings the full length of the board. As a bonus, I found wooden planes less tiring to use during long planing sessions. I was hooked.

Clearly, my assessment of wooden planes had been off the mark. And the more I studied and used them (including making some for myself), the more convinced I became that their apparent simplicity belied a well-developed and sophisticated design, one that embodied the woodworking lore of generations of woodworkers, including specialized plane-makers from about 1650 on.

Historic evidence for the range and quality of work these planes can perform is found in the extraordinarily fine furniture made during the 18th century – furniture that is commonly accepted to be the zenith of American furniture-making.

Wooden planes were involved in the surfacing, thicknessing and dimensioning of nearly every element of that furniture. Indeed, the achievements of the cabinetmakers of that period were made possible, in part, by similar levels of craftsmanship the plane-makers of that century exhibited.

In this chapter I hope to give you a broader appreciation of these tools and to provide some clues regarding the desirable features and characteristics to look for in older planes.

The Wood of Choice

Except for some early New England plane-makers who used yellow birch for a time, customarily, plane-makers have chosen beech. While beech is not a "perfect" wood for making planes, it combines a number of characteristics that make it the best overall choice for use in plane-making.

It is reasonably hard and dense, giving it decent strength and wear resistance. Yet it is relatively easy to shape compared to sugar maple, for example, rendering it more workable for day-to-day work by plane-makers. It is small-pored, not prone to splintering and has a relatively smooth, polished surface. Despite an unfortunate tendency to check while drying, it is not particularly

Cutter   Wedge

Adjusting a wooden plane's cutter isn't mysterious. To advance the cutter for a deeper cut, simply give it a light tap. Then, a quick hammer tap to the wedge will lock in your adjustment.

To make a lighter cut, tap the heel of the plane with your mallet and then tap the wedge. Some planes have a "strike button" on the top of the stock in front of the blade. You also can tap the strike to reduce the cut.

83

A properly tuned wooden plane is a joy to use. Nearly every surface of traditional 18th-century furniture was shaped or smoothed with a wooden plane.

Rings not parallel to sole

Nearly parallel to sole

Traditional wooden planes are made from quartersawn beech with the plain-sawn side acting as the sole, as seen at right. However, some exceptions do occasionally surface. In the compass plane at left, the plain-sawn side is not parallel to the sole.

"rivable," thus it resists complete failure. Also, beech is readily available in an appropriate form and size for plane-making, so it is relatively economical.

Other woods – such as apple, boxwood and rosewood – have some features suitable for making planes and sometimes were chosen for use in special planes. But none of these woods had the combination of characteristics and availability to unseat beech as the customary wood of choice.

In addition to choosing beech, the best plane-makers exhibited their skill in the way they made use of it. For example, they selected straight-grained material that was relatively defect-free. This helped minimize any tendency of the tool to bow or distort through environmental changes.

Additionally, they almost invariably used quarter-sawn beech – orienting it so the annual rings of the stock were roughly parallel with the sole of the plane. One outcome of this is that the plane's body (commonly referred to as the stock) is much less likely to "cast," or go out of square, through seasonal changes.

Another result of the use of quarter-sawn stock in this orientation was that the overall dimensional movement of the stock was minimized. This brought about much less distortion of the plane's bed over time.

This orientation also resulted in a "plain-sawn," or tangential, surface serving as the sole of the plane. I believe this was done because plain-sawn surfaces are more resistant to wear. In my experience planing beech I have noticed that the plain-sawn surfaces are noticeably more recalcitrant – though I don't have technical data to back this up. Also, plane-makers used the "sap-side" surface as the sole. Some writers have claimed this surface was more wear-resistant than the "heart-side" surface, but I haven't seen any formal documentation of this.

Finally, if there was any noticeable grain run-out in the plane blank, plane-makers customarily oriented the toe and heel of the plane so that any downward inclination of the grain was

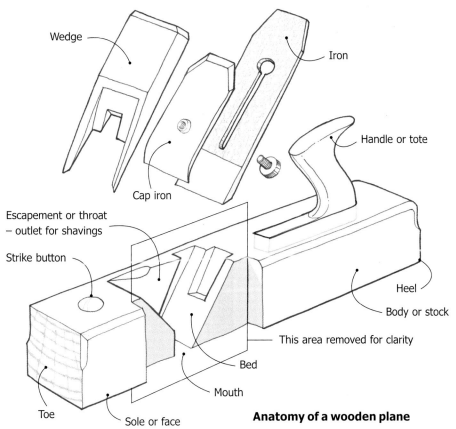

Wedge

Iron

Handle or tote

Cap iron

Escapement or throat
– outlet for shavings

Strike button

Heel

Body or stock

This area removed for clarity

Bed

Mouth

Toe

Sole or face

Anatomy of a wooden plane

ILLUSTRATION BY MATT BANTLY

toward the heel. Thus, any abrasion of the sole would tend to smooth the grain rather than lift and roughen it.

Adjusting the Cutter

There are several other aspects of traditional wooden planes that exhibit the same sense of refinement as the stock. But I thought it might be more useful to turn our attention to the perception that setting and adjusting the irons seems primitive and imprecise. This, in turn, gives rise to a common suspicion that wooden planes aren't intended for fine work.

While the means of adjustment seem mysterious, once understood they are both simple and capable of increasing the control and precision. Adjusting the plane can be a bit of an acquired skill, but in experienced hands, a wooden plane is capable of very fine work.

With wooden planes, it's important that the wedge, which secures the iron in the stock, fits well. If properly fit, this wedge will hold the iron with a surprisingly light tap of a mallet or hammer. (It's really best to watch someone with experience to get a clear idea of the amount of force involved.) This avoids distorting the plane stock, minimizes the chance of splitting the abutment cheeks and allows for more controlled adjustment.

Adjusting the iron is achieved through the simple physics of inertia. If you need to advance the set of the iron to take a deeper cut, use a hammer to tap the upper end of the iron. It then moves down relative to the stock.

If you wish to back off the set of the iron, you have a couple of choices. You can tap either the heel of the plane or the upper surface at the front of the plane (probably best if there is a "strike button," as shown in the illustration above) with a mallet.

Loosening the iron for sharpening is accomplished with somewhat sharper mallet raps in the same locations.

Lateral adjustment is a simple matter of tapping the iron sideways as necessary. In each case, because the iron and wedge are both tapered along their lengths, you need to reset the wedge with another light tap before checking the set and putting the plane to use.

Perfectly Simple

Perhaps it's fitting that these traditional wooden planes exhibit a certain elegance of design we normally think of as a modern industrial-design sensibility – a sensibility that stresses a straightforward and functional use of appropriate materials.

It's an elegance summed up by Antoine de Saint-Exupery (who was not only an aviator and author, but also an aircraft designer in the early 20th century): "A designer knows he has achieved perfection not when there is nothing left to add, but when there is nothing left to take away."

There are some long-term issues that arise because the stocks of these planes are wood, such as wear and dimensional changes caused by changes in environment. Also, because of the taper of the irons and the configuration of the throat of the escapement, the mouth opens as the iron gets shorter as it's sharpened and the sole is jointed.

While wearing of the sole is something of a reality, its significance is often exaggerated. Soles need to be jointed more often because of frequent changes in environment – not because of wear.

In any event, after the sole of the tool has been jointed many times, the mouth will open enough to degrade the performance of the plane. But that can be remedied with a wooden patch using simple woodworking skills.

One of the best reasons to consider using wooden planes is the wide variety of specialized planes available that can be useful for virtually any woodworking operation you can imagine. While they are not as easy to find as they once were, they continue to reappear for sale and can be very affordable.

85

17

EVEN IF YOU OWN A POWERED JOINTER, YOU CAN GET A SUPERIOR FIT WITH A LONG HAND PLANE.

edge jointing by hand

BY DON MCCONNELL

I imagine a good percentage of you are wondering why in the world you should learn to joint a board's edge with a hand plane. After all, most woodworkers own a machine jointer and have gotten by without this hand skill.

However, having jointed edges by both hand and machine, I've found it requires a good deal of care to tune

a machine jointer for precision edge-jointing. And it's almost always possible to improve the jointed edge by planing it by hand – even those edges from well-maintained machines.

Additionally, there are circumstances where a hand plane is the only way to achieve a true edge. A particularly long or heavy board can be too cumbersome to pass over a machine jointer. In this

Learning how to joint a board by hand pays great dividends when you need a perfect fit or you are dealing with boards that are too long for your powered jointer. With a little practice, almost anyone can do it.

instance, the most effective method would be to hold the board stationary and shoot the edge by hand – if you have the planes and you know how to use them.

Some of you may already know the value of this skill, but you are not sure how to proceed and think it might be a bit too tricky to learn this technique. Or you may have already taken a stab at it and met with some frustration.

This chapter will show you an approach to edge-jointing by hand that is clear and basic enough to help anyone with average hand-eye coordination to begin mastering this fundamental skill. Specifically, the focus will be on the planes and edge-planing techniques involved, as I believe this to be the keystone to edge-jointing by hand.

Getting Straight and Square

At its most basic level, this is the goal when shooting the edges of boards: Create two surfaces that will mate well enough so the glue will create a joint that will not fail under normal circumstances.

It's not accidental that the effort to gain this desirable proximity in edge-jointing involves the quest for straight, square edges. Rather, it flows directly from the critical functional characteristic of the planes woodworkers have used for millennia: The cutting action of the plane iron is regulated by the flat sole of the plane that's in contact with the surface of the wood.

If it were possible for the cutting edge to lie at the same height as the flat sole of the plane, every bench plane would cut in a straight line. However, things are not that simple. Because the cutting edge projects below the sole to take a shaving, bench planes tend to cut in a shallow, concave arc.

Many factors enter into the magnitude of this arc, but it's roughly a function of the length of the plane and the depth of the iron. The shorter the plane and deeper the cut, the more pronounced the arc. Conversely, the longer the plane and finer the set of the iron, the more closely its cutting action will approximate a straight line.

Even if you don't have a jack on your bench for supporting long boards, you can use handscrews. Clamp one end in your face vise and the other end in handscrews that you rest on your benchtop.

That's why longer bench planes (20" to 24" try planes, 26" to 30" jointers) are typically used for final truing of surfaces and edges. Their length, in combination with irons set to take a light shaving, regulates the cutting action to closely approximate a straight line.

Properly Applied Pressure

Throughout history, woodworkers have developed the following simple strategy for taking advantage of the cutting characteristics of these long hand planes.

The technique involves concentrating downward pressure on the toe of the plane as the cut commences and transferring that downward pressure toward the heel of the plane as the cut continues. The pressure is concentrated toward the heel as the cut ends. This helps ensure that the weight of the plane hanging off either end of the board doesn't interfere with the sole maintaining uniform contact with the material.

When edge-jointing, the principle of maintaining uniform contact between the sole of the plane and the edge is sometimes lost sight of. Often that's because some people think the plane needs to be tipped, laterally left or right, to correct an edge that is out of square. The unwanted consequence of this tipping is that it tends to defeat the self-regulating nature of the plane, causing your edge to have several

surfaces, or facets, none of which are straight or square.

To plane straight edges, I recommend taking advantage of the inherent control of the plane by maintaining that uniform contact. By shifting your hand pressure as I describe in the photos on the next page, you get a great deal of control, especially on boards that are $3/4$" thick or more. (For thinner stock, you can use an appliance known as a shooting board to great advantage.)

Surprisingly, when using this technique to shoot an edge with my try plane, if a straightedge indicates that the plane has left it very slightly hollow in the middle of the board I take it as a sign that the plane is functioning properly and my technique is sound. Though this idea may seem at first at odds with the purpose of edge jointing, that largely proves not to be the case. We'll get back to this point in just a moment.

Fix a Crooked Edge

First let's deal with the question of how to correct an edge that is out of square if we're not going to tip the plane laterally. The key is using a plane iron with a cutting edge that is slightly cambered. In other words, the cutting edge has a slight convexity.

A slightly cambered iron (only a few thousandths of camber is necessary) will take a slightly thicker shaving where the curvature is at its maximum, namely the middle of the cutting edge.

When preparing a board for edge-jointing, I typically take a couple of strokes in the middle of the edge – starting and stopping before the ends. This slightly hollow edge is actually easier to put the final edge on.

We take advantage of this feature to correct an edge that is out of square by shifting the plane sideways (but keeping the sole in contact with the surface of the edge) so that the middle of the cutting edge is taking a heavier shaving at the high side – or arris. This allows you to bring an edge into square one shaving at a time.

Controlling the lateral position of the plane to correct for square is the main aspect of edge planing that differs from face planing. Rather than gripping across the top of the stock of a wooden plane, or the knob of a Bailey/Stanley plane, place your thumb on the top of the plane and curl your fingers under to grip the sole of the plane (as shown in the photo above).

This technique allows you to use your fingers as a fence to control and influence the lateral position of the plane, while still using your thumb for downward pressure at the beginning of the stroke.

When edge-jointing, it's important to pay attention to your body mechanics. At the beginning of your pass, apply considerable pressure to the toe (front) of the jointer plane and push forward with your other hand.

In the middle of the pass, the pressure should be equal fore and aft on the plane's body. At the end of the pass, as seen here, all of your downward pressure should be applied to the heel of the tool.

Use your fingers as a fence when edge-jointing. With your hand wrapped around the plane as shown, you can keep the plane registered on the edge and positioned laterally where you want the cut to occur.

A slight hollow in the middle is preferable. A hump in the middle of the board will likely result in joint failure.

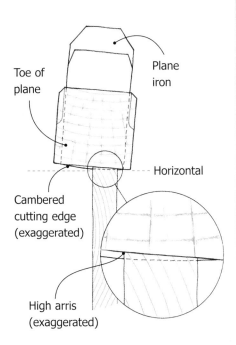

Toe of plane

Plane iron

Horizontal

Cambered cutting edge (exaggerated)

High arris (exaggerated)

ILLUSTRATION BY MATT BANTLY

The final test is to lay the board's mate on the edge you just planed. The top board should not pivot easily or rock on the board. If it does, you have a convex edge that needs to be removed.

After a pass or two, check your edge to see if it is square to the faces of the board. You can use the cambered iron of your plane to adjust an edge that is out of square, as shown in the illustration at left.

Begin With a Slightly Hollow Edge

Edge-jointing generally takes place after at least one face of a board has been trued up. It's a good idea to mark the true face to ensure it is consistently used as the reference surface when checking the edge for square.

If an edge is in the rough or has a significant fault, a jack plane with a significantly cambered cutting edge can be used at the outset. A heavier shaving and more pronounced camber allow it to remove saw marks and major faults quickly. This will need to be followed up with a try plane or jointer, depending on the length of the edge.

In either case, the approach is the same. In my experience, it's desirable to remove any convex bow by beginning and ending a couple of strokes short of each end. Next, full-length strokes can be taken, following the basic techniques already described, continuing until full-length shavings are produced. This can be followed by, or combined with, manipulating the lateral position of the

plane to square the edge up. Finish by taking one full-length shaving while keeping the plane centered on the edge.

When both edges are to your satisfaction, one edge can be offered up to the other to test the fit. If it rocks, swivels in the middle or if the reference faces don't create a flat panel, adjustments will need to be made.

On shorter pieces, the slow arc of the cut of the longer try plane or jointer so closely approximates a straight line that it is possible to directly achieve a "perfect" fit. In fact, woodworkers have traditionally made use of the rapid adhesion of hot hide glue to do "rubbed joints" in these circumstances. In other words, the two pieces were rubbed together momentarily until the hide glue began to congeal and grab, eliminating the need for any clamps. I've successfully done this with aliphatic resin glue, but I feel safer using at least one clamp.

On longer pieces, woodworkers traditionally have made use of the slight concave arc produced by their planes to execute a "sprung joint." The ratio-

nale for leaving this slight hollow in the middle of the joint (to be pulled together with clamps) rests on the observation that the ends are subject to more stress through dimensional changes because of the more rapid moisture movement in the exposed end grain at the ends.

This rationale seems to have some merit, and generations of woodworkers have successfully used sprung joints. However, I am unaware of any research testing this rationale and it seems safest to minimize the clamping pressure required to pull any joint closed.

Edge-jointing by hand is not as difficult or mysterious as many might believe. While it takes some experience to feel comfortable with it, and every situation is slightly different, anyone can have early success at this task by making use of the control inherent in their planes.

TUNE UP A SMOOTHING PLANE AND YOU WILL GREATLY REDUCE THE AMOUNT OF SANDING YOU DO. HERE'S HOW TO SELECT, FINE-TUNE AND USE THIS OFT-NEGLECTED TRADITIONAL TOOL.

18

using a smoothing plane

BY CHRISTOPHER SCHWARZ

In the days before sandpaper was common, fine furniture was prepared for finishing using planes, scrapers and little else.

Smoothing wood surfaces with a handplane is a skill, and doing it well takes practice. But the rewards are substantial. With a well-tuned smoothing plane, you can quickly take a piece of flattened wood to a ready-to-finish state. In fact, I find that in many situations, using a smoothing plane can be faster than using a modern random-orbit sander.

Also, surfaces that have been smoothed are different than surfaces that have been sanded. The wood fibers have been sheared cleanly instead of abraded. So the wood looks – in my opinion – luminous after it has been smoothed.

And finally, smoothing is healthier. It's a mild upper-body workout, though nothing like running a 5K. But more important, smoothing is better for your lungs. You're not producing clouds of the unhealthy lung-clogging dust that power sanding kicks up.

But before you can start smoothing, there are three important hurdles: selecting the right plane, tuning your tool and learning the basic strokes.

Picking a Plane

For some, choosing a smoothing plane is like picking a computer operating system, spouse or a religion. It's per-

Smoothing planes – when set up and used properly – can eliminate a lot of sanding. Here's a tip for planing doors: Don't assemble the door and then plane it; you'll have to plane around corners and that's tricky. Instead, before assembly, plane the rails down so the stiles will be a little proud when the door is assembled. Then glue up the door and plane the stiles flush to the rails.

sonal, and people tend to get worked up and argumentative about it.

So let me say this: All good-quality smoothing planes can be tuned to handle most workaday smoothing tasks. Each kind of plane has its strengths and weaknesses; and in the end, you'll probably end up owning several smoothers.

But before we talk about the different varieties of smoothing planes, let's look at the factors that make smoothing planes work well.

A Well-bedded Iron: Without a doubt, the most important characteristic of any plane is that the iron be firmly fixed to the body of the plane

90

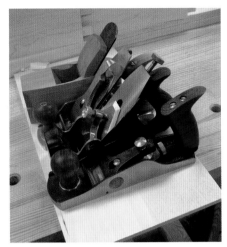

Here you can see the different angles that smoothing planes commonly come in: a low-angle, a Norris 47½° pitch, 50° and 55°. The higher the pitch, the better the performance on tough-to-plane woods (but the harder the tool is to push).

and not rock or vibrate in use (even the tiniest bit). If the iron isn't seated well, it's going to chatter.

The Angle of the Iron: Garden-variety Stanley smoothing planes have the iron bedded at a 45° angle to the work. This angle allows the plane to be pushed without too much effort and handles most straight-grained domestic woods without tearing out the grain. Some smoothing planes have irons bedded at 47½°, 50°, 55° or 60°. The higher angle makes the plane harder to push, but it increases the plane's performance on some tricky woods such as curly maple and situations where the grain is interlocked or wild. You'll get less tear-out with a high angle.

Other smoothing planes have an angle of attack that's lower: usually 37°. These low-angle smoothing planes work great on end grain, pretty well on straight-grained species and have mixed utility on the wild stuff. Sometimes a low-angle plane is the only plane that will work on a weird piece of wood. So they're good to have in your arsenal.

The Throat Size: This is a matter of some debate in the world of handplanes, but many woodworkers contend that a tight throat (the opening between the cutting edge and the plane's sole) is another key to reducing tear-

out. There are a lot of physics involved in the reason why. But the dime-store-novel explanation is that a tight throat keeps the wood fibers pressed down before they are sheared by the iron so tear-out is less likely to start and then progress along the grain. I've found that a tight throat seems to help sometimes; and other times it doesn't seem to make a difference at all. It depends on the wood.

For many of the planes on the market, the throat is adjustable so you can try it either way and decide for yourself.

There are basically four different kinds of smoothing planes available: wooden-bodied planes, Bailey-style planes, low-angle planes, and infill planes. See the sidebar on page 95 "Choosing a Smoothing Plane" for a discussion of the strengths and weaknesses of each type of plane.

Sharpening for Smoothing

Without a sharp iron, smoothing is impossible. You must learn to put a keen edge on your iron and shape the edge for smoothing.

For a basic lesson in sharpening, check out "Sharpening Plane Irons" on page 25. For a complete education on the topic, read Leonard Lee's *The Complete Guide to Sharpening* (The Taunton Press).

Unlike a chisel or the iron for a block plane, the cutting edge of the iron for smoothing planes needs to be shaped differently. With a chisel, you want a straight edge that's perfectly perpendicular to the sides. With a smoothing plane, you want the edge to have an ever-so-slight curve.

Here's why: If you smooth a piece of wood with a perfectly straight iron, the corners of the iron cut a small shelf in the wood. These are called "plane tracks," and they are undesirable. They feel like small ridges to your fingers and they can be noticeable after you finish your project.

To reduce or eliminate the plane tracks, I like to do two things to the plane's iron. First, I clip the corners of

All planes smooth wood to some degree, but not all planes are "smoothing planes." Smoothing planes – or smoothers as they are sometimes called – put the final finishing cuts on your work. Typically, they are 6½" to 9" long and 2¼" to 3¼" wide, according to R. A. Salaman's *Dictionary of Woodworking Tools* (Astragal).

In the common Stanley plane-numbering system the No. 2, No. 3 and No. 4 planes are considered smoothing planes. Wooden smoothing planes that have been made since 1700 are typically coffin shaped. Infill smoothing planes – which are based on Roman planes believe it or not – are usually the most expensive planes and are highly prized by collectors.

The Clifton No. 4 smoother is an excellent modern-day handplane.

the cutting edge. I usually do this on a belt sander or with a file. You only want to take off about 1/32" of the corner or so. And you want it to be a smooth curve – like the radius of the smallest roundover router bit you can imagine.

Then you need to sharpen the iron so it has a slightly cambered edge – so the iron actually scoops out the wood. The tooling marks left by an iron sharpened this way are far less noticeable.

Luckily, it's easier to sharpen an iron this way than it sounds, especially with a honing guide. As you sharpen your iron, most people start with a coarse grit, move up to a medium grit and finish on a fine grit.

At the coarse-grit stage, finish sharpening at that stone by moving your hands' downward pressure on the iron to one corner of the iron and then making about a dozen strokes. Then shift your pressure to the other corner for another dozen strokes. Sharpen at the medium and fine grits the same way. When you hold up the iron against a square, you should be able to see a curve or belly in the edge of just a couple thousandths of an inch.

Other Tune-Ups

With your iron in good shape, make sure your chipbreaker (if your plane has one) is seated firmly on the back of the iron. Place it so its leading edge is $1/32$" to $3/32$" from the cutting edge. Placing it further back allows you to tighten up the throat more on planes that have adjustable frogs.

In general, the rest of the tuning is much like you would tune any plane. For smoothing, the sole of the plane should be as flat as you can make it. I flatten vintage plane soles on #120-grit sandpaper stuck to a flat piece of granite. Then I finish up on #220 grit.

The iron needs to fit perfectly on the plane and be secured as tightly as possible. For metal planes, this might involve tuning your frog: Flatten the face that contacts the iron, remove any burrs and make sure the frog attaches securely to the plane body.

With wooden planes and infills, this usually involves filing the wooden bed of the tool.

Then turn your attention to the device that holds the iron in place. On wooden planes, this is a wedge that might require a little sanding to seat just right. For infills and metal planes, the lever cap must be screwed down tightly.

Now set your iron square to the sole. For planes with adjusters, set the iron so it projects a little from the sole. Turn the plane upside down and look down the sole from the front of the plane. Adjust the iron until it projects evenly from the sole, then retract the iron. Now advance the iron until it takes the

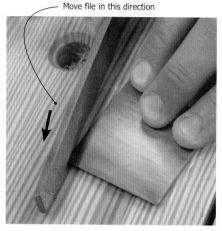
Move file in this direction

To avoid "plane tracks," clip the corners of your iron by filing a tight radius on the corners of your cutting edge.

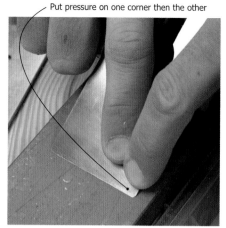
Put pressure on one corner then the other

To sharpen an iron for smoothing, work the corners on your sharpening stones. This will give your cutting edge a bit of a camber – which is perfect for smoothing.

lightest cut possible. Your wood should already be true – either from machining or earlier planing. Final smoothing removes just a few thousandths of an inch of wood.

A Stop Before you Start

The boards you plane need to be fixed on your bench so you can smooth them quickly. Some woodworkers use bench dogs and a tail vise equipped with a dog to secure the wood. This works, but it's a lot of trouble and should be reserved for times when your other efforts fail.

In my opinion, the best way to keep your boards in one place during planing is to use a "planing stop." This simple jig is a piece of hardwood that's $7/16$" thick, about 2" wide and as long as your bench is deep. My planing stop has a couple dowels screwed to it that allow

the whole thing to be slipped into two dog holes on my bench (see the photo on p.93).

Place the far edge of the wood to be planed against the stop. The downward and forward pressure of your plane will keep most work pieces in place against the stop. Very narrow wood or irregular shapes require some thought to clamp. This little jig works for about 90 percent of my needs.

One more thing you should consider as you set up your area for planing: A lower benchtop height (34") is better for planing than a higher bench (36" or higher). With a lower bench you can use your weight to hold the plane against the work instead of relying mostly on your arms. Old-time benches were 28" off the floor. People were shorter then, but you get the idea.

For smoothing work, position your chipbreaker between $1/32$" to $3/32$" from the cutting edge.

Take a look at the throat on this Clark & Williams coffin smoother. See it? Neither can we. This is a tight mouth.

Planing stop slips into dog holes in bench

A shop-made planing stop is a simple and effective way to hold your work for smoothing (left). The force you use to push your plane also holds your work down and against the stop (above).

Reading the Grain and Actually Planing

It's almost always best to plane with the grain. The illustrations at right show you what I mean better than words ever could.

Now rub some wax on the sole of your plane. I use squares of canning wax that I buy from the supermarket. It's cheap and effective. The wax cuts down on the effort required from your arms. Apply the wax again after a dozen or so planing strokes.

Grip the plane. Many smoothing planes require a three-finger grip on the rear handle. If your four fingers feel jammed in there, remove your index finger and wrap it on top of the iron.

The body mechanics you use when smoothing are the same as when you use a jack plane or other bench plane. Begin with the toe of the plane (the part below the front knob) on the wood with most of the downward force on that knob.

Start moving the plane forward. As you begin cutting, shift the downward pressure so it's evenly distributed between the front knob and rear handle (called the tote). At the end of the cut, shift your pressure to the rear handle or heel of the plane.

The shavings should emerge from the middle of the iron only. The edges shouldn't be cutting if you sharpened your iron correctly. To remedy this, you

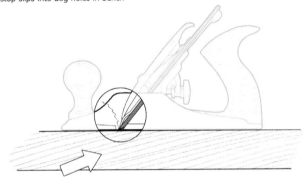

Planing against the grain — tear-out

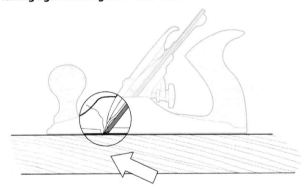

Planing with grain — no tear-out

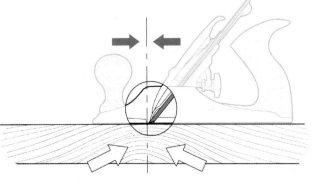

Reverse grain — plane both directions to avoid tear-out

ILLUSTRATIONS BY MATT BANTLY

A little canning wax on your sole makes the work easier and your cuts lighter. Some craftsmen prefer a little mineral oil.

See how the shaving emerges only in the middle of the iron? That's how you know your iron is sharpened and set correctly.

should tap the iron left or right to get it projecting squarely from the mouth.

Start planing at the edge of the board that's closest to you. After the first pass, make a second pass that slightly overlaps the first as you work your way to the other edge, and so on. Think of it like mowing a lawn. You want to avoid going over the same areas again and again.

I recommend that many beginning woodworkers start by planing Baltic birch plywood. I know that planing plywood sounds nuts, but it's good practice. The plywood has been sanded at the factory so it's easy to see where you are planing and where you aren't. Plus, the grain on this stuff is generally easy to plane.

When you have made it across your practice board, take a close look at the surface for tear-out and to make sure you're hitting everywhere on the face. A bright light at a raking angle helps this process. If the board looks good, run your fingers across its width to make sure you're not leaving plane tracks. If you are, it's probably one of three things:

• Your iron doesn't have enough (or perhaps any) curve at the cutting edge.

• You're taking too deep a cut.

• One corner of your iron is cutting deeper than the other; tweak the lateral adjuster.

Problem Grain

Of course, wood is cantankerous. Sometimes the grain in a board will switch directions. Or sometimes you'll plane with the grain and get tear-out. Or – even more frustrating – a small section of the board will tear out but the rest of the board will be perfect.

Tear-out can happen with every wood: domestics, exotics, you name it. What do you do? The trick is to try different approaches until you find one that works. You might have to plane most of a board in one direction and reverse direction for a small part of the board. Here are the things I do to tame tear-out:

• Try skewing the plane. Sometimes by angling the plane's body (which effectively lowers the cutting angle) magical things happen. But sometimes things get worse, too (black magic?).

• Try a different plane or reconfigure yours. Depending on the length of the plane's body, the mouth, the angle of the iron and the wood, some planes work better on some woods than others. If you can tighten up the throat of the plane, try that. Or switch to a different tool with a higher angle of attack or a tighter throat.

• Sharpen the iron. A sharp tool is always less likely to tear out the grain than a slightly dull one. If you are planing a board that refuses to be tamed,

try touching up your iron on a sharpening stone and then attacking your problem area immediately.

• Go against the grain of the board. Once in a great while I'll plane a problem board against the grain and it solves all or most of my problems. Wood, as I mentioned before, can be a vexing material.

• Shellac. Wipe on a spit coat of thin shellac to the problem area and let it dry for 10 minutes. Then give the area a try. This tip, which I picked up on the Internet, has worked for me. The shellac stiffens the fibers and allows you to shear them more easily. You only get a couple passes, though, before the shellac is gone.

• Scrape. My last resort is my scraper plane and my card scraper. The scraper

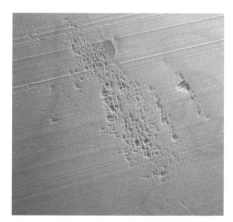

This is what tear-out looks like. Avoid it. When a finish is applied, it looks terrible.

choosing a smoothing plane

There are lots of brands of smoothing planes available, especially if you start adding in all the vintage flea-market specimens available.

I do have some old smoothing planes, but for budding hand-tool users, I usually recommend they buy a new, premium smoothing plane. Restoring a plane is a separate skill unto itself, and smoothers are tricky enough to tune anyway. Here are some of the smoothing planes I use in my shop, and their advantages and disadvantages.

CLARK & WILLIAMS 2¹⁄₄"
COFFIN SMOOTHER

Time for some honesty. I never liked wooden-bodied planes much until I tried those made by Steve Knight and Clark & Williams. Vintage wooden planes can be more difficult to tune than metal ones, in my opinion. These two plane makers have truly revived the art of wooden planes in this country. I'm partial to the Clark & Williams plane ($305, pictured) because of its particular ergonomics. The plane has no chipbreaker and a .005" throat. With the iron installed for a light cut, you can barely even see the throat. This is my plane of last resort. When I encounter grain that no other tool can tackle, the Clark & Williams with its 55° blade and tight throat has yet to let me down. Of course, because of the tight throat, it's good only for smoothing. These are beautifully made tools finished to a high degree. Other sizes are available.

Clark & Williams planes are available from Tools for Working Wood: 800-426-4613 or toolsforworkingwood.com. Knight's planes: Knight Toolworks: 503-421-6146 or knight-toolworks.com.

VERITAS BEVEL-UP SMOOTHING PLANE

Bevel-up (sometimes called "low-angle") smoothing planes are odd birds. Sometimes they are the only plane that will get the job done. Their advantages are that they have no chipbreaker to adjust, they work well on end grain (and miters) and you can adjust the throat as tight as you please – these tools have an adjustable throat like a block plane. The Veritas version is simple, well-made and costs only $169, a bargain in the premium-plane market. Veritas also makes a wider version of this tool that sells for $185.

One bonus is you can adjust the angle of attack simply by grinding a steeper bevel on the iron. That's because the bevel faces up in these planes. Grind the iron's bevel at 35° and you have a 47° smoother. Grind the iron at 48° and you have a 60° smoothing plane.

Lee Valley Tools: 800-871-8158 or leevalley.com.

RAY ILES A5 INFILL SMOOTHING PLANE

I recently finished building an infill plane from Shepherd Tool Co. and produced an excellent tool. If you don't want to build your own infill, I recommend the Ray Iles A5 ($899.95). It's a reproduction of the legendary Norris A5. Iles has made many improvements to the Norris design, including the excellent blade adjustment mechanism. He also makes a Norris A6, which has straight sides instead of the coffin shape of the A5. And a large panel plane is in the works as of press time.

The iron is bedded at 47¹⁄₂°, making it a bit better than the standard Stanley 45° angle for tricky grain. The Ray Iles plane looks and performs beautifully. I recommend you check it out.

Tools for Working Wood: 800-426-4613 or toolsforworkingwood.com.

LIE-NIELSEN NO. 4 WITH A HIGH-ANGLE FROG AND A LIE-NIELSEN NO. 3

These Bailey-style planes are heavy, expertly made and easy to tune to a high level for beginners. I used to use the No. 3 ($270-$300) for about 80 percent of my smoothing. But since Lie-Nielsen has come out with a No. 4 plane with a 50° blade angle ($250-$325), I now turn to that for problem-grain boards, too.

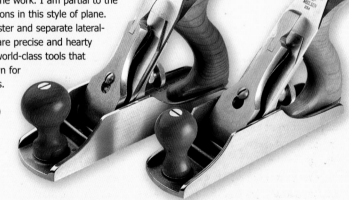

The nice thing about Bailey-style planes is you can adjust the size of the throat so the planes can be used for rough and fine work. I am partial to the way you adjust the irons in this style of plane. The Bailey-style adjuster and separate lateral-adjustment controls are precise and hearty systems. These are world-class tools that you'll be glad you own for the rest of your years.

Lie-Nielsen Toolworks: 800-327-2520 or lie-nielsen.com.

To tame difficult tear-out, I turn to my scraper plane, the Lie-Nielsen No. 85. This plane and the No. 80 cabinet scraper are the two easiest types to sharpen and use.

plane handles the larger problem areas (half a board). The card scraper is for the small sections that refuse to behave.

Finally, just keep at it. Refuse to give up. Smoothing is one of those skills that seems to develop in fits and starts. Don't be ashamed if you have to resort to sandpaper or power sanding.

Another suggestion I give beginners is to begin developing their planing skills by smoothing the interior parts of their casework. If you botch things there, it generally won't show.

Then, when you think you've got that down, I encourage you to plane all the parts of a project and then power sand it with #220-grit paper. This will quickly point out where you planed too little or too much. Depending on how messed up things are you can continue with the sandpaper or go back to the plane.

Just remember: Sometimes a plane is the right tool for the job, and sometimes you need to resort to the random-orbit sander or the scraper. But as you get more experience with a smoother, I think you'll find your power-sanding equipment sitting dormant for longer periods of time.

Skewing the plane body during the cut can help in tricky grain situations.

A little shellac on a problem tear-out will stiffen the wood fibers and allow them to be sheared cleanly – sometimes.

19

A WELL-TUNED JACK PLANE CAN QUICKLY **TRIM DOORS, FIT DRAWERS AND ELIMINATE EDGE-SANDING FOREVER.** IF YOU'VE NEVER SUCCESSFULLY USED A PLANE BEFORE, HERE'S HOW TO BUY ONE, SET IT UP AND USE IT.

metal-bodied jack planes

BY CHRISTOPHER SCHWARZ

Let's be honest: Teaching yourself to use a hand plane without guidance is a challenge. It's like trying to teach yourself to drive an 18-wheeler. Don't let anyone tell you different.

Back in the day – before the apprentice system was disbanded – journeymen cabinetmakers showed their apprentices how to properly sharpen the iron, how to adjust the tool and how to cut paper-thin shavings. Perhaps most important, the master was there to tell the apprentice what he was doing

wrong when the plane stopped working well. "Your iron is dull; your frog is too far forward; your chipbreaker is set too far back. Here, this should fix things."

These days, unless you take a good class, you're on your own. So it should come as no surprise to you if you've had terrible luck using a hand plane. Unlike many power tools, there are myriad adjustments that must be made to adapt the tool to different planing situations. A plane set up to cut perfect shavings on sugar pine might not do so well on ash, white oak or hard maple.

Now before you give yourself up to a life of power sanding, let me tell you this: Learning to use a plane is worth every minute of agony and puzzlement. In fact, I personally couldn't imagine woodworking without hand planes – or without my table saw and jointer, for that matter.

The jack plane was once reserved for rough work in a shop with a full array of job-specific planes. But if you have just a few planes (or even just one) you should probably get a jack plane. With

Some of the jack planes we've used in our shop. Inexpensive ones are OK (barely) for coarse work, but you generally get what you pay for.

the jack of all planes?

Many hand planes have nicknames that describe what they're used for: smoothing planes for smoothing, jointer planes for jointing, shoulder planes for trimming shoulders etc. But what does "jack" have to do with a "jack plane?"

Ever since I got into woodworking, people have told me that the "jack" refers to the expression "jack of all trades." The jack plane, it was explained, was a good all-around plane, so that's its nickname.

So I asked Graham Blackburn, the author of *Traditional Woodworking Handtools* (The Lyons Press) and a longtime hero of mine, about jack planes. According to Blackburn, "jack" is an expression used since the Middle Ages to describe something that is common, such as jack boots or a jack knife. The jack plane is indeed one of the most common sizes you'll find on the shelves of hardware stores. However, it could be argued that the "jack" refers instead to the most common sort of carpentry and construction work performed with this plane.

Indeed, Blackburn explained how carpenters called the plane a "jack plane" while cabinetmakers called the same instrument a "fore plane." And to make things even more complex, the premier English plane manufacturers of the day tried to separate their products from the common ones by calling the same-size plane a "panel plane."

But in the end, the people spoke, and in this country we call it a jack plane – no matter if the tool is used for the coarse surfacing of a piece of rough lumber, for fine furniture work or for trimming an interior door to fit its jamb on the job site.

Lap the sole with the plane fully assembled (but with the iron retracted into the body). I start with #90-grit silicon carbide powder and kerosene. Rub the sole on your flat surface in a figure-8 pattern, being sure not to concentrate your efforts in one certain place on the sole or on the surface (above). It's like a big sharpening stone, and you don't want to dish the center.

Turn the plane over after a few minutes and check your progress. You can see the red marks at the toe and heel of the sole. This is the point where I'm ready to move up to a finer-grit powder or call it done.

some tweaking, it can be used like a short jointer plane, or even as a longish smoothing plane.

Equipped with a fence, my jack plane cleans saw-blade marks off the edge of boards. I never worry about rounding over edges with a random-orbit sander. This isn't about "hand-tool heritage." It's simply a better and faster way to do things.

The same goes for trimming doors and drawers. The inset doors I fit with my jack plane fit better than those I've fit with a power jointer or table saw. Why? I have more control over where the cut stops and starts, so things are less likely to spiral out of control.

Finally, my jack plane excels at cleaning up band-sawn edges. I'll taper table legs on my band saw and clean up the tapers with a jack plane. Again, I have more control, and the tapers need no sanding when I'm done.

First, Learn to Sharpen

Before you'll have any luck with a jack plane, you need to get familiar with

sharpening. The iron's edge must be keen, or the plane won't work. All the sharpening systems work; you need to find one that's right for you. Also key is choosing the shape of the cutting edge of your jack plane. You can sharpen it straight across for general work, or with a slight curve (just .002" at the edges) for fine smoothing work, or a large curve (an 8" radius) for coarse stock removal.

Once you learn to sharpen, you need to purchase a decent plane. Some years ago, I reviewed all of the jack planes then available on the market. Bottom line: the ones from the Far East had a lot of problems. If you want to buy a new tool that requires no tweaking, I recommend you buy a premium plane from Veritas, Lie-Nielsen or Clifton. If you're short on cash and have some free time, I recommend one of Stanley's classic 100-year-old planes, which you'll see at flea markets almost anywhere. See the story "The Venerable and Affordable Stanley Type 11 Jack Plane" on page 100.

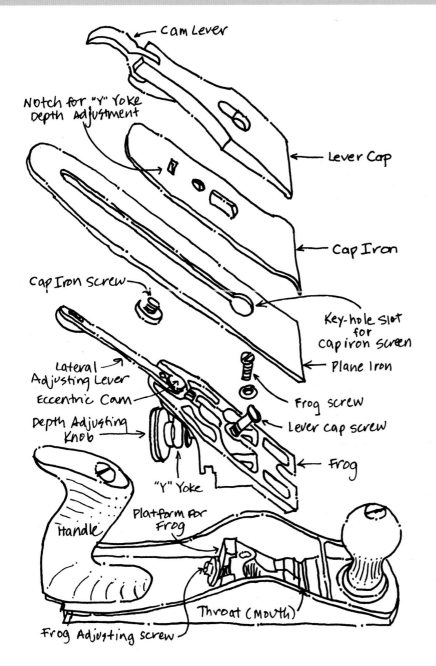

Cam Lever

Notch for "Y" Yoke Depth Adjustment

Lever Cap

Cap Iron

Cap Iron Screw

Key-hole Slot for cap iron screw

Lateral Adjusting Lever

Eccentric Cam

Depth Adjusting Knob

Plane Iron

Frog Screw

Lever cap screw

Frog

"Y" Yoke

Platform for Frog

Handle

Throat (Mouth)

Frog Adjusting Screw

ILLUSTRATION BY KRISTI CULLEN

Set Up Your Jack Plane

All planes require some degree of "fettling," also called tuning. In general, the more money you pay up front for your plane, the less fettling you're in for. On average, expect to spend anywhere from one to six hours to fettle a plane.

If you've bought an old plane, you might need to work on the sole if you cannot get the tool to take a consistent shaving. But if you've bought a new plane and the sole isn't flat, send it back.

There are people out there who insist the sole must be lapped dead flat and be as shiny as a mirror. Others say that sole flatness is overrated

and you need only to be worried about major warps.

It's been my experience that the truth is somewhere between. If you are going to use the tool for coarse work, the sole doesn't have to be even close to flat. If you're going to use this as a precision tool, sole flatness is a factor. In general I lap my soles so that the area in front of the mouth is flat. And I make sure that most of the sole (especially the edges) is flat behind the mouth. I don't worry much about the extreme front and rear of the sole. These are more likely to be out of kilter, especially if the plane has ever been

dropped. And as to the required final sheen on the sole, I'm not much of a purist here, either. I've made a few soles look like a mirror, but it didn't seem to boost performance much. Lap until the tool works.

There are several ways to lap the sole, but the most important thing to remember is that the surface for lapping must be flat. Your choices include thick glass, a marble pastry slab or a metal casting – usually the wing on your table saw.

Sandpaper or Silicon Carbide?

Next you have to choose an abrasive. Most people use either sandpaper or silicon carbide grit. In sandpaper, the choice product these days is called Alumina-Zirconia (and sometimes it's called Zirconia Alumina). This light blue-colored sanding belt is used for thicknessing wood in belt sanders and abrading stainless steel and titanium; so it's fine for a plane's sole. You can purchase it in belts from a home center ($6 for two belts; get some medium- and fine-grit belts to start), or order it from Klingspor (800-645-5555). Attach the belts to a flat surface using a spray adhesive.

The other option is silicon carbide powder. You sprinkle a few pinches of powder along with a light-bodied oil or kerosene on your flat surface and rub the sole until it's flat (see photo at left). You can buy a 4-ounce jar of #90-grit powder for $4.95 from Lee Valley Tools (leevalley.com or 800-871-8158). Or you can buy a kit of five grits for $15.95. One thing worth mentioning is that if you use the powder on your table saw wing it will lower the sheen of the cast iron to a dull grey.

Usually, I prefer the sandpaper over the powder. It makes much less mess and leaves a shinier surface on the sole of your plane.

No matter which abrasive you choose, the method is essentially the same. Affix the sandpaper to your flat surface, or mix up a slurry on it using a few pinches of powder. Put your plane together as if you were going to plane wood, but

the venerable and affordable stanley type 11 jack plane

The low knob is an immediate clue that the plane you're looking at may be a Type 11, a desirable and inexpensive option to many modern-day planes.

I'm sorry to say it, but Stanley just doesn't make hand planes like it used to. Though the new English-made Stanleys can be tuned to perform adequately, you can easily purchase a plane from the Stanley Works' glory days for less. The only catch is that you might have to do a lot more tuning and cleaning than you would on a premium plane. But the results are worth it.

Without a doubt, the best bench planes that Stanley ever produced were the Bed Rock line of professional planes, which began production in 1902 and were discontinued after World War II. These planes are different than other Stanley planes in the way the frog mates with the base casting. Simply put, there's a lot more contact between the frog and base, so there's less opportunity for blade chatter. It's such a good idea that Lie-Nielsen Toolworks and Clifton use that same 100-year-old technology on their premium planes. But trust me, it's tough to afford a Bed Rock plane (unless you're prone to dumb luck at yard sales). They can be as expensive as a new Clifton or Lie-Nielsen.

In my opinion, the next best thing is a Stanley Type 11 plane. These planes,

produced between 1910 and 1918, are common sights at flea markets. I've fixed up four of these planes and find them excellent. Here's why: The face of the frog of the Type 11s (and earlier planes) is a flat casting. Properly prepared, this frog will give rock-solid support to your iron and chipbreaker. Modern-day frogs have small ribs on the face of the frog that support the iron, so blade chatter is more likely.

So how do you know if you have a Type 11? It's pretty easy. Type 11 planes have three patent dates cast into the base behind the frog: March 25, 1902; Aug. 19, 1902; and April 19, 1910. As far as I know, it's the only Stanley bench plane with three patent dates. Additionally, the front knob is a low mushroom-shaped thing. Later planes have the same "high" knob as on planes today. There are some other trademarks of planes of that era, including the fact that the lever cap does not have "Stanley" cast into it, a feature found on planes made from 1925 until today.

Sometimes you'll find a plane that has some Type 11 characteristics, but the plane might have a high knob or a lever cap with Stanley's logo cast into it. Likely you have a

plane that has been assembled from parts from different eras. If the frog still has the solid cast face, it's worth considering. However, be sure to ask for a discount.

So how much should you pay for a Type 11? That depends on how pretty you like your tools. Nice examples fetch $30 to $40 on eBay. Planes with defects, such as a split in the handle or rust pitting on the iron, can be had for as little as $7.50. I've bought all mine for between $12 and $15, but each one needed a little work.

Many of these Type 11 planes have corrugated soles. The thought was that the corrugations would reduce friction while planing. The corrugations do make it easier to flatten the sole of the plane. You have to remove only about half the metal as you would on a sole without the corrugations.

Finally, I recommend you purchase a new iron for your Type 11. Hock Tools (hocktools.com or 888-282-5233), Lee Valley Tools and Woodcraft (woodcraft.com or 800-225-1153) all manufacture or sell aftermarket irons that are thicker and better made than stock irons. You'll be glad you did.

I use a DMT diamond stone to flatten the face of the frog, but any medium-grit stone will do. You'll have to work around the lateral adjustment lever, but you'll get most of the frog flattened this way.

Here you can see the difference a little stoning makes to your frog. Your iron is going to seat much more firmly against the frog once it's flat.

Take a few minutes to polish the top hump of the cap iron. Anytime you can reduce friction you'll improve planing performance.

retract the blade into the body. This is critical because the lever cap exerts pressure on the base casting and it can affect the shape of the sole slightly.

Now take a permanent magic marker and color the sole of the plane. I like red. Rub the plane for about 30 seconds on your abrasive surface and turn the plane over. The red spots are your low-lying areas. Continue rubbing the plane on the abrasive until you get as much red off as you can.

With the sandpaper, you will periodically have to use a brush to clean off the metal filings. With the silicon carbide, you will have to occasionally refresh the slurry with another pinch or two of the abrasive powder. When your sole looks good, move up a grit and continue your work. Keep doing this until you run out of finer grits or patience.

Fixing Your Frog

The frog is the soul of your hand plane. It holds the iron steady so it won't chatter and hop across your work like, well, a frog. Essentially, you want your iron to

You can stone the edge of your cap iron freehand, but a scrap piece of wood will make the operation foolproof and quick. Stone this edge until it seats tightly against the iron. A well-seated cap iron will save you from disassembling your plane every few strokes to clean out the shavings choking the mouth.

seat firmly against the frog and the frog to screw firmly to the base casting.

First, fix up the face of the frog. On a medium-grit sharpening stone, rub the face of the frog to remove milling marks and high spots. As with your plane's sole, you can check your progress with a magic marker. Move up in

Here you can see the rib between the two legs of the frog. If this protrudes past the face of the frog, your iron isn't going to seat properly. File it down or adjust your frog forward.

grits as you did with the sole. Unlike the sole, this is quick work. I find that vintage planes usually benefit from this tweak – premium planes are always good to go.

Now screw the frog to the base casting. Notice the black rib between the two legs of the frog. Keep an eye on

Hold the plane upside down and look at it head on as you tweak the lateral adjustment lever. When the cutting edge and sole are parallel, back the iron out and go to work.

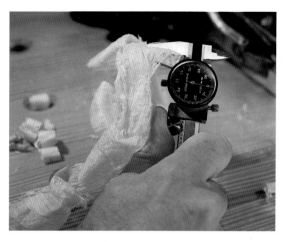

This is what your shavings should look like when your plane is properly set up for smoothing. This is the perfect setting for removing saw marks from the edge of a board or smoothing a board before finishing. If you want to hog off more wood in a hurry, advance the blade just a little more.

that rib. First position the frog about where you will keep it for general-purpose work. You want your mouth to be about 1/16" wide, perhaps smaller if you're going to use this occasionally as a smoothing plane.

Put the iron and cap iron in place and lock the lever cap. Check the mouth. If it's about the right size, remove the lever cap, cap iron and iron. Rub your finger over that rib. If it protrudes past the frog, you've got trouble. A protruding rib prevents your iron from seating against the frog. File the rib.

You also want to make sure that the base casting isn't interfering with the mating of the iron and frog. If your frog is set too far back, the blade will rest against the base casting and some point at the back of your frog. The result will be chatter. So move the frog forward a bit.

Quick Cap Iron Fix

Another oft-neglected part of the plane is the cap iron, also called the chipbreaker. There are two common problems with this part. First, it doesn't mate tightly with the cutting face of the iron. And second, it doesn't have any

"spring" to it. Luckily, both are simple fixes on new and vintage planes.

If you screw the cap iron to the iron and the cap iron doesn't have to bend even a little, that's usually a problem. If the cap iron bends so much that the iron bends, that's also a problem. Put the cap iron in a vise and bend it using your hands to increase or decrease the amount of spring in it. It's easy.

Now, screw the cap iron to the iron and hold the assembly up to a light. If you can see light between the cap iron and iron, you need to stone the edge of the cap iron. This is a quick fix, and I've found it necessary for all planes, regardless of the price tag. Put a scrap of wood next to your sharpening stone and stone the leading edge of the cap iron. It shouldn't take a lot of time; cap irons are made from soft metal. The scrap of wood keeps your cap iron at a consistent angle.

Reassemble the iron and cap iron and check your work. When the fit is tight, you're done.

Finally, while you're working on the cap iron, polish the top of the curved edge, too. Anything that reduces friction between the plane and the shavings will make your tool work better.

Tricks for a Perfect Setup

The hard part is over; now it's time for a test run. Attach the cap iron to the iron. Set the cap iron so it's a little less than 1/16" back from the edge of the iron. This is a good, all-purpose setting. For rough work, set the cap iron back a little more. For fine work, move the cap iron forward slightly.

Put the iron assembly in place on the frog and put the lever cap in place. Now is a good time to check the setting of that screw in the middle that holds everything together. The screw should be tight against the lever cap but you should still be able to smoothly adjust the iron's cutting depth by turning the wheel behind the frog.

Turn that wheel until the iron protrudes from the mouth just a bit. Now hold the plane as shown in the photo at left and move the lateral adjustment lever until you can see that the cutting edge and sole are parallel. Now, without touching the lateral adjustment lever, retract the iron so it's almost protruding from the sole.

Get a piece of scrap. Try something easy at first, like poplar. Just like with your woodworking machines, you need to read the grain direction on a board when deciding which direction to plane. You want to plane with the grain. The wood fibers will likely tear out if you plane against the grain.

Turn the iron adjustment knob just a bit to advance the iron. It's important to note that you should always adjust the iron by increasing the depth of cut. This avoids what is called "backlash." If you retract the blade and then start cutting, the blade can back up during use because there is slack in the adjustment mechanism.

Push the plane over the board and see what happens. How you hold and push the plane is important. Skew the body of the plane about 5° left or right as you push it forward; this will almost always improve your cut. When you

With your jack plane set up for smoothing, you can easily trim fitted drawers to a perfect flush fit. If you have to plane the end grain of the drawer front and the grain direction of the sides dictates that the drawer front is at the end of your cut, be sure to clamp a back-up block to the drawer front (not shown). This will help prevent you from blowing chunks out of your drawer front.

begin the cut, keep most of the downward pressure on the front knob. In the middle of the cut, keep the downward pressure even on both the front knob and rear handle. As you finish the cut, most of the downward pressure should be on the rear handle. This takes a bit of practice, but it's worth it because your boards will remain true as a result.

After your first stroke, advance the iron in tiny increments until the plane starts to cut. If the plane seems to be cutting on one side only, tweak the lateral adjustment lever left or right. Just like with a ham radio, it's all about small adjustments. In a perfect world, shavings for a highly tuned smoothing plane should be the width of the blade (2"), about .001" to .002" thick and fluffy.

You'll also know if you're in the ballpark by the sound the plane makes. When things are going well, it sounds like "swish." When your cut is too heavy, the sound will have a grinding quality.

Using machinery to trim inset doors so you have a perfect 1/16" gap all around is a real skill because it's easy to go too far. With a jack plane and the Veritas jointer fence, you can sneak up on the perfect fit. This method also removes any milling marks from your doors' edges, so you don't have to sand the edges once the door fits.

Troubleshooting

Lots of things can go wrong for the beginner, so here are some things to think about. If the plane chatters or skips across the work, look for something loose. Is the frog screwed tightly to the base? How about the iron? Is it seated correctly on the frog? Is the screw that comes up through the iron assembly tight enough to keep everything in place? Have you checked for backlash?

Another common problem is shavings choking the mouth. Check the location of the frog. If it's too far forward for the cut you're making, the shavings will bunch up in the mouth. Next, check the fit between the cap iron and the iron. If it's not airtight, chips will bunch up there.

If the plane seems to cut inconsistently – that is, it cuts in some places on a board but not in others, you need to check two things. First, the board might be twisted, so you're only able to plane the high spots. Second, your lateral adjustment might be out of wack. Try adjusting the lever this way and that a bit.

The Veritas jointer fence is a great accessory. It really shines when it comes to removing machinery marks from the edges of your boards. With the fence attached to a well-tuned plane, you'll produce shimmering straight edges that are ready for finishing. No more edges rounded by your sander, and no more toiling over the edges with a sanding block.

Finally, just keep at it. Start working with some pine 2 × 4s. Pine is a forgiving wood that begs to be planed. Then try some poplar, which gives up wispy shavings easily. Then move on to oak, maple and cherry. With practice, all your common cabinet woods will do as you please.

And when you're ready to be humbled again, move on to the exotic woods. That's a bit like teaching yourself to steer the QE II, and that's another story.

Supplies

Lee Valley Tools
800-871-8158 or leevalley.com

1 • Veritas Jointer Fence
    #05P30.01, $34.50

• Silicon carbide grit, 90x
    #05M24.01, $4.95

• Silicon carbide grit,
    set of five grits
    #05M01.01, $15.95

1 • Glass lapping plate
    #05M20.12, $10.50

Prices correct at time of publication.

20

block plane basics

BY LONNIE BIRD

My tool cabinet contains a number of planes – bench planes for smoothing, shoulder planes for trimming and even a full set of hollows and rounds. But the planes I use most often are block planes. I own a number of block planes and I reach for them several times a day to smooth away saw marks, level intersections at joints, trim miters and even create simple shapes such as chamfers.

What makes the block plane so versatile? Well, it has several features that distinguish it from other planes, such as its small size, adjustable mouth, low bed angle and a unique bevel-up blade. Let's take a closer look at each of these features.

Small and Adjustable

Most block planes are compact so they can easily plane small parts or maneuver in areas that are too tight for a bench plane to reach. This is a great advantage when leveling joints in frames and casework. Additionally, the short length, dimpled sides and domed lever cap make the block plane fit easily in the hand and ensure a firm grip and good control in the cut.

For tear-out free cuts, the mouth of a plane must be as small as possible. It works like this: As the edge lifts a shaving, the sole of the plane directly in front of the edge presses the shaving down. This helps break the shaving

There are many different styles of block planes. Some are new, others are vintage. Some are small, others are large. From left: Lie-Nielsen 60¹/₂ low-angle block, Lie-Nielsen 62 low-angle jack (essentially an oversized block plane), Stanley 60¹/₂ low-angle block, Lie-Nielsen standard-angle block and Lie-Nielsen 102 low-angle block.

and prevent tear-out. If the mouth of the plane is adjustable, it can be set for either a coarse or a fine shaving.

To adjust the mouth, bench planes use a movable frog – the casting that supports the iron. Adjusting the frog of a bench plane is a bit tedious. However, the toe of the sole on most block planes is a separate casting that slides in a machined recess in the front of the plane. This design makes mouth adjustments quick, easy and precise.

Standard or Low-Angle?

Another feature that distinguishes block planes is that they're available in standard and low-angle versions. This allows you to select a plane for the type of cut you want – face grain or end grain.

The angle refers to the bed angle. Standard-angle block planes are typically 20°, while the low-angle planes feature a bed angle of 12°. Realize, though, that the bed angle is not the cutting angle. Because the blade of a block plane is bedded bevel-up, the cutting angle is the sum of the bed angle and the grind angle. On a standard block plane, the cutting angle is typically 45°, the same as most bench planes. Low-angle block planes have a cutting angle of 37°. Which one is best for you depends upon the planing you plan to do. You'll probably want both. Here's why:

When planing end grain, a low cutting angle works best. End grain is tough, and a low cutting angle shears the fibers. But face grain requires a different approach. Although a low cutting angle will give good results on face grain much of the time, especially when the wood is moderately soft and straight-grained, it has a tendency to

lift and tear out hard and highly figured wood such as curly maple. Here's where you need a higher cutting angle. In fact, the higher the better. The steep bevel of a higher cutting angle breaks and curls the shaving, which limits its tendency to splinter and tear.

That's where a block plane's bevel-up design is an advantage. The cutting angle can be altered simply by changing the grind angle on the blade. You can't do that with a bench plane; because a bench plane's iron is bedded bevel down, the cutting angle is determined by the bed angle of the frog.

On my standard block plane with a 20° bed angle, I've ground the iron to 30°, which yields a cutting angle of 50°. This steeper cutting angle, sometimes referred to as a York pitch, is quite effective at smoothing highly figured, difficult woods such as tiger maple.

105

When I need to trim the end grain on a miter, I use my low-angle block plane. The sum of the 12° bed angle and a 25° bevel angle yields a low 37° cutting angle – just what's needed for shearing tough, fibrous end grain. In fact, you can lower the grind angle another 2° for a 35° cutting angle. Any lower, however, and the edge becomes too fragile.

Finally, the bevel-up blade also means that the bed of the plane can support the blade much closer to the edge. This stiffens the blade where it needs it most and virtually eliminates chatter.

Other Block-plane Styles

Although the 6"-long block planes are most common, there are other styles you may want to add to your tool kit. Remember: Any plane with the iron bedded bevel-up is, technically, a block plane.

For example, take a look at a low-angle jack plane (page 105). At first glance it resembles another bench plane. It even features a wooden handle and knob like a bench plane. But the iron is bedded bevel-up at a low, 12° angle. Mouth adjustments are made with a movable toe piece. Although it resembles a bench plane, it functions as a low-angle block plane. And its large size gives it lots of mass for clean slicing through tough end grain.

Some plane makers feature a small, 5"-long block plane. Although the throat isn't adjustable and it is somewhat large for fine work, the tool's small size and comfortable shape make this plane feel like an extension of the hand. This plane is one of my favorites for light trimming and other less-demanding tasks during a project.

Tuning Your Block Plane

New planes vary widely in quality of workmanship and design. All new block planes require tuning, although the best ones require only honing the blade and adjusting the mouth. But many less-expensive planes require reworking to function. If you've been frustrated by your new (or old) block plane, you may find that it just needs a tune-up.

Start by examining the sole of the plane. It must be flat to provide support to the blade. A warped sole or one that was sloppily ground can be flattened by rubbing it on coarse sandpaper. The sandpaper must be supported by a flat, stiff surface such as a granite plate or the cast-iron top of a machine. I start with #100 grit and finish with #320.

The next step is to flatten the bed. On a quality plane the bed is large and dead flat. But less expensive block planes feature a small bed just behind the mouth and the surface often has burrs or a glob or two of paint. Although you can't increase the bed size, you can use a small, flat mill file to smooth away any defects. Be careful, however, and don't be overzealous with the file.

Next, turn your attention to the lever cap. The lever cap applies pressure to the iron just behind the cutting edge. To perform properly it must also be flat and free of leftover burrs or traces of excess paint. You can easily flatten the cap with a coarse, flat bench stone.

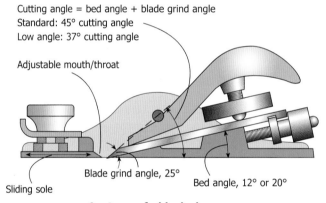

Cutting angle = bed angle + blade grind angle
Standard: 45° cutting angle
Low angle: 37° cutting angle

Adjustable mouth/throat

Blade grind angle, 25°

Sliding sole

Bed angle, 12° or 20°

Anatomy of a block plane

The sole of a block plane can be trued on sandpaper (#100 to #320 grit) supported on a granite reference plate.

A small mill file can rescue the bed of an inexpensive plane by ridding it of any defects. However, a light touch is key. You can easily overdo it.

The next step is to sharpen the iron. Like all sharpening, it involves polishing the back and the bevel. Most new plane irons have coarse scratches in the back that remain from the manufacturing process. As each scratch intersects the edge, it forms a tiny serration that resists cutting and will tear out fibers. Start with a coarse bench stone and work through to the finest stone until the back of the plane iron is absolutely flat and reflects like a mirror. Then hone the bevel to the angle you have decided is best for your work.

Finally, install the iron in the plane and adjust it for a very fine cut. Then close the mouth of the plane so that a thin shaving can barely pass through. A tight mouth is critical, especially when planing face grain.

Proper Technique

A sharp, finely tuned low-angle block plane can remove ultra-thin shavings from tough end grain. I often use a plane to skim the mitered surface of mouldings; the plane will smooth away all saw marks, ensuring a tight, gap-free fit. With the workpiece secure in a vise, I grasp the plane with one hand and apply firm pressure to the toe with the thumb of my other hand. A sharp plane iron and a light cut are the key to a clean cut here, along with smooth, positive strokes.

When planing the end grain of a board, you'll need to take steps to avoid splintering the grain along the edge. One approach is to clamp a backup board to the trailing edge of the workpiece. The backup board will apply pressure to support the grain and avoid splintering. Another method is to plane from both edges and allow your cuts to meet somewhere near the middle. I especially like this method when planing the end of a wide board such as a tabletop.

When fitting small drawers, such as those in a spice cabinet, the block plane is my favorite choice. I position the drawer against the bench stop and steady it with one hand while planing with the other. As I approach the intersection, I turn the plane 45° as I push

Block planes are ideal for working tough end grain. You must apply firm pressure to the toe of the plane for success, as shown above. The result should be a ribbon of end grain as shown at right. If you get dust, you've done something wrong.

Ribbon of end grain

When planing a drawer, be careful not to plane across the grain when turning a corner. To avoid this, just turn the plane 45° as you round the corner.

Chamfering is done easily with one hand. Simply follow the intersections at the corners.

the plane around the corner. This avoids planing across the grain and tearing the grain on either of the two pieces.

Chamfering can also be done one-handed. I usually chamfer the ends of chair legs, table legs and bed posts; this prevents them from inadvertently splintering as they're dragged across a floor. As with a drawer, you can position the leg against a stop while you

steady it with one hand and plane with the other.

Although you can pencil in layout lines to guide you as you plane, I never do. The intersections at the corners will show you where you need to adjust the chamfer. Besides, I like a small amount of irregularity that's often associated with hand planing. It gives the work a classic look that says, "handmade."

the essential
shoulder plane

BY LONNIE BIRD

I t's hard to imagine woodworking without planes; I use a variety of planes on almost every job for smoothing, shaping and fitting. A sharp, finely tuned bench plane will smooth away the mill marks left behind by machines and create a distinctive surface that says "handmade." A set of hollow and round planes will shape a large crown moulding that would otherwise require a heavy-duty industrial shaper and a power feeder. And when carefully fitting tenons to their respective mortises, I reach for a shoulder plane.

The shoulder plane is the only tool that will take thin, delicate shavings from the tough end-grain shoulders of tenons. But it's not limited to trimming shoulders. The shoulder plane's open sides, fine mouth and low bed angle make it useful for a variety of tasks – essentially anytime you might want to take fine, controlled cuts into a corner. Whether it's shaving the cheek of a tenon for a snug fit within a mortise or fine-tuning a drawer runner deep inside a case, a shoulder plane is up to the task and will give you good results every time.

It's Not a Rabbet Plane

I'm not one to get stuck on terminology, but it's pretty easy to get confused when shopping for a shoulder plane because many woodworking catalogs label these tools as rabbet planes. While rabbet and shoulder planes both

For fine-tuning joints, the versatile shoulder plane is a must-have tool in your shop.

have open sides for cutting into corners, there are some distinct differences between the two that affect how they are used in the workshop.

Basically, rabbet planes are designed for cutting rabbets while shoulder planes are designed for trimming. Rabbet planes usually come equipped with a fence and a depth stop to guide the plane and control the dimensions of the rabbet. Embedded in the sides of most rabbet planes is a "nicker" or spur that severs the fibers ahead of the iron when cutting across the grain. Shoulder planes lack these accessories. Because they are used for trimming, shoulder planes are guided by surfaces previously created by other tools.

However, the shoulder plane is a much more refined tool than its coarser cutting cousin. Don't forget: These finely tuned planes excel at trimming and refining surfaces. To perform these functions well, a quality shoulder plane has features that most other types of planes lack. First, the sole of a shoulder plane is ground exactly 90° to the sides. This helps ensure square, accurate cuts. The iron is usually bedded at about 20° and ground between 20° and 25°. This yields a cutting angle of 40° to 45°, effective for thin cuts on end grain.

Of course, like a rabbet plane, the sides of a shoulder plane are open. This unique feature allows the plane to trim into corners of rabbets, tenon faces, shoulders and practically anywhere else a fine, controlled cut is required. Some shoulder planes, such as the Stanley No. 92, also feature a removable front piece that quickly transforms the tool into a chisel plane, another useful tool.

To eliminate chatter, the bed of a shoulder plane supports the iron almost to the cutting edge. This feature, combined with the extremely narrow mouth, allows the plane to remove thin, delicate shavings – just what is needed when fine-tuning joinery.

Tuning a Shoulder Plane

For any plane to perform as expected it must be tuned properly and the shoulder plane is no exception. However, because a shoulder plane doesn't

Some shoulder planes, such as the Stanley No. 92 shown here, feature a removable front piece, that (when removed) transforms the tool into a useful chisel plane.

have nearly as many working parts as a bench plane, it's not quite as time-consuming to tune. Also, most shoulder planes are manufactured to more precise tolerances than bench planes, so they don't require the extensive reworking that many new bench planes do.

To begin tuning a new shoulder plane, first check the body of the plane to see that the sides are 90° to the sole. Fortunately most are, but if yours isn't, return it and request a new one. As you might imagine, reworking the sides to correct any deviancy from 90° is extremely difficult and labor intensive. Let the plane manufacturer correct this problem.

Next, check the sole for flatness. If the plane has an adjustable nose piece (which allows for adjustments to the mouth of the plane) make certain that the screw that fastens this piece is secure before checking the sole. If the sole of the shoulder plane is slightly out of true, you can correct the problem by lapping it on a diamond plate.

The next step is to sharpen the iron. It may be necessary to grind the iron; check to see that the edge is 90° to the sides. Unlike bench planes, shoulder planes don't come equipped with a lateral adjustment lever so there is little you can do to compensate for an edge that is out of square.

Although you can loosen the lever cap and pivot the iron slightly, this technique will allow for only a small adjustment. You're better off grinding the iron square to begin with. Grind the edge to a 25° primary bevel and, as always, make sure you don't let the steel overheat.

Because the sides of a shoulder plane are open, it's easy to trim into corners of rabbets.

Before honing the edge, compare the width of the iron to the body of the plane. The iron should be slightly wider than the sole, at the most .006" to .010" wider (.003" to .005" on each side). If the iron is too wide (as it sometimes is) it will gouge the face adjacent to the one you're planing. If necessary, slowly and carefully work the sides of the iron with a coarse sharpening stone. Be careful and don't overdo it. Otherwise the iron will not cut into the corners. A dial caliper works well to check your progress as you work.

After honing, install the iron and adjust it for a very light cut. Next, sight down the sole of the plane and slowly advance the iron until you can see only the edge. Finally, adjust the mouth of the plane so that only the thinnest of shavings can pass through. Your shoulder plane is tuned.

Using Your Shoulder Plane

Most shoulder planes, small or large, can be used one-handed. I use my other hand to grip the workpiece and position it against a bench stop. When planing

Your iron should be .006" to .010" wider than the sole. To get your iron to this width, carefully work the sides of the iron with a coarse stone. Check your progress with a dial caliper.

Once your iron is ready for cutting, install it in the plane and adjust it for a very light cut. Simply sight down the plane and slowly advance the iron until you can see just the cutting edge of the iron.

When planing end grain, as I'm doing here, be careful of splintering the grain at the trailing corner of the stock. To avoid this, simply plane from both directions and allow the cuts to meet near the middle.

long grain, such as when fitting the face of a tenon to a mortise, you can effectively plane all the way across the stock. However, when planing end grain, such as the shoulder of a tenon, planing all the way across risks splintering the grain at the trailing corner of the stock. Instead, plane from both directions and allow the cuts to meet near the middle.

When planing a wide shoulder, such as the end of a tabletop to receive a breadboard end, I reach for a large shoulder plane. Clamp the work to the benchtop and grasp the plane with both hands for the best control.

After a short time, you'll find the controlled, precise cuts from your shoulder plane to be addictive – and you'll find yourself using it often.

Sources

Lie-Nielsen Toolworks
800-327-2520 or lie-nielsen.com
• Large shoulder plane
No. O73, $225

Highland Hardware
800-241-6748 or
tools-for-woodworking.com
• Stanley No. 92 shoulder plane
#031804, $99.99
Prices correct at time of publication.

exotic infill handplanes

BY CHRISTOPHER SCHWARZ

There are times when I wish I could find my first handplane. It was, by most standards, an utter piece of junk. I had bought it after college during a late-night run to Wal-Mart, and my purchase was guided by the fact that it was blue, cheap and the only block plane I could find on the shelves that evening.

So it was surprising (then and now) that the tool actually worked quite well. It didn't have a blade adjuster, the sole was rough and the steel in the cutter was as gummy as Juicy Fruit. But when I put the tool to wood it made that sweet "sneeeeck" sound of a perfect curl of wood being sliced from its mother board.

It was the first step in my journey. In the last 13 years I've slowly upgraded my handplanes. After buying a Stanley jack plane, the blue plane went into my carpentry toolkit. Then it went into a box in the basement. And now I can't find it. Occasionally I do get a pang of longing for it. But never have I wanted that block plane more than the day I pushed a $6,600 Karl Holtey A13 infill plane over a piece of curly maple.

A custom-built Holtey A13 is for many handplane enthusiasts the pinnacle of the planemaker's art – perfect in form, function, fit and finish. And when I first used the A13 I got the same sort of heady feeling you get when you master a handplane for the first time. However, like any buzz, after about 20 minutes of work with the A13, the buzz wore off

and I began to think (somewhat) rationally about this beautiful piece of steel and brass under my command.

I set the A13 aside and picked up a plane made by James Krenov, the author of *The Impractical Cabinetmaker* (Linden) and planed the same piece of irascible maple. Then I tried a $2,800 Sauer & Steiner panel plane, a Bill Carter jointer plane, a $1,300 A13 from Darryl Hutchinson, a small $775 smoothing plane from Wayne Anderson and more infill planes from custom builders Robert Baker and Brian Buckner.

That Was a Very Good Day.

Before you wonder if I've won the lottery, let me explain. Many of these planes (and a dozen more) were loaned

to us by a generous and trusting man named John Edwards. Edwards, a retired automotive engineer from Detroit, amassed his collection of modern handplanes after years of saving and careful purchasing. He and I are both handplane geeks, and so we got together in the magazine's shop, tuned up these planes and put them to work, deliriously making shavings on boards both mild and wild.

After three days of using these tools, I recorded my impressions in a legal pad, took some photos and now am ready to share what we found. There were a few surprises, some disappointments and a small revelation at the end. If you've ever gazed longingly at some of these beauties on the internet

See the two steel pins in Holtey's A13? The iron is bedded against these and a steel plate at the throat – not the wood. Most unusual and interesting.

or at woodworking shows and wondered "But do they work well?" you're about to find out.

Holtey A13:
Perfect to the Nth Degree

I actually never thought I'd get to use one of these planes. In fact, this plane almost didn't make it here in time after getting tangled up in U.S. Customs for a breathtaking bit after its trip from Holtey's shop in Sutherland, England.

Holtey was one of the early pioneers of the modern infill makers. And his reputation, quality of work and prices all reflect the fact that most people see him as the top of the heap.

The Holtey A13 is based on a classic pattern of English plane made by the venerable Norris company. And it's one of Holtey's signature planes (his other, the No. 98, will be discussed shortly). Once you hold one of the tools you understand a bit of the Holtey mystique. The man is a perfectionist. No matter how closely you examine his tools, you cannot find cosmetic flaws. They are finished both inside and out to the highest degree. Here is just one example: Where some makers (both historic and new) will leave the bed of the plane with a few file marks (which you'll almost never see because the bed is covered by the iron), Holtey does not.

In fact, the bed of the tool is where we got our first surprise. Holtey secures his irons to the body in a way that's unlike any other infill toolmaker I know. In other infills the iron rests directly on the wooden infill below it. Sometimes there is a steel plate down by the mouth that offers support as well, but mostly it's the wood that's in charge. Some enthusiasts say it's this wooden bed that makes the tools special.

But Holtey's A13 mocks that assertion. His irons don't even touch the wooden infill. Instead, the iron rests on a steel plate by the mouth and two raised steel pins embedded in the tool's bed. What's the advantage? In my experience it made the cut much easier to adjust. Even with the tool's lever cap cinched down super-tight, the iron could still be adjusted with little effort – or risk. Many old Norris infill planes have adjusters that were stripped out by people who tightened down the lever cap too much and then adjusted the iron.

KARL HOLTEY A13

Sole length: 9"

Weight: 6 lbs. 2 oz.

Pitch of iron: 50°

Mouth opening: About $1/64$"

Iron: S53 steel, .183" thick, $2^1/4$" w.

Contact: holteyplanes.com or (UK) 01549 402500

KARL HOLTEY 11-S HIGH-ANGLE SMOOTHER

Sole length: $6^1/2$"

Weight: 2 lbs. 5 oz.

Pitch of iron: 60°

Mouth opening: About $1/32$"

Iron: S53 steel, .168" thick, $1^1/2$" w.

CLASSIC PLANES A13 BY DARRYL HUTCHINSON

Sole length: 9"

Weight: 5 lbs. 15.5 oz.

Pitch of iron: 50°

Mouth opening: Less than $1/64$"

Iron: A2 steel, .192" thick, $2^1/4$" w.

Contact: classicplanes.com or (UK) +44 01647 441015

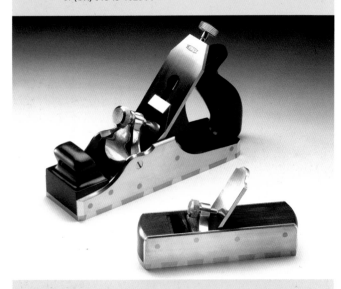

Karl Holtey's A13 (in the background) and his new 11-S both proved to be formidable planes when put to work.

Darryl Hutchinson's A13 (right) with a Ray Iles A5. Both are English makers and produce tools that very much evoke the classic infill planes of the 19th and early 20th centuries.

KARL HOLTEY NO. 98

Sole length: 9$\frac{1}{2}$"

Weight: 4 lbs. 3.7 oz.

Pitch of iron: 22°

Mouth opening: About $\frac{1}{64}$"

Iron: S53 steel, .176" thick, 2$\frac{1}{8}$" w.

My frustration with the No. 98 was in getting the iron to drop onto the pin shown here on the adjuster. It took much fiddling. Once in, however, the tool is a sweet user.

The Holtey A13 is surprisingly comfortable to use and has a wicked-heavy presence on the wood. What I didn't like about it was how uncomfortable it was to hold the tool upside down when sighting down the sole – a common operation when trying to center the blade in the mouth of the tool. The tool's front bun is hard to grasp in this position.

That's a quibble, really. I think I was looking for something – anything – to disappoint me on this tool. Not much cropped up. It's as close to perfection as you can get. If I had an extra $6,600 I'd love to own one.

Holtey 11-S: A High-Angle Solution

This new model from Holtey isn't based on an old plane – it's one of his original designs. When I first saw it I thought it looked as comfortable to use as a brick. And on that point, I was mostly wrong. The 11-S is easy to cradle with your hands and to control, thanks to its diminutive size. After a lengthy planing session my right hand began to rub on the back edge of the blade, which was annoying, but not awful.

The high cutting angle (called the "pitch") of the tool made it a remark-able smoothing plane. There was nothing in our shop that it couldn't handle with ease – and I rooted deep into our scrap pile. Unlike Holtey's A13, the iron is bedded directly on the wooden infill and the lever cap is removable; it hooks around a pin that passes through the sidewalls of the plane. This feature makes it easy to remove and install the iron.

The only disappointment with this tool is one shared by many of Holtey's tools, and that's the particular alloy of steel used in the plane's cutter. The alloy, called S53, wears astonishingly well. But I found it difficult to sharpen. Some of my stones wouldn't touch it, and I had to resort to diamond stones to get a keen edge. Even then, I wasn't confident I had gotten the best edge. This is a personal opinion, but I prefer steel that is easy to sharpen, especially with smoothing planes.

Compared to other Holtey planes, the 11-S is a bargain: about $1,500 with the way the dollar is trading. This is a sweet little tool that cries out to be used. I hope it doesn't sit on a collector's shelf.

Holtey No. 98: A Design That Changed the Rules

The No. 98 (about $2,900) is another of Holtey's original designs and it was a groundbreaking tool when he introduced it. It was one of the first modern "bevel-up" smoothers, and Holtey's trailblazing has led to a surge in the popularity of this style of tool.

That said, for a variety of reasons, the No. 98 was my least favorite of the Holtey planes I tested. The adjuster, while ingenious, is fiddly when it comes to installing the iron in the tool. The iron is bored with a series of holes. You drop the iron onto a pin that projects from the plane's adjuster. Because the hole and the pin have a tight fit, it took me a good deal of messing about to get the iron in place on the pin.

In use, the tool is remarkably balanced and has a sleek modern look that appealed even to my traditional tastes. And it performed admirably. With a steep 38° microbevel on the cutting

Here you can see the differences between the front buns of the two A13s – Holtey's is on the left; Hutchinson's is on the right.

edge, the resulting 60° pitch made it a formidable smoothing tool.

Classic Planes A13: A More Affordable Workhorse

Like Holtey, Darryl Hutchinson of Devon, England, also makes a version of the Norris A13. Hutchinson's plane is similar in form to the Holtey plane, but it's different in the details. Overall, the level of fit and finish and perfection is lower. But considering that Hutchinson's A13 costs about $1,300 – about one-fifth of the Holtey A13 – it's a value among premium tools.

The plane works remarkably well – as anything costing more than a grand should. It has a fine mouth and high pitch to the iron, which make it ideal for fine finishing cuts. Because of the vast price difference, it's not really fair to compare it directly to the Holtey, so here are my general impressions. The tote is pretty comfortable, though it had more flat areas than I like – I wished it were more sinuous. The front bun is sizable and I didn't find it as comfortable as an old-fashioned Stanley-style front knob during long planing sessions.

The adjuster works quite well and had little slop in its mechanism. I found it remarkably easy to get the plane running smoothly and making very sweet cuts. It's not a fussy tool.

There were some minor cosmetic things: The bed of the tool is essentially unfinished and is covered in file marks. Among its premium-priced peers this is unusual. And there were a few drips of finish in the channel for the adjuster. All in all however, the tool is quite solid, unpretentious and ready to go to work. I quite liked it.

BILL CARTER A1 JOINTER PLANE

Sole length: 28"

Weight: 12 lbs. 5.5 oz.

Pitch of iron: 47°

Mouth opening: less than $^1/_{32}$"

Iron: High-carbon steel, .169" thick, $2^1/_2$" w.

Contact: 98 Havencrest Drive Leicester, LE5-2AH United Kingdom

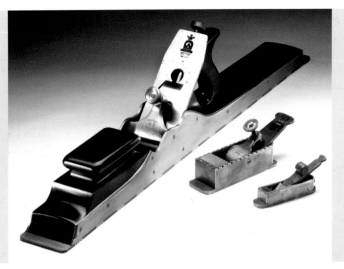

The Bill Carter jointer plane dwarfs two smaller Carter miter planes. Carter sometimes uses recycled materials – the little plane is made from a backsaw.

SAUER & STEINER PANEL PLANE

Sole length: $14^3/_4$"

Weight: 7 lbs. 15 oz.

Pitch of iron: 50°

Mouth opening: Immeasurably tight

Iron: High-carbon steel, .186" thick, $2^1/_2$" w.

Contact: sauerandsteiner.com or 519-568-8159

A Sauer & Steiner jointer plane (left) with two panel planes by the same maker. The Sauer & Steiner planes all have consistent lines.

Konrad Sauer made furniture before he made tools. And it shows here in the sculptural front bun on one of his panel planes.

Bill Carter A1: Beyond Massive

Bill Carter is another English tool maker, and he was probably the earliest of the modern infill makers. His hand-built infill planes have inspired toolmakers all over the world since he started building in the 1980s.

The jointer plane I used for this article is, like most Carter planes, a work of art. Carter has an excellent and eccentric eye: The dovetails in the sole are filed in the shape of a cupid's bow and he has a reputation for adding images of elephants to the sidewalls of his tools. Plus, though all his tools are new, Carter ages the metal and builds them with a decidedly old-world charm.

This jointer plane is as interesting as the man who built it. The story goes that Carter built it first as a 36"-long tool, but when he took it to auctions and tool sales to show it was simply too long to fit into the allotted space in his car. So Carter chopped a bit off each end. He sent the "offcuts" to Edwards when he bought it and suggested Edwards use them as (wait for it ...) sanding blocks.

This jointer plane has the presence of a museum piece. The metal is beautifully chamfered and the wooden infill is gracefully shaped. It is absolutely exquisite to behold. But pushing it is another matter. It is my opinion that infill jointers don't fit the American style of work. They are too heavy to wield for any length of time by mortals. After 10 minutes of pushing this tool up and

down my bench, I was ready for a nap. Also, the front infill is difficult to grip – or perhaps I never found the right grip.

I own a small Carter miter plane, and I have used several of his other planes so I know they are eminently usable tools. This jointer deserves a place above the mantle, or as part of an upper-body workout program.

Sauer & Steiner: New Kid On the Block

Konrad Sauer is a graphic designer turned furniture maker turned toolmaker. And all three of those traits are evident in his world-class workhorses. Sauer, who lives and works outside Toronto, incorporates classic touches from historic infill planes such as the venerable Spiers and Norris brands. But he blends them in a way that makes his tools both classic and distinctive. All of his tools look unmistakably like they are in the same vein, even his custom work.

As far as workmanship, Sauer's planes are at the top of the heap. I could find no flaws in the four bench planes that I inspected closely (two panel planes, one unhandled smoothing plane and a jointer plane). The metalwork was excellent. And the wood showed off Sauer's strengths as a furniture maker. The infill material he selected was itself astonishing, and the small details – fillets, curves and chamfers – were gorgeous.

But how do his planes function? Remarkably well. Everything clicks and fits together in a workmanlike manner. There's no fussing with this or that. The adjuster is precise yet not precious. The iron is well bedded on a massive steel throat plate and wooden bed.

And the tools (all of them) are a joy to push. Naturally, the high pitch and impossibly tight mouth relegate the panel plane I tested (about $2,800) for smoothing large surfaces, which it does with great aplomb.

Sauer's business, which has kicked into high gear in the last couple years, will surely flourish because of his energy and the exquisite finished product.

Sauer & Steiner No. 4: Finishing Magic

I'd really like to hold up this tool for special mention. It lacks a rear tote, which will turn off some users, but I found the plane a delight to wield. The coffin shape of the body and gracefully shaped infills conspire to make this a tool that you unconsciously reach for while working. Like the other unhandled tools I tried, there is a tendency for your hand to rub on the back edge of the iron a bit during long planing ses-

sions, but that's a small price to pay. Because of the No. 4's tight mouth (I tried to photograph it but failed because it was too small) and 55° pitch, it's for finishing cuts alone. This was, to me, one of the most appealing tools of the whole bunch.

Robert Baker Box Miter: Steeped in History

Baker has been making infill planes for a long time for builders of furniture and musical instruments. But his main line of business is in restoring old tools (and sometimes furniture). He's quite famous for his restoration work – many gorgeous and important tools have passed through his shop. I think it's clear that his link to tools of the past has heavily influenced the tools he builds today. They have an unmistakable old-school feel.

The enormous miter plane of his that I got to use was simply an awe-

SAUER AND STEINER NO. 4 SMOOTHING PLANE

Sole length: 7¹/₂"

Weight: 4 lbs. 4.7 oz.

Pitch of iron: 55°

Mouth opening: Immeasurably tight

Iron: High-carbon steel, .186" thick, 2" w.

The Sauer & Steiner No. 4 smoothing plane is unexpectedly comfortable. Note how the knuckle of my index finger rubs the back of the iron; this can be uncomfortable after hours of planing.

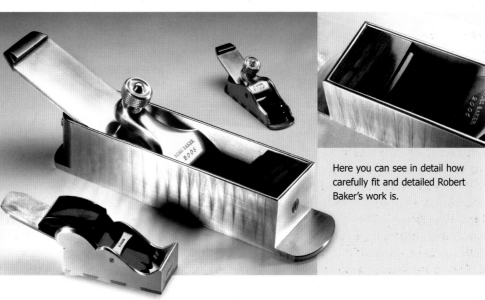

ROBERT BAKER BOX MITER PLANE

Sole length: 10¹/₂"

Weight: 6 lbs. 1.5 oz.

Pitch of iron: 20°

Mouth opening: Immeasurably tight

Iron: High-carbon steel, .180" thick, 2³/₁₆" w.

Contact: 1 Fieldstone Road, York, ME 03909 or HoltzGear@aol.com. (Note: Baker does not have a catalog or web site).

Here you can see in detail how carefully fit and detailed Robert Baker's work is.

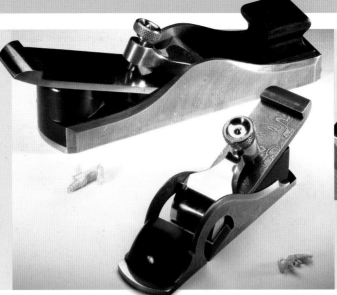

BRIAN BUCKNER DAMASCUS MITER PLANE

Sole length: 8$^{1}/_{8}$"

Weight: 2 lbs. 10.1 oz.

Pitch of iron: 20°

Mouth opening: Tiny

Iron: High-carbon steel, .182" thick, 1$^{5}/_{8}$" w.

Contact: sydnassloot.com/ bbuckner/tools.htm

Brian Buckner's improved miter (rear) and one of his unusual rabbeting infill planes – both with Damascus steel sides.

A detail of the outstanding woodwork on Buckner's miter plane. Ebony is absolutely no fun to shape in this manner.

WAYNE ANDERSON COFFIN SMOOTHING PLANE

Sole length: 5$^{1}/_{2}$"

Weight: 2 lbs. 1.7 oz.

Pitch of iron: 57°

Mouth opening: A sliver

Iron: A2 cryo-treated steel, .189" thick, 1$^{1}/_{2}$" w.

Contact: andersonplanes.com or 763-241-0138

Three Wayne Anderson planes: A rhino-horn shoulder plane (rear), a high-angle smoothing plane and chariot plane.

With no chipbreaker, shavings tend to collect in the mouth. However, the tool doesn't clog, it just doesn't eject shavings as quickly.

some piece of engineering and design. The decorative pattern worked into the sidewalls of the plane was something I'd never seen anything like before (and in fact a couple other toolmakers have wondered how he does it). The wood is finished to a high-grade furniture look. And the details are right-on. This tool was designed to be used on a shooting board and both of the sides were almost perfectly 90° to the sole (the right sidewall of the tool was an airtight 90°; the left just a smidge off). As someone who has tried to "fix" a misaligned sidewall on a few tools I can tell you that this is no small achievement for a handmade tool.

The weight of the plane made it a formidable shooting board plane; your fingers fill right in next to the lever cap like they should live there. The tool was not comfortable when used upright like a bench plane – but few box-shaped miter planes are.

Brian Buckner Miter: An Amazing Amateur

Buckner isn't a professional toolmaker – he does sell some of the planes he makes, but he also holds a high-tech day job in state government. What is particularly interesting about his tools is the level of detail he achieves because he doesn't have to put food on the table by selling his planes. As a result, everything is over the top. The chamfers he files into the steel sides are (I'll say it) downright sexy. He used Damascus steel for the sidewalls of this plane, which gives the tool an unmistakable graphic look. The ebony front bun has the presence and precision of a well-made chess piece.

This tool (photo, above) is what's called an "improved miter" pattern of plane. It's a form that is related to the box-shaped miter on page 115. What's improved about it? Well you can use it like a smoothing plane, which is something I've become comfortable doing. Buckner's tool fit in my hands and was effortless to get it set and taking beautiful shavings.

Wayne Anderson Smoother: No Two Alike

First, some full disclosure: I own this particular plane and have been using it regularly for several months now. Anderson's planes are all built with Swiss-watch mechanicals and European old-world flair. Every one of his tools is a little bit different than the ones he made before, even if it's the same basic form. They all have an organic and human-made quality to them that sets them apart from manufactured tools.

This tool, which was made in late 2005, has some unusual characteristics. First, there's no chipbreaker. This makes the tool simpler to set up – an errant chipbreaker can cause serious clogs. But it also makes the shavings bunch up in the mouth. Chipbreakers have one excellent benefit in bevel-down planes: they push the shavings up and out of the tool. With this smoothing plane (and others I've used without a chipbreaker) the shavings will never eject entirely out of the mouth. That said, this tool has yet to clog on me. The shavings simply pile up and come out of the tool in a less dramatic fash-ion – it's more like they foam up from the mouth rather than spit out.

The diminutive size of this tool would suggest it's only for makers of tiny boxes. Don't believe it. I've used this tool for smoothing large surfaces, even tabletops. And it's excellent for sneaking into small hollows to remove tear-out. As with the other unhandled smoothing planes, you will rub your hand against the iron during extended use. I've taken to putting a preventive bandage there before long planing sessions.

And in the End

The final revelation came when I put Krenov's handplane through the same paces as I did the other tools. By com-parison, Krenov's small polishing plane (7^1/$_2$" long) is crudely made – the wood-en stock looks like it was roughed out with a band saw and knife. The chip-breaker on the iron was roughly ground with many little facets. The mouth was tight (^{1}/$_{32}$") but not extraordinarily so. When I disassembled the plane I found that the bed down by the mouth had a layer or two of blue painter's tape affixed there, perhaps to close up the throat.

But the plane held its own with every other plane on my bench in terms of performance. As did my "work-a-day" tools from Veritas and Lie-Nielsen. The same goes for other high-end tools I've already written about: the Ray Iles A5,

A plane built by James Krenov (foreground) next to a plane made by Ron Hock from one of his plane-building kits (it also works very well).

the Clark & Williams smoothing plane and the new Bridge City variable-pitch plane, which I had only limited time with. Even my vintage Stanleys had nothing to be ashamed of.

I discussed this finding with several toolmakers, none of whom were sur-prised by it. Robin Lee, the president of Lee Valley Tools, summed it up this way: "The wood doesn't care." And he's right. Thomas Lie-Nielsen, founder and owner of Lie-Nielsen Toolworks, put it this way: "A plane is just a jig for a chisel." And he's right, too.

If your planes meet the minimum basic requirements of a plane: a sharp cutter that's firmly secured at an ap-propriate angle for the wood you're working, the tool will do an excellent job. So if you think that buying a very expensive plane will make all lumber bow down before you and your tool, think again.

But there are good reasons to buy custom planes – and they're the same reasons people buy custom furniture when they could go to a discount store and buy an entire bedroom suite for $500. Some people like handmade and exquisite things. And thank goodness, because our mass-manufactured world can use a few handmade touches.

These were the thoughts that were flying around my head as I packed up all the tools used for this article to ship them back to their owner. As I taped the last box and swept up the mounds of shavings we made, I resolved to tear apart our basement looking for my little blue $15 block plane. It just might have some high-end work ahead of it – until I win the lottery, that is.

23

WHY YOU SHOULD LEARN TO SHARPEN AND USE
THESE OFT-NEGLECTED HAND TOOLS.

the case for handsaws

BY GRAHAM BLACKBURN

Far from being quaint anachronisms or symbols of outdated and inefficient technology, handsaws are precision instruments that deserve a place in every contemporary shop.

There are several reasons for such a claim, including safety, convenience and economy, but of ultimate importance for most woodworkers – whether professionals or hobbyists – is the fact that there are things you can do with handsaws that you can't do any other way. Including handsaws in your tool kit gives you more choices and can produce better woodworking.

The most common and most useful handsaws are a dovetail saw, a backsaw (also known as a tenon saw), a rip saw and a crosscut saw.

The dovetail saw is your secret weapon for perfect joinery that lasts lifetimes.

The backsaw is an all-purpose saw for safe cuts on small workpieces – no one wants to push a small piece of wood (2" or less) through the table saw without all sorts of jigs and protection.

And crosscut and rip saws can be efficient alternatives to table saws and band saws when you don't want to change any of your jigs, blades or fences for a single cut. Plus, it's often

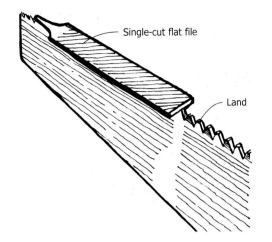

— Single-cut flat file

— Land

Jointing

Hold the file flat on the saw teeth and pass it the length of the blade from the toe to the heel until a "land" (a flat spot) is produced on every tooth.

easier to take the saw to the wood than vice versa.

Similar to all other tools, any handsaw must be properly tuned and skillfully used to be truly useful. But how can you tell a good handsaw from a bad one? How do you make sure it's in top condition? And what are the techniques to use it effortlessly and accurately in your shop?

There is very little that is inherently difficult about handsaw use, yet the answers to these questions – for people raised on tools that must be plugged in before anything happens – have become virtual secrets. What was once common knowledge has been largely forgotten.

The Tune-Up

The first requirement is a sharp and well-set tool. There are three components to tuning up a saw: jointing, filing and setting. And none of these tasks requires a time-consuming or costly trip to the old guy who sharpens saws on the other side of town.

• Jointing simply means running a flat file along the top of the saw's teeth. This ensures that all the teeth will be the same height (so they cut evenly) and provides a clear guide for the next step.

• Filing usually consists of no more than a couple of strokes with a triangular-shaped file placed between every tooth – in a particular manner and order. Three things make this process

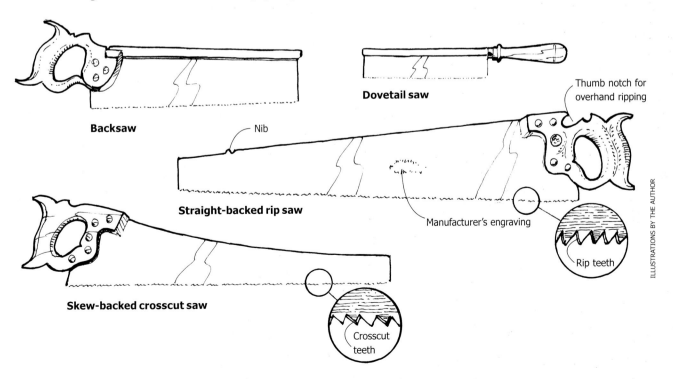

Backsaw

Dovetail saw

Nib

Straight-backed rip saw

Thumb notch for overhand ripping

Manufacturer's engraving

Rip teeth

Skew-backed crosscut saw

Crosscut teeth

ILLUSTRATIONS BY THE AUTHOR

119

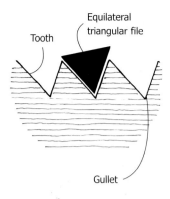

How a saw file should fit

easy: understanding the particular shape of a given saw's teeth, using the right size file, and using a saw vise or an improvised wooden substitute.

Saws designed to cut along the grain, such as rip saws, dovetail saws and many backsaws, have teeth formed like a row of little chisels, as shown in the illustration below. Saws used for cutting across the grain, such as crosscut saws, have teeth filed to look like a series of little knives.

The files used to sharpen Western saws (as opposed to Japanese-style saws) should be equilateral triangle files, because no matter how aggressive the rake of any given saw's teeth may be, the angles formed between the teeth and the angles formed by the teeth themselves are always 60°. The right-sized file is one that is small enough to fit into the gullet between two teeth and large enough to file the entire slope of a tooth.

When you file a saw, you need to clamp the saw in a saw vise (or between two pieces of wood held in a vise) so that the teeth of the tool are just visible above the vise. To position the file correctly, you need to pay attention to three things (which are shown in the illustration below at right):

First, hold the file horizontally.

Second, tilt the file so it fits down into the gullet and preserves the particular rake of the tooth. (This angle can be checked by dropping the file into a gullet at the extreme toe or heel of the blade where the teeth are unlikely to have been worn out of their original shape.)

Third, if you are filing a rip saw, hold the file perpendicular to the side of the blade. If you are filing crosscut teeth, angle the file back about 15°.

Now you are ready to file. If you abide by the following rules you'll never become confused when filing: Always start by clamping the saw so that the handle is to the right, then place the file to the left of the first tooth that is pointing towards you, at the toe of the saw. Hold the file as described above and take as many strokes as necessary to remove half the flat spot formed on the tip of the tooth when you jointed the saw. Remove the file and replace it to the left of the next tooth pointing towards you (this will involve skipping one gullet) and repeat the process until you reach the handle end. Then turn the saw around so the handle is to the left and place the file to the right of the first tooth pointing towards you at the toe of the saw. File until the remainder of the flat spot is gone from the tip of the tooth, then move the file towards the handle, skipping every other gullet. The whole process should take no more than a couple of minutes.

• Setting, the last operation, involves bending alternate teeth sideways so they cut a kerf slightly wider than the thickness of the saw blade. With no set, the friction caused by sawing heats up the moisture in the wood, causing the wood to bind on the saw. The wetter or softer the wood, the greater the set needed.

The tool used to bend the teeth, a sawset, is a small hand-held vise. Place the sawset on a tooth, squeeze the handle and it bends the tooth.

Modern sawsets can be adjusted easily to bend any size tooth correctly. Small saws with many teeth, such as dovetail saws, which are used for relatively small cuts in dry wood, need very little set. Large rip saws need considerably more set. However great the set, you should bend no more than half the height of the tooth – any more and the tooth may break off. This is not fatal, but like eating, the more teeth you have, the easier the process.

More important than the amount of set is the evenness of the job you do. If the teeth on one side of the saw are set out more than the other, they will cut faster and cause the saw to "lead" – a term used to describe the tendency of the saw to wander from the line you're trying to follow.

Sufficient and even set is therefore almost more important than actual sharpness. For this reason, set the teeth in the same way that you file the teeth: First set all the teeth that bend to one side, then turn the saw around and set the other teeth. This will tend to even out any differences.

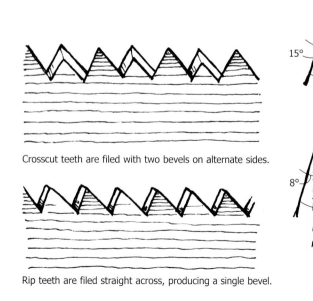

Crosscut teeth are filed with two bevels on alternate sides.

Rip teeth are filed straight across, producing a single bevel.

Filing crosscut and rip teeth

If, after setting, the saw still leads, simply dress down the teeth on the side to which the saw is curving by running a flat file along the side of the teeth. Then check your saw to see if it still leads by making a test cut.

Quality Tips

Even cheap saws can be tuned so they perform well, but quality saws will have more comfortable handles, better balance and superior blades that will stay sharp longer. Clues to finding a superior saw, old or new, include:

• Nicely formed wood handles (the more screws that hold the blade to the handle the better).

• A skewed back, rather than a straight back. This indicates a hollow-ground blade, which means the blade is thinner as you move further away from the teeth, thereby necessitating less set and a smaller kerf.

• Manufacturer's pride, which can be seen in items such as a brass back instead of a steel back on a backsaw, or fancier engraving (sometimes called the "etch") on the face of the blade.

The Basic Technique

Also essential for efficient handsaw use is learning correct technique. Even the best saw will prove disappointing if you don't understand how it should be used. A lot of this is common sense, but to avoid reinventing the wheel, you need to know the basics.

First, understand that handles are not designed to accommodate your entire hand. The idea is to insert only the lower three fingers of your hand into any saw with a closed handle; the index finger should be held alongside the handle, pointing forward.

Second, if you hold the saw like this while aligning yourself with the cut so that your eye is directly above the back of the blade, favoring neither side, you will take advantage of your natural ability to recognize verticality. Unless we are sick or drunk, most of us can tell more easily what is straight up and down than we can judge any other angle.

This basic positioning remains true whether you're sawing down an 8'-long oak board on sawhorses or making a 2" cut in a small workpiece held on your benchtop.

Next you need to know how to start a cut and at what angle the saw teeth should be presented to the work. Whether you're using a small dovetail saw or a full-size, 26"-long rip saw with four teeth per inch, start the kerf by placing the saw on the work near the heel of the blade (the end nearest the

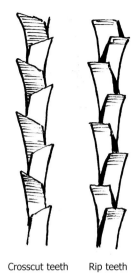

Crosscut teeth   Rip teeth

Tooth set

handle) and drawing backward for a few strokes. Resist the temptation to push until the kerf has been cut sufficiently deep for the saw not to jump out of it.

Guide the saw for these first few backward strokes by holding the work near the blade so the side of the blade rests against your extended thumb, as shown in the illustration on the next page. It's very difficult to cut yourself as long as you're pulling the saw backward, but when you start to push forward, you must move your thumb.

Filing positions

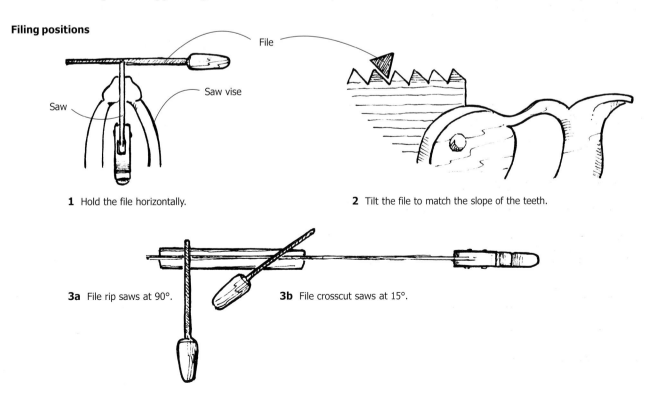

1 Hold the file horizontally.

2 Tilt the file to match the slope of the teeth.

3a File rip saws at 90°. **3b** File crosscut saws at 15°.

Keeping the line visible

1 Tilt the workpiece so that the layout lines across the top and down the front side are visible.
2 Then turn the workpiece around so the layout line on the back side is visible – the previous kerfs will guide the saw.

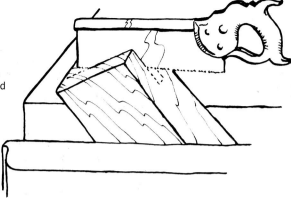

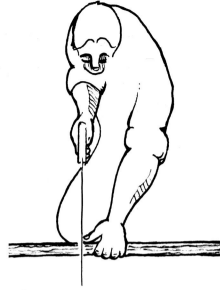

Hand and eye position

1 Hold the saw vertically.
2 Position your eye above the blade.
3 Use your thumb to guide the saw for the first few backward strokes.

The initial back cuts and the first few forward cuts should be made with the saw at a fairly low angle to the work, about 20° or so. Once the kerf is well established you'll work faster if you raise the angle. Especially long cuts may require you to insert a wedge or screwdriver into the kerf to prevent it from closing up and binding on the saw if the board has been cut from wood that has grown under compression. When using a dovetail saw or a backsaw, the situation may demand a more horizontal stroke, especially if the workpiece is small and you're using a holding device such as a bench hook.

Remember to use the whole length of the blade instead of short strokes. This is a more efficient use of the entire saw and will demand less effort. In any event, you shouldn't have to push the saw with a great deal of force – if the saw is properly sharpened and set it should be able to cut through the wood under its own weight – if held at a steep enough angle.

Also, always saw on the waste side of the layout line. This sounds obvious, but it implies that you position yourself and the workpiece so that you can always see the line you're attempting to saw on through the entire cut. It's easy to secure a piece of wood in the vise, align yourself carefully with the cut, then saw past the point where you can see the line.

Guaranteeing Accuracy

In addition to the above techniques, remember that in traditional high-end woodworking, the use of hand tools is rarely synonymous with freehand hand-tool use. In the same way that you would be ill-advised to attempt to push something through your table saw without the aid of fences, miter gauges, hold-downs or sleds, it also is risky to

use a handsaw without taking advantage of the shop-made jigs and guides that have been developed over the centuries to guarantee accuracy.

The most useful sawing aid for small workpieces is undoubtedly the bench hook. Easily made in a variety of sizes (sometimes in pairs), the bench hook functions as a third hand for holding a workpiece securely. Also, if the hook is affixed and kerfed accurately, it works as an accurate miter block.

A metal miter box is useful, but typically requires an especially large backsaw. You can use a dovetail saw or a regular backsaw with similar accuracy if you make your own wooden miter box, providing it has stops and wedges for complicated angled cuts.

When using either of the above devices, how you position the work determines if you'll get tear-out on the

Sawing angles

20°

45°

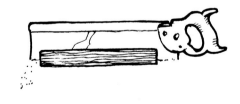

1 At start of cut the saw should be at a low angle.

2 Increase the angle once the cut is established ...

3 ... unless you're using a backsaw for joinery cuts.

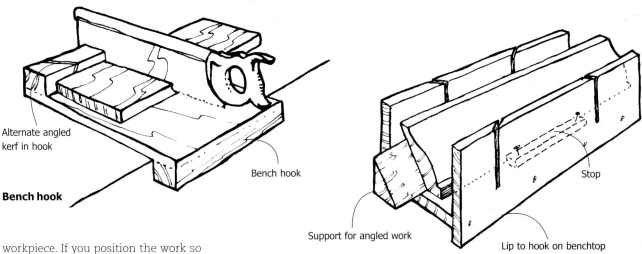

Alternate angled
kerf in hook

Bench hook

Bench hook

Support for angled work

Stop

Lip to hook on benchtop

Shop-made miter box

workpiece. If you position the work so
that the shaped part of the moulding
faces you as you work, the tear-out will
be on the backside of the cut and then
hidden from view. This is called "sawing
into the cut."

While bench hooks and miter boxes
can quickly become standard equipment in many shops, there are numerous other jigs and guides that can be
made easily as the specific need arises.
A side guide, for example, can be cut
with a face at any angle to provide a
foolproof method for you to make wide,
angled cuts in your work.

One of the easiest mistakes to make
when using a handsaw is to saw deeper
than intended. This kind of mistake
can ruin tenon shoulders, dovetails,
housed joints and many other cuts.
Metal miter boxes usually are fitted
with depth stops, but there is no reason
not to clamp your own depth stop to
the side of whatever saw you may be
using, thereby guaranteeing a consistent depth of cut. You will frequently
find old saws with a pair of holes bored
through the blade – these once held
screws that were used to attach a strip
of wood that functioned as an adjustable depth stop.

Also, you should take advantage
of quickly made auxiliary vise jaws
to hold unusually shaped workpieces,
such as round or curved sections, and
remember whenever possible to position the workpiece so the cut you make
is vertical.

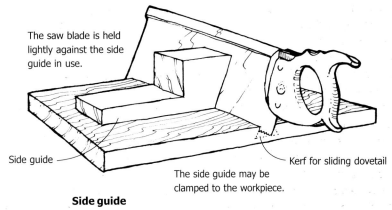

The saw blade is held
lightly against the side
guide in use.

Side guide

Kerf for sliding dovetail

The side guide may be
clamped to the workpiece.

Side guide

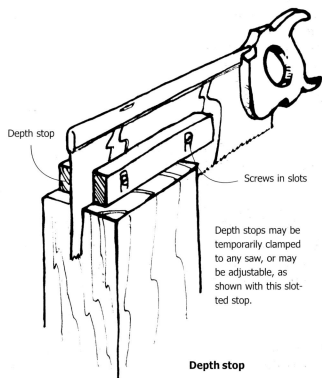

Depth stop

Screws in slots

Depth stops may be
temporarily clamped
to any saw, or may
be adjustable, as
shown with this slot-
ted stop.

Depth stop

24

WHEN COMPARING JAPANESE SAWS TO WESTERN SAWS, THE DIFFERENCE IS MORE THAN JUST PUSHING OR PULLING.

handsaws: east vs. west

BY CHRISTOPHER SCHWARZ

It might shock you to hear this, but in the last decade or so more than three centuries of a Western tool-making tradition has been almost completely undone.

The Western handsaw, a tool that cuts on the push stroke and was the pride of the English-speaking world, isn't the tool most woodworkers now reach for when they need a handsaw.

It has been replaced by the Japanese saw, which cuts on the pull stroke and once was mocked by Westerners as "backwards."

The numbers tell the story best:

• Sixty percent of the saws sold by Lee Valley Tools are Japanese style, says Rob Lee, president of Lee Valley, one of the world's largest hand-tool catalogs, which sells both styles of tools.

• Woodcraft Supply Corp. sells 100 Japanese saws for every Western saw, says Peter Collins, a product manager for this large catalog, Internet and retail company.

• And Japan Woodworker, which sold many Western saws 30 years ago, now sells 1,000 Japanese saws for every Western saw, says Fred Damsen, the owner of the catalog company.

What caused this shift to Japanese saws? While some say it's because sawing on the pull stroke is superior to sawing on the push stroke, the issue actually is more complex.

And which saw is best? The prevailing wisdom says Japanese saws are su-perior and easier for beginners to learn. But if you've ever worked with a sharp, well-tuned Western saw, you know this can't be entirely true.

To answer these questions, we decided to scrutinize the two types of saws to learn their true differences, beyond the information in catalogs. Armed with this knowledge, you can choose a saw that's right for your woodworking and your budget. Our journey begins in ancient Egypt.

The First Handsaws

Modern woodworkers would almost immediately recognize the first known metal saws, which were excavated in Egypt.

They had a long, knife-like blade, a straight grip and cut on the pull stroke, like a Japanese saw. Why the pull stroke?

Early Egyptian saws were made with a thin sheet of copper (as thin as 0.03") and had no rigid spine like the modern backsaw.

"(If they had been used) on the push stroke, the saw would have buckled and bent," according to Geoffrey Killen, author of numerous books and articles on Egyptian woodworking and the head of faculty at the Design and Technology Department of the Stratton Upper School and Community College in England.

One unusual aspect of these early saws is that all the teeth were set (meaning they were bent) to only one side of the blade. This makes the saw quite difficult to steer, and the Egyptians had to come up with ingenious ways of wedging the saw kerf open during each cut, according to Killen.

The advent of bronze tools brought some refinements, as did the iron saws developed by the Romans. But the form of the tool itself was still a pull saw with a thin blade.

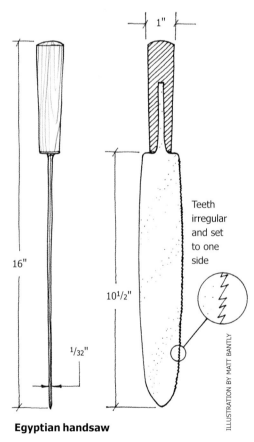

Teeth irregular and set to one side

1"

16"

10¹/₂"

1/32"

Egyptian handsaw

ILLUSTRATION BY MATT BANTLY

A Japanese-style dozuki

A Western-style dovetail saw

The West Stumbles

The 19th and early 20th centuries were the golden age of Western handsaws. There were hundreds of saw manufacturers, fierce competition, high-quality tools and a very hungry market.

But as the demand for quality hand tools declined, so did the number of manufacturers. And quality slipped dramatically.

"Western manufacturers thought it was OK to ship a saw that was poorly set, dull and had a handle that looked like it was made by a third-grade art student," says Thomas Lie-Nielsen, owner of Lie-Nielsen Toolworks. "You couldn't use the saws right out of the box. It's no wonder the Japanese ate their lunch."

When Western saws suitable for cabinetmaking disappeared off the shelves, the Japanese saws quickly picked up the slack.

"In Japan, the product lines have not been cheapened," says Lee of Lee Valley Tools. "Even products that have been mass produced have not been cheapened."

So while it was tough to find a decent new Western saw at almost any price, the Japanese exported saws to the West that were sharp, straight, perfectly set and inexpensive. A good Japanese backsaw still costs only about $40. So it's little wonder that the Japanese saw now is in many North American workshops. It was, in many ways, a simple matter of economics.

It was the invention of the frame saw (which put the thin blade under high tension in a wooden framework) that finally allowed these thin metal blades to be used on either the push stroke or the pull stroke – much like a modern coping saw or bowsaw, according to *The History of Woodworking Tools* by W.L. Goodman (G. Bell & Sons). The frame saw might not have been invented by the Romans, but they certainly refined the form and produced a wide variety of them.

This is an important fork in the road in saw history that affects us to this day. The Japanese culture developed pull saws like the Egyptians, but they never seem to have developed frame saws, according to several students of Japanese history (although a Chinese frame saw did come into use in 15th century Japan).

So the Japanese, with their scarce metal resources and their traditions of working low to the ground, stuck with the pull saw and refined it to a high art.

In the West, most of the European continent stuck with the bowsaw. But the Dutch and English took a different path. In the mid-17th century, wider steel blades became possible thanks to water-driven mills, and the modern handsaw that cuts on the push stroke was born.

The Western handsaw, shown here being used by Don McConnell with an overhand rip grip, cuts on the push stroke.

Facts About Japanese Saws

Japanese craftsmen would be quite curious about the way Westerners use their saws. For one, we work on a high bench and clamp our work when sawing. The Japanese furniture maker works on a low sawhorse (6" high or so) and does not generally have a vise.

"(Westerners) tend to clamp everything," says Harrelson Stanley of JapaneseTools.com. "The Japanese don't clamp unless they have to. They do some wedging. Mostly they saw in toward a solid object," such as the work, which is secured by their foot, he says.

A second difference is that many Westerners use the crosscut dozuki saw (a saw with a rigid spine) for cutting dovetails, which is primarily a ripping operation.

The Japanese woodworker instead uses a rip-tooth dozuki (which is less common in the West) or a rip saw without a back, says Damsen of Japan Woodworker. That's because the Japanese philosophy on dovetails and tenons is, at times, different than the Western approach.

"When (Japanese woodworkers) cut dovetails they don't want the cut too smooth," he says. "They compress the joint before assembly and let it expand and lock the joint."

Westerners want a smoother cut and are willing to sacrifice the speed of a rip tooth. Many Japanese dovetail saws for the Western market have some sort of combination tooth, in some cases a tooth that was designed to cut plywood that also works quite well for dovetails, Damsen says.

Types of Japanese Saws

But one thing Japanese and Western craftsmen share is having to choose

advantages of japanese saws

• Thinner kerf removes less wood, which means less effort.
• The inexpensive saws are of high quality and work very well right out of the box.
• The teeth are generally harder and can go longer between sharpenings. The best Western saws are 52-54 on the Rockwell "C" scale. Japanese saws are 51-58 for the handmade saws, and 61 and higher for the machine-made impulse-hardened saws. While the harder teeth stay sharp longer, they also are more brittle and prone to break.
• There are many manufacturers who sell a wide variety of saws with different teeth configurations (more than 100 kinds, by Harrelson Stanley's count) for every woodworking task and every type of wood.

disadvantages

• It's almost impossible for a woodworker to sharpen a Japanese saw. The teeth are too complex on handmade saws and too hard on the impulse-hardened ones. Handmade saws usually go to Japan for sharpening. Impulse-hardened saws become scrapers or go in the garbage.
• The crosscut teeth are more delicate. If you hit a knot or cut quickly into particularly tough wood, you could lose a tooth or two.
• The saws are easier for the inexperienced sawyer to ruin. Because the blade is thin, you can bend it on the return stroke if you push too hard and the saw isn't aligned properly in the kerf.
• Japanese saws pull sawdust toward you, obscuring your line.
• Japanese saws made for dimensioning lumber (not joinery) have shorter blades than full-size Western handsaws. Depending on the saw, the pull saw might require more strokes to do the same amount of work.
• Japanese saws are designed to be used in traditional Japanese fashion on low benches. When used in Western fashion, some Japanese saws are not always as effective as they should be.

Instead of benches, Japanese craftsmen use low trestles. Sawing a tenon with a Japanese saw this way is efficient and requires sawing at a less awkward angle than at a high Western bench. However, you need to be in good shape to work this way.

advantages of western saws

• The teeth are more durable than those on Japanese saws and are highly unlikely to break, even under the worst conditions. The blades themselves are thicker and less likely to buckle in use.
• They will last you a lifetime. The teeth can be resharpened many times. Saws can even be refiled by the user to a different tooth configuration if their needs change.
• With a little practice, you can sharpen a Western saw with inexpensive and easy-to-obtain tools.
• Western dovetail saws that are properly filed for a rip cut will cut more aggressively than the crosscut-filed dozuki that's commonly used for dovetails in the United States.
• They push the sawdust away from your cut line.
• High-quality secondhand Western saws are both plentiful and inexpensive in most areas.

disadvantages

• High-quality new or restored Western saws are more expensive than their Japanese counterparts. Japanese joinery saws average about $45; the equivalent quality Western saw costs $125.
• Inexpensive new Western saws are – in general – dull and poorly set compared to similarly priced Japanese saws. Learning to saw with these less-expensive tools frustrates many beginners, causing them to swear off Western saws.
• While vintage Western saws are plentiful in most parts of the United States, you must first learn to restore them before putting them to work: straightening the blades, fixing the teeth and sharpening.
• The teeth are softer and require more frequent sharpening, although it is a task you can do yourself after a little education and practice.
• In general, the saws are heavier and have a thicker kerf, so they require more effort to use.

For crosscutting in joinery, the Japanese will use a dozuki saw (which means "shoulder of a tenon"). There are various ways to grip the saw.

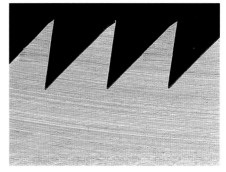

Japanese Rip Teeth ■ The length of the rip teeth are graduated on Japanese saws. They start small near the handle and get larger.

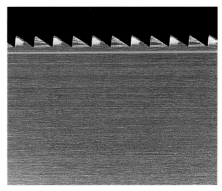

Western Rip Teeth ■ Rip teeth work like chisels, levering out the grain. Crosscut teeth work like knives, severing the fibers on either side.

what type of Japanese saw to buy: a machine-made saw or a craftsman-made saw. There are important differences:
• A good-quality machine-made Japanese saw costs about $20-$50. The price of a craftsman-made saw averages $150, and the premium tools are about $250 or more.
• Generally, craftsman-made saws have softer teeth than the machine-made saws, which are typically impulse-hardened. Impulse hardening is a fast, high-voltage process that hardens only the teeth. While the machine-made saws stay sharp longer, they cannot be resharpened without totally retoothing the blade.

Craftsman-made saws can be resharpened and even customized to the way you work. But this is meaningless to Western woodworkers, says Frank Tashiro, owner of Tashiro Hardware, which sells the line of impulse-hardened ZETA Saws.

"(The sharpener) doesn't know your work so he does the best he can, so it doesn't work out," says Tashiro, who adds that the best value and performance come from a Japanese saw with replaceable impulse-hardened blades.

But replaceable blades rankle woodworkers who don't believe in disposable tools.

To counter that, Japanese saw manufacturers say that once your impulse-hardened saw becomes too dull for woodworking, it is still plenty sharp for work in the garden as a pruning saw.

"You can make a nice scraper out of the blade, too," Damsen says of the saws.
• Another difference is that many craftsman-made saws are more delicate because of their thinner blades. Even the most robust craftsman-made saw should not fall into the hands of a beginning woodworker.

"Just because you have a $200 saw doesn't mean you will saw better," says Stanley. "It's important to practice the technique. Start with impulse-hardened saws. Don't get a $250 saw and break it. As your skills improve you can use thinner saws."

When using Japanese joinery saws, most everyone agrees that you shouldn't be aggressive or saw at a radical angle. Just a bit of downward pressure on the pull stroke is all it takes, and you shouldn't apply any downward pressure on the return push.

Facts About Western Saws

No one can deny that Japanese saws cut very well, but so do Western saws that are sharp and properly set. The problem is finding Western saws suitable for woodworking. There are still some manufacturers of full-size Western saws that do a decent job for woodworking, including E. Garlick & Son, Pax, Paragon, Sandvik/ Bahco, Lynx and Augusta. Some of them also make joinery saws – backsaws with a rigid spine on the blade. And companies such as Lie-Nielsen and Adria now make premium joinery saws that are equal to the outstanding saws of the 19th century.

But by far, the biggest sources of quality Western saws are flea markets and auctions. Top-of-the-line Disston, Simonds and E.C. Atkins saws can be purchased for $5-$25. These, however, can be rusty, dull and bent. If you have no desire to restore one of these old saws, there is an alternative.

Pete Taran runs the web site VintageSaws.com, which is a sawyer's paradise. He takes classic handsaws and backsaws and returns them to their former glory by making them sharp, properly set and ready to cut. A vintage highly tuned handsaw or backsaw will cost between $85 and $200 at Vintage Saws.

The site also is a treasure trove of good historical information on saws. One of Taran's primary goals is to teach woodworkers how to sharpen their Western saws, which is easier than you might think.

He sells the files and saw sets you need, plus there is a fantastic tutorial on his web site that explains the process from start to finish. And if you just want to get your feet wet, Taran even offers a saw-filing kit to get you started. The kit comes with a user-grade saw with freshly cut teeth, a file, a file handle and complete instructions. When you're done, you'll have some more confidence and a saw that cuts very well.

Sharpening a Western saw is probably one of the biggest stumbling blocks for woodworkers.

"No one knows how to sharpen Western saws," says Graham Blackburn, author of *Traditional Woodworking Handtools* (available with his other books at blackburnbooks.com) and an instructor at Marc Adams Woodworking School. "I ask the students to bring in their worst plane and their worst saw. Once they sharpen their saws they never go back to Japanese saws."

But if you don't want to learn to sharpen, you still can get a flea-market saw professionally tuned.

We recommend Daryl Weir of Knoxville, Ill. Weir has tuned up a few handsaws and backsaws for us over the years and does a nice job, and his prices are reasonable. (See the "Saw Sources" box for contact information.)

Western Saw Tips

Once sharpened, a Western saw is easier to use than you might think. Here are a few tips:

• Though it sounds obvious, use a rip saw for rip cuts, such as dovetailing. Some dovetail saws are filed for crosscut. They work OK, but not as well as a rip saw.

• Let the saw do the work. Don't use a lot of downward pressure on the kerf – this is surely the No. 1 problem faced by beginners. The saw will wander and you'll never cut straight.

• Don't clench the handle tightly. Hold the saw with just enough pressure

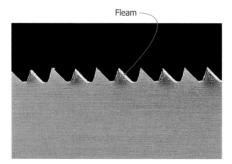

Japanese Crosscut Teeth ■ Note the long slender teeth and three bevels filed on each tooth. The tips are discolored from impulse-hardening.

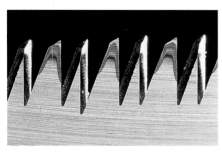

Fleam

Western Crosscut Teeth ■ You can see the simpler secondary bevels (called the "fleam") filed on every other tooth.

Some students of woodworking history think the push stroke was developed in the West because we work on high benches, unlike Japanese craftsmen who work near the floor on low trestles or beams.

This $18 Disston No. 4 backsaw cuts incredibly well now that it has been properly sharpened. The handle on a vintage Western saw will fit your hand like a glove. Later handles are uncomfortable to use and look crude by comparison.

to keep it under control. And use only three fingers – your index finger should point down the blade.

Worst of Both Worlds?

All this has to make you wonder why someone hasn't built a saw that merges the best qualities of both traditions. Well, a few companies have tried, though nothing has been able to challenge the dominance of the pure Japanese-style saw.

And the reason might be illustrated by the experience of one veteran woodworker.

A few years ago, Blackburn was poking around a flea market and discovered a beautiful old Spear & Jackson backsaw.

The saw had a perfectly shaped handle, much like the one on the outstanding Lie-Nielsen dovetail saw. But the blade of this Spear & Jackson was horribly bent. So Blackburn hung it on his wall.

One day a friend noticed the saw and offered to send it to Japan to see if they could straighten it out. Blackburn agreed. The saw came back a few months later straight as an arrow but with one major and shocking change.

They had filed Japanese-style teeth on the blade. Trying to keep an open mind, Blackburn gave it a try. "It cuts well," he says, "but it feels wrong to me. So it still hangs on the wall."

Chalk it up to this: When it comes to traditional hand-tool skills, it's hard to defy tradition. Now you just have to decide which tradition is best for you.

Saw Sources

Adria Woodworking Tools
604-710-5748 or adriatools.com
- Premium Western joinery saws

BlackburnBooks.com
- Books and videos on traditional Western woodworking

DisstonianInstitute.com
- Detailed information on Disstons

EuropeanHandTools.com
888-222-8331
- E. Garlick and Lynx saws

Geoffrey Killen's Egyptian Site
geocities.com/gpkillen
- Information on Egyptian woodworking tools and furniture

Hida Tool
800-443-5512 or hidatool.com
- Range of Japanese saws

Japan Woodworker
800-537-7820 or japanwoodworker.com
- Full range of Japanese saws and some Western saws

JapaneseTools.com
877-692-3684
- Range of Japanese tools, including some hard-to-find types

Lee Valley Tools
800-871-8158 or leevalley.com
- Impulse-hardened Japanese saws
- Wide range of Western saws

Lie-Nielsen Toolworks
800-327-2520 or lie-nielsen.com
- Premium Western joinery saws

Tashiro Hardware
206-328-7641 or tashirohardware.com
- Impulse-hardened Japanese saws

Daryl Weir
weir@gallatinrivernet or
781 S. Market St,
Knoxville, Il. 61448
- Western saw sharpening

VintageSaws.com
- Restored vintage Western handsaws and sharpening supplies

Woodcraft Supply Corp.
800-225-1153 or woodcraft.com
- Impulse-hardened Japanese saws and some Western saws

25

THE TRADITIONAL HAND SAW (WHEN WIELDED CORRECTLY)
CAN SIZE ALL YOUR STOCK. HERE'S A BASIC PRIMER.

secrets to sawing fast

BY ADAM CHERUBINI

Ripping at the horse is surprisingly fast and effective. Here (dressed in the traditional garb I wear at Pennsbury Manor) I'm using the more heavily raked teeth at the toe of the saw to help start the cut.

Hand saws were used to make some of the finest furniture ever built. They are very clearly capable of producing accurate cuts. Hand saws require little shop space, and produce little appreciable noise or dust.

These facts conspire to allow work in environments or at hours otherwise inhospitable to modern means. Please don't underestimate the advantage of working outside, late at night, in the living room or kitchen, etc. Likewise, the elimination of the table saw – or even the reduction of its use – frees up precious workshop floor space, allowing room for other tools, workbenches, finishing areas, etc.

So it appears in advantage after advantage that hand saws are effective if not superior tools. Clearly only 220-volt speed stands in their way of becoming the one essential tool in every woodworker's shop.

In this chapter we'll investigate the secret tricks period woodworkers used to saw quickly. Let's begin by examining basic technique:

How to Rip Efficiently

Ripping at the horse is performed using one or more sawhorses. Boards can be placed across two horses (typically 20" to 24" high), or supported by the broad top of a single horse. Because ripping is defined as sawing along the grain, the cut is started at one end of the board.

The cut is started with the finer, heavily raked teeth, at the toe of the rip saw. Using the knuckle of your thumb or forefinger to steady the blade, draw the saw backwards to create a small nick. Use very light strokes for the first cuts. Don't allow the full weight of the saw to rest against the board. These first motions can be very short, using just the fine teeth at the toe.

Once the saw starts cutting, full strokes can be used. The saw should be held more vertical than horizontal, say 45° to 60° with respect to the board's face. Don't force the saw into

the cut as if it's a knife. Let the saw's weight provide the force for the cut. Relax your grip. Focus on placing your effort behind the teeth. These strokes are performed with the arm only. The shoulders must remain fixed, as twisting moves the hand sideways. The hand should move from armpit to full extension, in a nice straight line. In time, this motion will become second nature.

To correct a wayward cut, lower the angle the saw makes with the board. The saw will now ride in a much longer kerf. Push the heel of the saw sideways, ever so slightly back to the line with each passing stroke. The effort of sawing will likely be increased as the blade is forced into a curved shape. If the effort becomes too great or the miscut too severe, return the saw to the previously straighter section, and lay it down. Lay a new kerf through the miscut area. See the photo on page 132 for more details.

If the cut is not perpendicular through the thickness, there's no way to fix it during the saw cut. Resist the temptation to twist the saw or bend it sideways to correct. This won't help. This must be fixed later with a hand plane, but then nearly all long rip saw cuts must be cleaned up regardless of the tool that does the ripping. Next time, leave a little extra room to the line. Leaving a little extra beyond the line is no great sin in rip sawing. The planing goes so quickly, one can't honestly say it's a waste of time, only a waste of wood.

Crosscutting Wide Boards and Panels

Because crosscuts are often related to the long edge (often perpendicular) they are typically performed after ripping

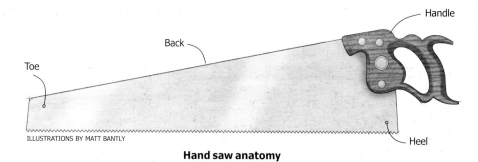

Hand saw anatomy

ILLUSTRATIONS BY MATT BANTLY

and edge planing is finished. The resulting cut is often the finish cut (not like a rough cut with a rip). Moreover, planing end grain is difficult. For these reasons, extra care should be taken to produce a straight and square crosscut.

Depending on the length of the resulting scrap or offcut, crosscutting is performed either using the bench hook or using a pair of sawhorses. The line to be cut should be carefully knifed across the face of the board. A square mark is then knifed through the thickness with the try square. Make this mark on the far edge of the board (where the cut is about to begin).

Drawing the saw back slowly at a 45° angle to the work, nick the far corner. Begin the saw cut with light, careful

strokes. Advance on both lines (across the face and through the thickness) simultaneously. This is a critical skill worth practicing, as it will be later used for all crosscuts and many joinery operations, including dovetailing. When the cut through the thickness is complete, lay the saw down and advance the cut only on the face line, using the existing kerf to guide the saw. Maintain this relatively low angle (maybe 30°) until a sizable kerf is created. With a good-sized slit to guide your saw, begin incrementally raising the angle as you saw through the stock. Your saw should make a 45° angle when you reach the end of the cut. As always, make sure the scrap is well supported before finishing the cut.

good grips

All hand saws are held in a similar manner. Three fingers and the thumb grip the handle lightly. The index finger points, laying along the side of the handle or blade.

Most rip saws with closed or ring-type handles have enough room for four fingers. These handles allow a two-handed grip. You can pass the thumb of the offhand through the space not used by your dominant hand's forefinger. The other fingers wrap over the top of the handle. You will likely find the handle has been specially designed to permit this grip.

The overhand grip, while it looks uncomfortable, is highly effective. I find it is especially helpful when sawing thick stock as it limits the number of teeth in the kerf and keeps the kerf free of tooth-clogging sawdust.

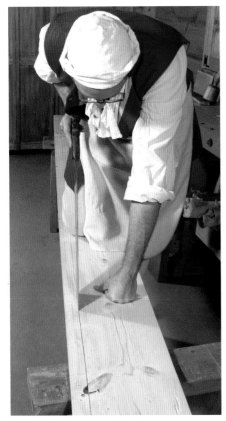 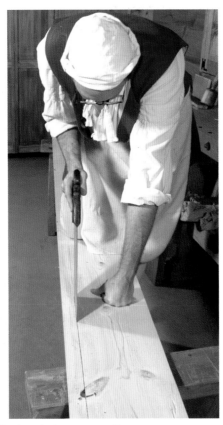 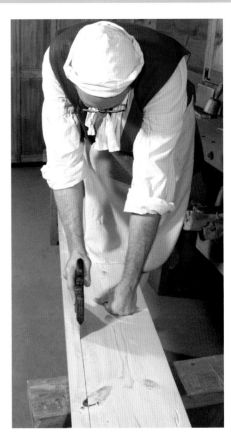

Try to limit the amount of motion in your upper body when ripping or crosscutting.

Picking Up Speed

I find a sharp saw cuts faster than a dull one (not hard to believe). Sharpening a saw isn't as difficult as honing a plane iron, though it takes about the same amount of time to learn and perform. Selecting the right saw for the job (see "Good Saws" on the next page) is a major contributor to sawing speed. In general, saws with lower rakes cut faster. Even faster than a low rake is a saw with no rake or negative rake (forward-swept teeth). Handles that focus all effort behind the teeth seem more efficient to me and thus make sawing faster. Of course, these benefits come at some price. But generally, learning more about how saw teeth work, and optimizing your saws for your work, is an important first step to learning to saw faster (and a topic worthy of another article).

In addition to a good saw, good technique makes a significant contribution to speed. With proper technique and practice, you'll be able to rip 4'-long 4/4 stock in a few minutes. The ripped edge will need to be planed to achieve a

straight, square edge, but that process goes quickly and would be performed regardless of the voltage of the saw used. But good saws and technique can take you only so far. There is a limit to the speed achievable. I believe that limit is still far below the reasonable expectations of modern craftsmen.

Correct a miscut by lowering the angle as shown above. This angle puts more of the saw in the kerf. We see this philosophy again and again in the period shop. Long tools make straight cuts.

Before we reject our hand saws it may be helpful to look back in history (as is our custom in this column) to see what we might learn from 18th-century craftsmen.

Eighteenth-century account books indicate craftsmen sometimes purchased lumber in "scantlen." This may provide some explanation for pre-industrial woodworkers' productivity. Scantlen was a term used to describe boards purchased at some desired dimensions straight from the mill. Craftsmen could purchase stock in the sizes they needed to limit the amount of sawing required in-house. Mills at the time, not unlike modern lumberyards, had specialized machinery and personnel that could dimension lumber faster than individual shops. Some 18th-century mills in Philadelphia advertised that they had lumber sized for certain industries in stock and ready for immediate delivery. Surely this was done in response to a demand from area craftsmen who found such a service cost-effective.

Modern period woodworkers rely heavily on project plans made from extant pieces. Unfortunately the original builders' plans are lost. It could be that the plans were drawn on scrap wood that later fueled the shop's heating system. Or perhaps we have failed to recognize their plans simply because their plans don't look like plans we use today. Artists generally don't care if their canvas is 12" tall or 200". Beauty isn't contained in these numbers. The proportions are what we see, not inches. Period craftsmen may have worked parametrically, using existing stock to define key dimensions. In this way, they could use their materials more efficiently, limit the labor required and work directly to the desires of their customers.

Now you know a secret I've spent years learning. If you don't understand this mystery, unplug your table saw and start relying on your hand saw. After you've learned to sharpen and use it correctly, you too will find clever ways to keep it hanging from the nail in the wall. No saw can cut as fast as that.

good saws

Choosing the right saw for the job at hand is an important first hurdle.

Rip Saw ▪ A good rip-saw blade should be as long as your arm. For work with 4/4 to 8/4 softwoods, I recommend a coarsely toothed saw. Teeth should vary from 5 tpi at the heel to 7 to 8 tpi at the toe. Similarly, the rake angle should vary from nearly 0° at the heel to 20° or even 30° at the toe. A "salmon belly" is an advantage, though I'm not sure I understand exactly why. A salmon belly – sometimes also referred to as a "breasted" saw is when the blade is a bit convex at the toothline. For ripping hard wood, the saw can be finer pitched. Six to 8 tpi at the heel makes a good hardwood ripper. If you can have only one, always choose the finer toothed saw.

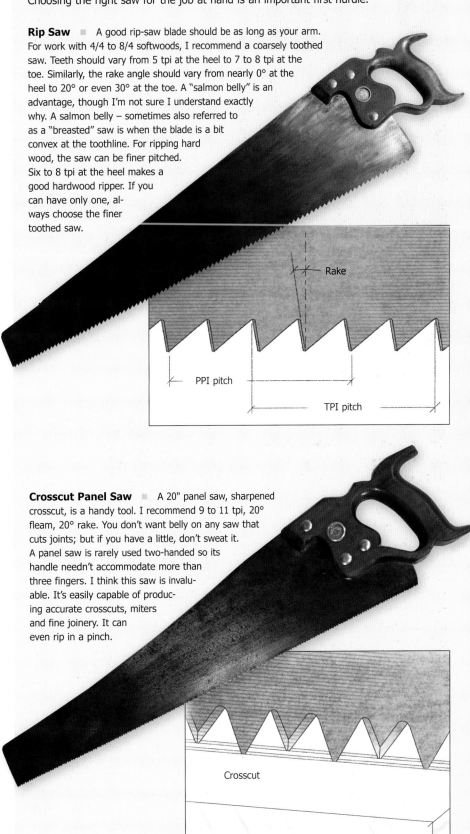

Crosscut Panel Saw ▪ A 20" panel saw, sharpened crosscut, is a handy tool. I recommend 9 to 11 tpi, 20° fleam, 20° rake. You don't want belly on any saw that cuts joints; but if you have a little, don't sweat it. A panel saw is rarely used two-handed so its handle needn't accommodate more than three fingers. I think this saw is invaluable. It's easily capable of producing accurate crosscuts, miters and fine joinery. It can even rip in a pinch.

26

**STOP MEASURING AND SIMPLY LEARN
HOW TO SAW STRAIGHT.**

the final word on dovetails

BY FRANK KLAUSZ

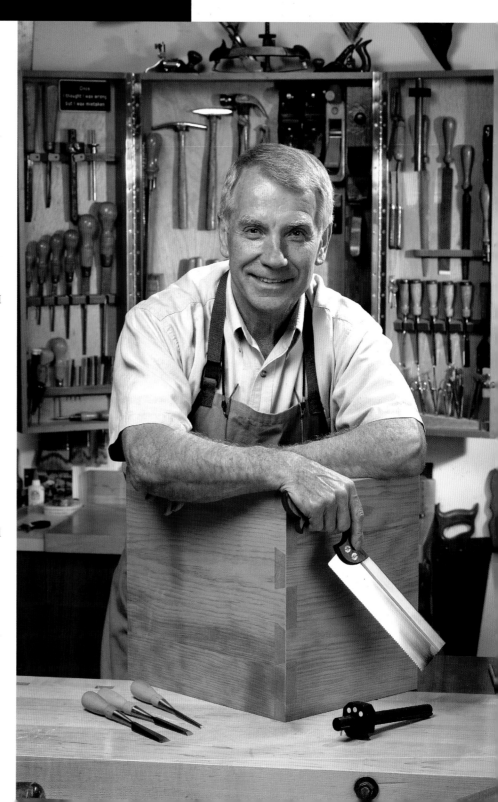

The dovetail is an ancient joint widely used in cathedrals, barns and Egyptian furniture. It is the right joint for many items including fine furniture, carcases, drawers and jewelry boxes. They are all dovetailed together.

I was only 27 years old when I came to this country in 1968 from my native Hungary. Although I had a piece of paper that said "master cabinetmaker," I was still very eager to learn more about my trade.

Where I came from I was happy if I could carry a white-haired master's tool chest to the job site because I knew I would learn a thing or two that day working with him. Now I am that white-haired master with 45 years of experience in the trade.

In the early 1970s I went to a lot of seminars. Some were on dovetailing with well-known teachers in the woodworking world. Some cut the tails first; others cut the pins first. They used tools that I didn't own, such as a dovetail marker. They measured the size of the pins and tails, which is completely different from my method. The more I studied, the more confused I became. I decided to find the best way to cut tight dovetails quickly.

A Search for the Best Method

I owned an antique restoration shop. I had a chance to study a lot of antiques from around the world. Each time a piece of furniture came to the shop, the first thing I looked at was the dovetails. I studied hundreds of them and made tracings of dozens of unusual pieces. I tried to find an answer for my methods. I learned in Hungary, I worked in Vienna, and I was looking for someone from a different part of the world than Eastern Europe to do dovetails. I found Hector, from Guatemala, a master cabinetmaker.

"This is great, Central America!" I said. I asked him to make me dovetails. He said, "You cabinetmaker, you make dovetail." We had a language problem. I had a hard time explaining to him my intentions. I replied, "I know how to cut dovetails, I want to see how you do it." "OK," he said. He grabbed some chisels, a dovetail saw, a marking gauge, some scrap wood, set up the marking gauge to the thickness of the wood, marked the wood, clamped it into a vise and started cutting. He cut the pins, chiseled the pins; from the pins he marked the tails, chiseled the tails and put it together. "How is that?" he asked. I was as happy as can be! "That is exactly the way I do it," I replied.

After my experience with Hector, and my 10 years of researching dovetail techniques, I came to the conclusion that Grandpa wasn't a bad craftsman at all and my father taught me well.

Later on, I wrote some articles for different magazines and I made some videos – one of them is *Dovetail a Drawer with Frank Klausz*. Before I knew it, I was teaching the craft throughout America. I taught hundreds of people how to dovetail. A lesson took plus or minus one hour with a 99 percent student success rate (let's face it, some of us are born with two left hands).

Anyone Can Do It

If you already know how to make hand cut dovetails, and you are happy with your method, I am happy for you and don't mean to change your ways. If you are a beginner or learning about new methods, you can do it my way. I know you can do it!

How do you know how to write? You learned in school. You made a whole

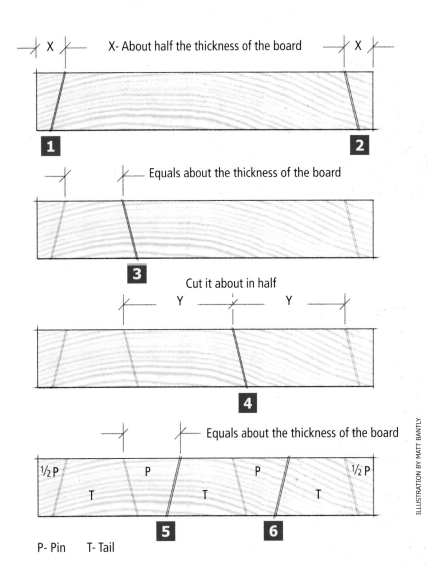

1
2
X- About half the thickness of the board

3
Equals about the thickness of the board

4
Cut it about in half   Y   Y

5   6
Equals about the thickness of the board
½ P   P   P   ½ P
T   T   T

P- Pin   T- Tail

ILLUSTRATION BY MATT BANTLY

row of A's. You made a whole row of B's. Before you knew it, you were writing words and sentences. That's how I learned to do dovetails. In school, I cut a whole row of straight cuts without marking, checked it often with a square, and improved the next row. In the next lesson, I cut angles approximately 10° to 15°, all to the left, the next row all to the right, and before I knew it, I was cutting dovetails.

Companies sell router bits from 7° to 18°, so the angle you use is a personal choice. The strongest dovetails have equal-sized pins and tails, like machine-made drawers. Pope John Paul II's coffin had approximately 3" pins and 3" tails. The choices are endless.

cut dovetails easily on bigger boards

When cutting dovetails on a wider board, use the same method as I describe in this article. You have to divide the remaining space after your third cut in half and half again, or ⅓. With practice it will come naturally. The thicker the wood, the bigger the pins and tails. For example, a 1"-thick board for a blanket chest should have 1" to 1½" tails. It both looks good and is very strong. When I was an apprentice watching my father work, I asked him, "How can you do this so fast?" He replied, "Don't worry, after 10 to 15 years you will be a good beginner yourself."

Cutting Dovetails My Way

So how do you make dovetails my way? Make yourself a cheat sheet (see the drawing on page 135) or look at some dovetails to copy. Get some scrap wood. Mill them to the same size: 3½" to 4" wide, ½" thick and cut them 5" to 6" long. Mill five, 10 pieces, whatever it takes. Set up your marking gauge exactly to the thickness of the wood. Mark the face of the wood. Clamp it into your bench vise, and start cutting with your dovetail saw. (I hope you already practiced your rows of straight and angled cuts.)

Every dovetail starts with a half pin. On the other side is another half pin. Cut them. Next to the half pin you need a full tail. Cut it. Cut the remaining distance in half with the same angle, turn it around, make two more cuts and you're done. Cut only pins, and cut as many as you need until you are pleased.

There's no marking involved – use your eyesight and judgment, and use the thickness of the wood for the width of the tails by judging distances. Make them to your liking. My pins are a little smaller than the tails. That's the way I like them. You may make them the same way or you may make small pins such as ones found in English furniture. They are all good. You are cutting hand-cut dovetails; there should be some variation. Hand-cut dovetails have character and Mrs. Jones likes that.

Once you're happy with your pins, chisel the pins. Put the chisel on the marking gauge line and tap it. Take out a little "V" cut. Now chisel deeper, taking out chips. Undercut just a very little. Flip the piece over and do the same on the other side.

Next, use your pins to make the tails. Hold all three sides even with the edge and the end. With a sharp pencil, mark it from the inside. Here is the hard part: When you cut the pins a little this way or a little that way, it doesn't matter because you're making a template. But when you cut the tails, you have to be accurate and cut that pencil line in half. To understand which side of the pencil line you are cutting, you have to mark the half pins and pins with an "X." That will be your waste. When you chisel out your waste, the "X" will become sawdust and chips. Cut off your half pins; chisel your tails (you are chiseling out the space for the pins).

Here comes the fun part: Try fitting it together. If it doesn't fit, try to find out why, but don't fix it. Cut your next piece. You may have to go closer to the line if it is too tight or leave more of the line on to make it tighter. Make a new one using the same pins until you are happy with a snug fit.

You are ready to make a jewelry box for your mother-in-law. Good luck trying, I am sure you can do it! Happy woodworking.

cutting dovetails the klausz way

Set up the marking gauge exactly to the thickness of the wood.

Next, mark the wood.

Cut a half pin.

4

Cut another half pin.

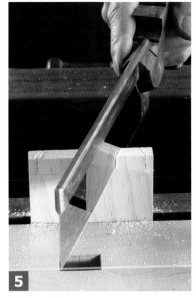

5

Define a tail.

6

Divide the distance in half between the two saw kerfs and cut it.

7

Go back to your first angle and cut another pin.

8

Cut one more pin. You're done cutting pins.

9

Put the chisel into the marking gauge line and tap it.

10

Do the same on all the tails.

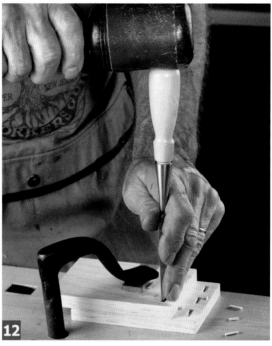

11 Tilt the chisel forward to take out a little piece.

12 Put the chisel back up and tap it more. Undercut a little bit, approximately 2°.

13 With a smaller chisel, chisel into the corners. Chisel about halfway.

14 Flip your stock and chisel from the other side.

15 From the pins, mark the tails. Hold the pin board flush on the outside and on the edges.

16

Mark your waste (the bits of wood you will be cutting out) with an "X."

17 Line up your saw with the pencil line. Use your thumb for a guide and cut on the "X" side.

18 Here you can see what it looks like to leave the lines on the tails.

19 Cut off the half pin. The saw kerf should be outside of the marking gauge line.

20 Chisel the tails the same way you chiseled the pins.

21 With the edge of your chisel, push out your waste.

22 If you did everything right, it should easily tap together.

23 Here you can see the finished practice piece.

27

THREE PIECES OF WOOD **MAKE CROSSCUTTING AND PLANING EASIER** – NO MATTER WHERE YOU WORK.

the basic bench hook

BY DON MCCONNELL

It's difficult to imagine the wooden bench hook without its almost constant companion, the backsaw. Indeed, this association is so strong that an alternative name for this useful hand-tool appliance is "saw rest."

For lighter sawing in the shop, the bench hook excels in effectiveness and convenience. The lower extension, or stop, "hooks" against the edge of the bench, and the material being sawn is held against the upper stop, as shown in the photo at left. Because Western saws cut on the push stroke, the thrust of the saw helps hold the material in place. As a result, the bench hook and the material can be moved around at will, without any need for clamping or fastening.

Typically, the bench hook has a notch at the end of the upper stop (or a kerf is sawn into the stop) to allow the material to be fully supported while it is being cut. This arrangement also protects the benchtop from being damaged as the saw blade breaks through the work. The notch (or kerf) is located to the right of the stop for right-handers and to the left for left-handers.

The squared end of the stop can serve as a guide for the saw. For example, with the addition of a secondary "length stop" (which can be as simple as a strategically placed handscrew clamp), you can make repeated cuts of uniform length by using the squared end of the stop as a guide. This is a safe

and effective way to cut short lengths of dowel stock, as shown on page 142.

However, I tend not to use the end of the stop as a saw guide. Rather, I work to knife lines on the material itself and use the notch as a "safe" area where saw cuts can be made without damaging the stop or the saw.

Building a Bench Hook

As with all shop-made appliances, bench hooks can be constructed in any number of ways, depending on their intended usage and available materials.

The simplest, and possibly earliest, type of bench hook can be cut from a single piece of 4/4 material by drawing the shape of the two stops and the bed on the face grain and sawing them out. The hook will be quite narrow (the 1" thickness of the stock it was cut from) and you will need a pair of them to adequately support your work. Although this type of bench hook doesn't provide the same protection for the benchtop when cutting and isn't as adaptable, it is compact and portable.

The bench hook most commonly encountered today is constructed using three pieces of wood – a main bed piece of some length and width (10"-12" long and 7"-8" wide, typically), and two narrow projections, also known as "stops." These pieces are attached in various ways to the bed of the bench hook, depending on circumstances, available materials and intended use.

Because bench hooks are often used in a somewhat sacrificial manner, they often are made without regard for the long-term effects of cross-grain construction. Indeed, a perfectly usable bench hook can be temporarily constructed simply by nailing the stops to the bed piece. A more common method is to affix the stops to the bed using glue and wooden pegs. If it isn't too wide and the bench hook isn't subjected to extreme environmental changes, a hook made this way will remain viable for a long time.

If you have suitable material and want a wider bed piece for your bench hook, it is possible to use slotted screw hole construction to attach the stops, as

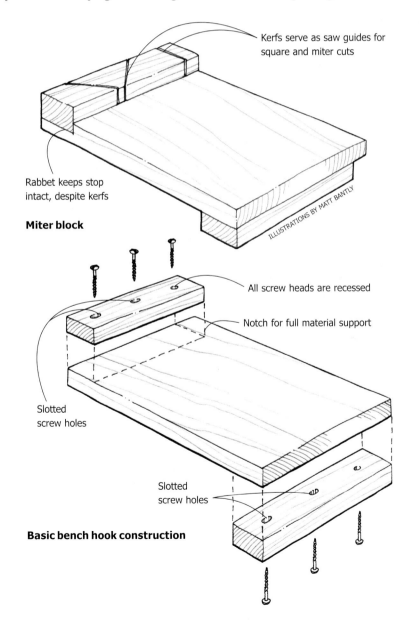

Kerfs serve as saw guides for square and miter cuts

Rabbet keeps stop intact, despite kerfs

Miter block

ILLUSTRATIONS BY MATT BANTLY

All screw heads are recessed

Notch for full material support

Slotted screw holes

Slotted screw holes

Basic bench hook construction

Bench hook   Handscrew serves as length stop

Cutting short pieces to accurate length is a tricky operation with a miter saw. The bench hook, back-saw and a handscrew clamp make the job safe and efficient.

bench hook history

Some readers might be surprised to learn that Joseph Moxon, in his *Mechanick Exercises or the Doctrine of Handy-Works* (published serially between 1678-1680), uses the term "bench hook" to describe a device we know today as a bench stop or a bench dog. In other words, a device that is installed in a recess in the benchtop, that projects just above the surface and that prevents material from moving forward while being planed. The type of "bench hook" illustrated by Moxon has a lateral projection at its upper end that gives it the appearance of a hook. This usage is largely obsolete now, though it continued until at least the middle of the 19th century.

Because the wooden shop appliance we now know as the bench hook is closely associated with backsaws, it is tempting to hypothesize that it arose as a common shop accessory in conjunction with the emergence of backsaws. Because backsaws first appeared about Moxon's time, it seems likely that the wooden bench hook first emerged not long after. However, the first illustration of a wooden bench hook that I'm aware of isn't until in Peter Nicholson's *Mechanical Exercises*, published in 1812.

shown in the illustration on the previous page. The actual construction method can vary, but it is best to recess the screw heads to eliminate the possibility of running the teeth of your saw into them. The location of the fixed screw on the upper stop isn't important, but it can be critical on the lower stop if you are planning to use the bench hook as a shooting board and need the end of the stop to remain flush with the edge of the bed. This form of construction is secure enough for most uses, while the slotted holes for the screws allow for the cross-grain movement of the wider bed piece.

Miter Block for Precision Sawing

Though usually treated as a separate subject, the miter block (page 141) can be seen as a specialized form of bench hook. This has both square and miter kerfs sawn into one of the stops that serve as effective guides for a backsaw.

Each kerf can be made with the aid of an accurately placed guide block,

being sure to use the saw (preferably with minimal set) that will be in service for the subsequent work. When kerfs are made in a stop in this manner, it's desirable to glue the stop into a shallow rabbet in the end of the bed. This allows the stop to retain its lengthwise dimensional stability, and the integrity of the kerfs, despite the cross-grain construction.

The miter block is a useful alternative to a miter box when working with small pieces. If maintained and used with care, it is capable of precise work because it fully supports the material being sawn and the location of the cut can be precisely predicted. Its utility is especially apparent with short pieces, which can be difficult or dangerous when being cut with a power miter saw.

Particularly when making miter cuts, it's often best to quickly secure the lower stop of the miter block in your bench vise to keep it from sliding sideways during use.

Bench Hooks and Planing

As already mentioned, a bench hook can be used in conjunction with a hand plane. For example, it can be turned over lengthwise so that the full length stop is at the top. In this orientation, it serves as a short shooting board to true the ends of smaller pieces. Sometimes it's desirable to place a thin scrap below the plane for it to run on, which protects the plane and adjusts its height so the cut takes place near the center of the iron.

Also, if you add a secondary "bed" that is slightly thinner than the stop, the bench hook can be used to plane

Scrap protects side of plane and raises its cutter

The bench hook makes an effective shooting board for truing the ends of small pieces. The piece of scrap below the plane protects the side of the tool and centers the tool's cutter on the work.

thin stock of short lengths. Most of the time, this secondary bed can simply lie on the main bed with its end against the stop. In this usage, the bench hook serves as a small planing board.

The versatility of the bench hook also makes it a prime candidate for various kinds of on-site work. As long as there is a surface on which to place the bench hook, plus an edge that you can rest the lower stop against, it can be used for all of the above-mentioned functions – all while protecting the saw or plane and the surface on which the bench hook rests. I've used bench hooks on the top tread of a staircase, the edge of a porch and on the tops of table saws and jointers.

Especially for shorter, thinner, narrower or awkward pieces, a bench hook and backsaw can provide a safe and versatile option for any woodworker, either at the bench or out on the work site.

Scrap raises work above stop

Bench hooks can be used almost anywhere (such as on the bed of this jointer) and can do some surprising tasks. Here it is being used as a small planing board. The light-colored scrap below the work raises the work above the bench hook's stop.

28

AN EASY GUIDE TO WHETHER YOU SHOULD BE **PUSHING, PARING OR POUNDING YOUR CHISELS,** IN ANY GIVEN SITUATION.

chisel use

BY JIM STUARD

Back when I started as an apprentice cabinetmaker, a chisel was something to be beaten with a large hammer. That was before I learned how to properly sharpen and use these tools. Since then it's become apparent there are three distinct chisel operations that every woodworker should know: paring, light chopping and heavy mortise chopping.

There's a right way and a wrong way to make these cuts. This chapter will show you how to use your chisel with the least amount of effort, damage to the chisel and damage to your work.

Before I begin, there are a couple things to mention about safety. One nice thing about chisels is you don't have to wear hearing protection. But there are safety issues. Wear safety glasses when chopping or mortising, and I mean that. A chisel breaking can send pieces of metal flying, possibly causing an eye injury.

Second, if you have any reservations about using the sharp end of a chisel while paring, consider using a Kevlar protective glove, which is routinely used by carvers. The glove will dull the impact of a slipped chisel and reduce your chance of injury. Finally, never use a chisel that's pointing toward your body. Always be mindful of the direction a chisel is going and where your hands are. This is the first thing to check before making a cut of any kind. The last thing you want to do on a Sunday afternoon is explain to an emergency room physician how you almost gave yourself a home appendectomy while working on Aunt Betty's blanket chest.

Paring

The one thing that amazes most beginning woodworkers is how seldom you really need to hit the chisel to get it to work right (the exception to this is, of course, mortising). Paring is a process of using the knife edge of a sharp chisel to slice small amounts of wood off. With a little technique and a sharp chisel, you can get into places inaccessible to a plane or knife.

Paring is basically the finest work you can do with a chisel. Some examples of paring include:

One hand determines force and direction of the cut

One hand holds the chisel on course

Paring: One Hand Steers, the Other Pushes ■ To do this properly, you need to use both hands on the chisel to get the most control. One hand is on the chisel blade as close as you can get to the edge. The other hand is firmly on the handle. How much you push down on the blade as you push forward determines the amount of wood removed. You can also angle the chisel into the wood to get a more aggressive cut. That is where having a flat face on your chisel is important.

145

1. TAP THE CHISEL WITH A MALLET TO DEFINE THE LINE OF YOUR CUT.

After defining the pins with your dovetail saw, start chopping the waste out by chopping to a line approximately $^1/_{32}$" away from the actual marked line. What happens when you chop with a chisel is the bevel will push the chisel toward the line as it's struck. You have to compensate for this by starting in a little from the line, then remove the waste.

2. PUSH THE CHISEL FORWARD TO REMOVE THE WASTE

Use a combination of paring and light chopping technique to remove the waste. The procedure is to chop a line, across the grain, then remove the waste by pushing into the end grain down to the cut line. Depending on the wood, you may or may not need to tap the chisel with a mallet. Re-cut another line and repeat till you get down to the marking gauge line.

3. ANGLED CUTS HELP BREAK UP THE WASTE

To remove the rest of the waste up to the gauge line, start by pushing a series of angled cuts into the waste up to the line. Yes Virginia, you can pare end grain but only with sharp tools.

4. FINALLY, PARE THE WASTE OUT

Proceed to pare or gently chop out the waste, cutting across the end grain. Some light paring is required to get into the corners along with a sharp, pointy knife.

• Trimming the cheeks of a mortise to fit a tenon that's too large.

• In the absence of a shoulder plane, paring the tenon to fit the mortise.

• When you lay out a hinge mortise, after chopping the mortise sides, you basically have to pare the waste out to the edges of the hinge layout.

• If the space between dovetails is large enough (i.e. the pins) for a chisel, they can be pared, on their sides, to fit.

Before beginning, make sure your work is secured on your bench or in your vise. This will impart more of the force of your pushing into the work, thereby giving you more control of the cut. Paring requires pushing a chisel while it lies flat on a surface, slicing into the wood grain. This can be either with or across the grain. When you pare, you're generally not taking off large amounts of wood. Just gently slicing little shavings off.

To pare well, the chisel needs to have a flat face and a sharp edge. See the story below on flattening for more about this. You can generally tell when your edge isn't cutting the way it should when paring end grain. If the grain starts to collapse and bend over from the chisel pushing through, the chisel needs sharpening. I won't go into a long diatribe on sharpening here, but suffice it to say that if your chisels are coming up dull, you either need to increase the frequency or quality of your sharpening.

Light Chopping

At some time you'll have to do some chopping with a bench chisel. A half-blind dovetail joint is a good example of

in defense of a flat chisel face

Did you ever wonder why sharpening experts tell you that your chisel face has to be flat? Well, if your face isn't flat, one of two things will occur. If the chisel face is bowed you'll start digging into the wood; if the chisel face is bellied, you'll need to lift the chisel to get it to start cutting.

Either condition requires lapping. I like to use a coarse diamond stone, and then work up to a couple of finer grits. There's lots of other lapping equipment out there, but one of the cheapest alternatives is to use dark gray wetsanding paper (start with 150 grit and move up gradually to 400 or 600) on a flat surface. A thick

piece of glass does nicely. Just soak the paper in water before use. Lay it down on the flat surface and the surface tension of the water will adhere it to the surface fairly well. Rub the chisel until it is flat at least two-thirds of the way up. This might take a while. Consider it paying your dues before you get into the high-falootin' chisel-use party. Get as fine a polish on your chisel face as you can to eliminate catches or nicks. It also helps to finely sand the edges of the chisel face. If you pinch your finger between a piece of wood and the edge of the chisel, you'll stand less chance of scissoring a cut on your hand.

how to use chopping to remove wood. Other uses for chopping are defining a hinge mortise, low relief carving and through-dovetails.

When chopping, you can use the same force you would use when mortising — just not as often. Bevel-edged bench chisels shouldn't be used for mortising. They aren't designed for this purpose. Mortise chisels have a steeper cutting angle ground on them: 30° compared to 25° for bench chisels. Their blades are thicker with square flat sides to stand up to a pounding. Bench chisels are thinner and beveled on the sides to get into tight spaces.

Most bench chisel chopping consists of light tapping of the chisel to define a cut line or remove a small amount of waste. Chopping is the most vigorous use that a bench chisel should see. Only about half of the chisels available commercially will stand up to repeated medium/heavy chopping. If you plan on heavy use for your chisels, check around (magazine reviews or the internet) to find a bench chisel that will hold its edge longer.

Before beginning, make sure your work has a direct connection with the ground. That is, place the work directly over the leg of a bench or table. This imparts all the force of the blow directly into the cut and not into flexing your bench's top.

Mortising

I'm sure that back in the days when all mortising was done with manual labor, there were large muscular blokes all hammering and chopping away. This is certainly the woodworking equivalent of heavyweight boxing. The chisel and the wood both take an incredible pounding.

Mortising has one purpose: to make a square flat-sided hole in a piece of wood to receive a tenon. To that end, mortising chisels are the beefiest chisels you can buy. They have a steep grind (30°) and high flat sides to take a beating and guide the chisel while mortising. A bench chisel, with its thin profile, is likely to wander in your cut, ruining your mortise. Not to mention that if you hit a bench chisel as hard

1. DEFINE MORTISE BY TAPPING

First, lay out a mortise and start by lightly chopping a series of lines, inside the layout lines, across the grain.

2. PUSH CHISEL THIS WAY TO REMOVE WASTE

Next, using the bevel side of the chisel, remove the waste and repeat. After you get the first couple of layers knocked out, it's easier to just wail away and start taking large amounts of waste out of the mortise. When you get to the bottom of the mortise, start checking the depth with a combination square. When you get towards the finished depth, it's easier to just reach into the mortise with the chisel, bevel side down and pare out fine amounts of wood till you get to the finished depth. If necessary, use a wide bench chisel to pare the cheeks of the mortise.

as you hit a mortising chisel, especially the small sizes like 1/2" and 3/8", they might actually fracture. Also, repeated pounding of a bench chisel will either roll or collapse the cutting edge.

If you own only one mortising chisel, I recommend a 3/8" tool. Tenons are typically half the thickness of your stock, and most stock is 3/4" thick. Make sure the mortising chisel you buy has a long handle because you're going to hit it pretty hard. If the handle is too short, it's your hand that will take the abuse.

Mortising has three parts. One, light tapping. This defines where the mortise will go and begins the mortise. Two, heavy pounding, which is what most of us think about when we talk about mortising. Three, paring. This is the only time you should use a bench chisel while mortising: to pare the sides of a mortise after chopping.

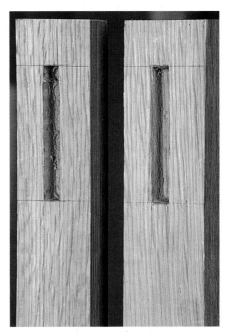

Here's the finished results of using a mortising machine (left) and a hand cut mortise (right). The hand-chopped mortise is prettier, right?

147

29

WHEN YOU KNOW WHAT YOU'RE DOING, **CHISELS CAN BE WONDERFULLY HELPFUL TOOLS.**

advanced chisel techniques

BY ADAM CHERUBINI

If all you want to do with your chisels is adjust machine-cut joints or slice glue drips, any technique or tool will work. This sort of work is occasional in nature, and not particularly strenuous. But chisels offer woodworkers the opportunity to do much more.

For machine-using woodworkers, chisels provide the opportunity to explore new possibilities. You can cut shapes with a chisel that are not achievable by other means. For the beginner lacking specialty machinery, chisels can be used to cut all manner of joints quickly and efficiently. But this work requires more effort than the occasional paring of a joint.

For this sort of work to be practical, we need much more thoughtful tools and techniques. The trouble is, neither the tools nor the traditional techniques are well-understood. What we need is a professional to show us his tricks and the tools we'll need to perform them. That's where I come in. Oh, no, I don't mean me. See, the guy we need died more than 300 years ago.

In this article on working wood quickly and efficiently with hand tools,

Christopher Schwarz makes a rabbet using an 18th-century chiseling technique: After scribing the lines for the joint, you can quickly rough out the rabbet by wielding the tool as shown. Then come back with a rabbet plane and clean up the joint to your scribed lines.

we'll look back in time in hopes of discovering the effective and efficient use of chisels.

Paring

"This way of handling may seem a preposterous Posture to manage an Iron tool."
— JOSEPH MOXON, *Mechanick Exercises*

When examining period chisels, one can't help but notice the strange design of their handles. Surviving examples and period illustrations from the 17th, 18th and early 19th centuries indicate chisels typically had tapered or wedge-shaped handles.

Holding such a chisel is like pinching a watermelon seed. It's difficult to hold at first, then it grows increasingly slippery the harder you squeeze. The rationale behind the design of these handles is unknown to me.

But rather than immediately tossing out the design as 18th-century muddle-headedness, which is clearly what modern toolmakers have done, we might assume the design served a purpose we do not yet fully understand.

"With pressing the shoulder hard upon the [handle], the edge cuts and pares away Irregularities."
— MOXON, *Mechanick Exercises*

Joseph Moxon, a chronicler of woodworking techniques in the 17th century, describes a technique in which one's shoulder is used to drive the chisel. The chisel's blade is held a bit like a pencil with the heel of the hand resting upon the work. The pinky must be behind the blade so it cannot be cut, and doesn't obstruct the view of the edge. The other hand guides the chisel handle to the shoulder where it can be pushed with great force.

I tried this technique with my beloved Hirsch firmer chisel. Its downright pointy handle wore a hole in my shoulder in minutes and left a bruise that lasted for days. What I needed instead was a chisel with a much wider butt end. Hmmm.

Creating Joints With Chisels

With the proper chisel, this technique can be used whenever a low angle or paring cut is desired. We usually associate paring with fine cuts, but this technique can produce chips that would make a scrub plane blush.

Paring Grooves

Grooves can be created quickly using this technique. In the example shown on the next page, a groove in a drawer's front is pared to accept the drawer bottom. A marking gauge establishes the top of the drawer bottom. A sharp firming chisel, usually $^1/_4$" to $^3/_8$" wide, is used. With the board well clamped, start at the far end and begin paring, bevel down, with a few degrees of clearance between the bevel and the work. The edge of the chisel must rest against the marked line to ensure a straight groove. You needn't mark out both sides of the groove because the width of the chisel dictates the width of the groove.

Paring Dados

Dados can be similarly pared out, but both sides of the dado must be marked to prevent fiber break out. I typically strike the first mark with my striking knife (see "The Striking Knife," page 174), square to the edge (using a large square). I reposition the square for the second mark using an appropriately sized chisel to establish the distance between the lines (and the width of the dado). When it's time to make the mating part, I simply set my marking gauge to the width of the chisel I used and transfer that measurement to the edge of the board. Planing to that line on the mating part is then a simple procedure.

Paring Rabbets

This same technique can be used to make rabbets or fillisters (sometimes called fillesters or cross-grain rabbets) quickly without adjusting any planes or temporarily attaching a batten. Because of the grip I described, it's easy to work right to the scribed line and leave a nice straight edge behind. The rabbet plane can then use that straight shoulder to

Socket firming chisel

Shown here are tanged firmer chisels with traditional octagonal handles scaled from those found in the famous Benjamin Seaton chest. Also shown is a socket firming chisel that is also a copy of one found in the Seaton Chest.

Shown here are handles of German firmer chisels. The handles' shape makes them unsuited to the traditional paring technique that uses your shoulder to drive the tool.

clean up the bottom of the rabbet and bring it to final depth.

Raised Panels

What is a raised panel but a board with angled rabbets and fillisters? This technique is a good match for roughing-in

A groove for a drawer bottom can be created quickly with one scribed line and a chisel that is the width of the desired groove. Use the paring technique described in the article to cut the joint.

To pare a dado with your chisel, first strike a line on the workpiece using a knife and your square. To set the width of the dado, use the chisel's width to properly position a square and straight-edge. Then scribe your second joint line.

raised panels; it's a sensible approach when the panel has an arched or otherwise curved top.

Mallet Work: Embrace the Bevel

In Moxon's day, the standard all-purpose bench chisel was called a "forming" chisel or "former." This later became the "firming" chisel or "firmer." Today we define firming chisels as general-purpose chisels suitable for use with a mallet and this was probably true in Moxon's day as well. We shouldn't look at mallet work as brutish. In fact, using a mallet with a chisel requires a fair bit of skill. Moxon illuminates a little-discussed technique worthy of your consideration:

"...you must bear the [handle] of the Former a little inwards over the stuff."
— Moxon, *Mechanick Exercises*

When chopping straight down, you must be cognizant of the fact that the wood sees the chisel's blade as a wedge. As such, the wood wants the direction of the cut to be the bisection (center) of the chisel's bevel angle (the 25° to

30° you honed on the edge). Driving the chisel straight down typically results in an undercut. Thus, to produce a 90° cut you must pull the handle back ever so slightly away from the scrap side. This is precisely what Moxon meant in the quote above.

Chopping Dovetails

When chopping out dovetail waste, the tendency for the chisel to undercut can be used to one's advantage. Begin by placing the firming chisel 1/16" to 1/32" on the scrap side of the scribed line (base of the dovetails) exactly as Moxon described:

"...set the edge of the Former, a little without the scribed Stroak, with its (bevel) outwards..."
— Moxon, *Mechanick Exercises*

Holding the firmer as vertical as possible by eye, strike the chisel two or three times, not more. Each blow drives the chisel's edge back toward the scribed line. Embrace this.

Now pare away the waste material starting 1/8" from the edge of the board to the depth of your chopped line using the shoulder-powered paring technique discussed earlier. Always leave behind the full thickness at the extreme edge of the board.

With the wedge-shaped chip removed by paring, repeat the process until you are halfway through the board. When you flip the board over and work the opposite face, the force of chopping will not simply break the waste, as a portion of it still touches the bench. When the waste is removed you will notice the material you have removed has left an undercut or "V" shape through the end grain of your tail board.

No further work is done to this half of the dovetail joint. This tail board can now be knocked onto its mating pin board. The little extra material created by the initial placement of the chisel will simply yield away as the joint is assembled. With experience the initial placement of the chisel will be governed by the hardness of the stock and exactly how you transfer marks and saw.

I find this only helpful with the tails. The pins should be chopped exactly as Moxon said, with the chisel leaning away from the waste slightly to create a perfectly square edge.

While we're on the subject, another trick I use is to lay out my dovetails using the chisel I want to chop them out with. Now my chisels have square sides and my initial placement is not right on the line, so the width of the waste must be slightly greater than the width of the chisel. Theoretically this should be a problem, but in the many years I've been chopping dovetails this way, a problem has never arisen. It may be worth mentioning that although bevel-edged chisels were known in the 17th century, they were not generally used by Anglo-American cabinetmakers in the 18th century. Our modern partiality for them may be arbitrary.

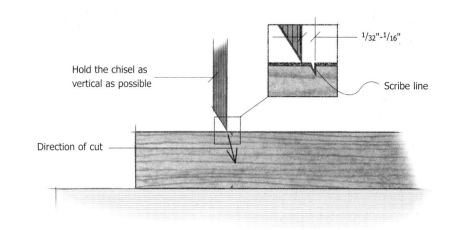

Hold the chisel as vertical as possible

$1/32"-1/16"$

Scribe line

Direction of cut

Chopping Mortises

My mortising technique is a bit unorthodox. It uses portions of both of the advanced techniques we've discussed so far. Begin the mortise with a single marking gauge line representing one wall of the mortise. The chisel's width will determine the width of the completed mortise. Place the chisel $1/8"$ from each end, and with the chisel leaning slightly away from the center of the mortise (to make a square cut), apply no more than three mallet blows.

Using the mortise chisel in precisely the same technique as the firmer was used to make a groove, pare a shallow groove between the chopped ends, carefully aligning the chisel's edge to the marked line. Repeat the mallet blows at the ends of the mortise, and remove the waste between them as before. As the mortise gets deeper, the paring can become more aggressive. The low angle of the chisel during the paring will allow the walls of the mortise to guide the chisel, keeping the mortise nice and straight. Finish the mortise by lightly chopping the ends to the desired length.

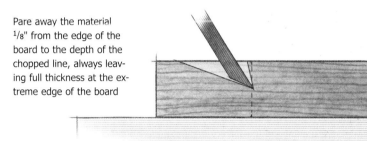

Pare away the material $1/8"$ from the edge of the board to the depth of the chopped line, always leaving full thickness at the extreme edge of the board

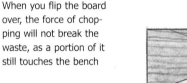

When you flip the board over, the force of chopping will not break the waste, as a portion of it still touches the bench

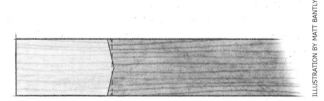

You will notice the material you have removed has left an undercut or V-shape through the end grain

Choosing the 'Right' Tool

The 18th-century toolmakers offered a variety of chisels. In addition to the standard firming chisel, tool dealer Christopher Gabriel offered a heavy-duty version of this tool called the strong firmer. Socket firmers were known and used by carpenters and wheelwrights. But their use was not exclusive to any single trade. Mortise chisels were available in both socketed and tanged varieties, but we shouldn't confuse these with the large socketed firmers used by carpenters for framing.

The dizzying array of chisels is no mere testament to personal preference. Substantive differences between seemingly like tools indicate a degree of optimization long since lost. For example: Socketed firming chisels weren't generally available in sizes smaller than $1/2"$ or so. It's also notable that tanged firmers were generally available in $1/8"$ increments while socketed chisels were not.

True mortise chisels, socketed or tanged, were rarely available in widths over $5/8"$, while socketed firmers

(framers) were available in widths exceeding 2".

In addition to the variety of patterns, chisels were available in a wide range of sizes. The standard 18th century set of firming chisels included 12 to 16 tools. Such a set would include chisels from $1/8"$ to 1" wide, roughly in $1/8"$ increments, then 1" to 2" by either quarters or eighths. Artisans would likely add to this basic set a set of eight joiner's mortise chisels sized $1/8"$ to $1/2"$ or $5/8"$ by $1/16"$ increments, a few paring

a proper set of chisels for hand joinery

If you want to be able to make furniture with traditional joinery by hand here's what I think you need:

Firmers: $1/8$" to 1" by eighths. I grind the small chisels pretty low, maybe 20° to 25°. Hitting one with a mallet is like driving a nail. Edge retention isn't usually a problem. I grind larger chisels, $7/8$" and larger, pretty low as well. The edge is so long that it spreads out mallet force and is thus well retained. (Don't ever compare the edge retention of two chisels of different sizes. The larger one will always win!) The chisels in the middle receive the majority of punishment, so I grind these close to 30°.

It's nice to have one really big chisel. A really sharp $1 1/4$" to 2" framing chisel will suffice. There are plenty of good blades on the market. Trouble is, they are often paired with unfortunate handles. If you love the steel but hate the handle, consider immediately re-handling it.

If you can only have one mortise chisel choose $5/16$" – it'll work for most materials roughly 1" thick. The larger sizes are only helpful for the larger stock found on chairs and large tables. When you start getting into mortises over $1/2$", I think you are better off to first bore holes and use a framing chisel to clean out the waste. Mortises this big aren't typical in furniture I'm familiar with. This is more like general carpentry.

A paring chisel with a long blade, and possibly a curved edge is nice to have. A 1" tool of this form is a nice size. Besides that chisel, it's nice to have one or two paring chisels in the $3/8$" to $5/8$" range because those firmers see so much use, they may not be quite as sharp as you'd like when you need to take a small shaving.

Here you can see cabinetmaker's or joiner's mortise chisels.

"Joiners use (mortise chisels) of several Breadths according as the Breadth of their Mortesses may require."

— MOXON, *Mechanick Exercises*

By carefully applying a chisel to a board, one can make a cut of a consistent and repeatable width. With regard to mortising, one chooses the width of the chisel based on the stock size: Use a $1/4$" chisel for $3/4$"-thick, 4/4 surfaced stock, a $5/16$" for 4/4 rough or 5/4 surfaced, and a $3/8$" for 6/4 and so on. In these instances we can create mortises of very uniform width with no extra effort on our part.

Similarly, we can "custom design" projects to match our tools. Dovetail layout, for example is a highly arbitrary process many woodworkers fuss with. During carcase joinery, through-pins and tails can be sized and laid out using one or preferably two firming chisels. The chisels themselves can be used to make the marks. Dovetails could be one firmer chisel wide and one firmer chisel (usually a smaller one) apart. Just remember to leave a little extra space between the marks to account for the thickness of the firmer blade and the dovetail saw kerf.

Conclusion

I hope I've convinced you that there are things we can learn about using hand tools quickly and efficiently by investigating historical methodologies. Did you

ever think to push a chisel with your shoulder? It's wild isn't it? And I think it could be useful. But I don't think this specific technique alone will be responsible for a dramatic increase in your efficiency.

But the ancient and forgotten "Arts & Mysteries" are much more than a mere collection of hand tool techniques. They encompass hundreds of years of industrial evolution and are characterized by consistent philosophical approaches to solving workshop problems.

We have our own "Arts & Mysteries" today such as "measure twice, cut once." By measuring carefully, we create accurate pieces that fit together. We are aided by a slew of tools that were generally unavailable in Moxon's day. One can't help but wonder how craftsmen managed 300 years ago without tape measures, dial calipers and (my favorite) the micro-adjustable marking gauge – if only it had a digital display.

Through our examination of chisel technique, we have discovered the answer and one of the most important of the "Arts & Mysteries." It allows accurate work to be performed very easily. Like any other technique, it must be practiced to be mastered.

"...This Posture, all workmen are at first taught, and Practice doth so inure them to it, that if they would, they could not well leave it."

— MOXON, *Mechanick Exercises*

chisels, and several firming gouges (for coping). The total cost of these tools could approach a week's pay. It can be difficult for those of us who have only four chisels, ($1/4$", $1/2$", $3/4$" and 1"), to understand the sense in having so many chisels.

But the rationale behind these large sets is probably the single most advanced chisel technique we can learn. It is directly responsible for making the use of chisels efficient and productive, while at the same time is not limited solely to the use of chisels.

OLD CHISELS CAN BE BROUGHT
BACK TO LIFE USING THESE SIMPLE STEPS.

30

resurrecting chisels

BY PAUL ANTHONY

If ever there was a type of used hand tool that was a good candidate for restoration, it's a chisel. Lots of good deals on old chisels can be found at flea markets, garage sales and auctions. And while many old tools – such as kinked hand saws or badly warped planes – may be hopelessly damaged, it's usually not hard to bring a chisel back to a working life.

The process of restoring a chisel back into working order involves four basic steps:

1. Flattening and polishing the back
2. Grinding the edge square to the sides
3. Grinding the bevel
4. Honing the bevel

These steps ensure that the cutting edge will consist of two polished intersecting surfaces, which is the essence of any sharp, durable edge. And a flat back is important because it serves as a directional reference in many paring and chopping operations.

In this chapter, I will take you through these processes step by step, including the nuances that can make all the difference in getting a frighteningly keen edge. Although the following approach – arrived at after years of teaching sharpening and testing products – is certainly not the only way to sharpen, I think you'll find that it yields great results. For most chisels, it's the blade that needs work, not the handle. Most wooden handles can be sanded

and refinished. If you need to replace yours, I recommend you read "Make Your Own Chisel Handles" on page 162.

Working With Waterstones

Thirty years ago, I was sharpening with oilstones, like everyone else I knew. But after Japanese waterstones hit the market, a friend brought his over for me to try, and I was sold in about three minutes. Unlike oilstones, waterstones cut quickly because the surface particles on these soft-bond stones break free in use, exposing new, sharp particles for continued aggressive cutting. However, the cost of this is that the stones must be dressed, or flattened, frequently during use because dips or humps in the surface would compromise the flatness or straightness of the tool being sharpened. You can easily dress a stone by rubbing it on #220-grit silicon carbide paper glued to a sheet of plate glass with spray adhesive. A more convenient, but expensive, alternative is to use a coarse diamond plate like I do.

Waterstones are available in a variety of grits: typically #220, #800, #1,000, #1,200, #4,000, #6,000 and #8,000. Grits #4,000 and up are considered finish stones, which impart the final polish to the metal. Expect to pay about $20 per stone except for #6,000- and #8,000-grit stones, which can cost twice as much.

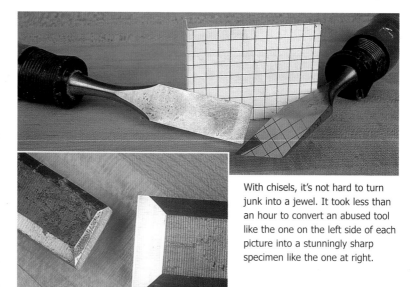

With chisels, it's not hard to turn junk into a jewel. It took less than an hour to convert an abused tool like the one on the left side of each picture into a stunningly sharp specimen like the one at right.

Metal particles

Dress a waterstone flat by rubbing it on a diamond plate or sheet of #220-grit silicon carbide paper on glass until the entire face of the stone is clean. The small dark area of metal particles near the end of this stone shows that it needs just a bit more dressing.

a sharpener's best teachers

Sharpening is a tiny art. It's impossible for the naked eye to detect progress on the scale that really matters. For that you'll need two very important helpers: light and magnification. To best learn sharpening, inspect your work closely after every step, viewing it under a strong light with an 8x or 10x magnifying loupe. (A $6 slide viewing loupe from the photo store works fine.) You'll be amazed what your naked eye doesn't see. And if a cutting edge looks good under strong magnification, you can bet it will cut well.

When flattening the back, orient a chisel diagonally to the stone, then aggressively rub the full length of the stone, moving slightly to the left or right after every few strokes to avoid creating a furrow in the chisel, especially from the edge of a coarse #220-grit stone like this.

Rub the back aggressively on the #1,200-grit stone, letting the gray slurry of metal and stone particles build up. The slurry serves as a finer grit that will begin to polish the back, as seen in the inset.

After aggressive rubbing on the #8,000-grit stone, the chisel back should be flat and have a near-mirror polish. The angle of reflection shown here shows virtually no scratches, but you would see a very light scratch pattern if you were looking straight at it.

Tending to the Back

The first step – flattening the back – often requires removing a fair amount of metal. Performed by rubbing the chisel against a stone, this step is also necessary on new chisels to remove the manufacturer's grinding marks. For this, you really need an aggressive cutting method that doesn't distort the flatness of the back. After trying everything from coarse silicon carbide paper and diamond stones to ceramic stones and silicon carbide waterstones, by far the best product I've discovered for the job is the #220-grit waterstone made by Norton. This $25 soft-bond stone wears down faster than any other stone I've used and requires frequent dressing, but the labor saved is well worth the cost of buying a new stone occasionally.

So begin flattening the back on the #220-grit stone. Apply strong pressure with your fingers spread out across the endmost $1^{1}/_{2}$" or so of the chisel. Be careful not to lift up or you'll round over the area near the cutting edge. To help prevent lifting, keep your hands away from the handle. It also helps your leverage if your work surface is just about wrist height.

It's very important to rub the tool over the entire surface, turning the stone end-for-end occasionally in order to work both edges. The purpose is to

For restoring a blade, I use grits #220, #800, #1,200 and #8,000.

If you're on a budget, I recommend as a starter set a Norton #220-grit stone (discussed in a moment), an #800-grit stone and a #4,000-grit stone. The last stone will give you a perfectly serviceable edge, although not what you could expect from an #8,000-grit stone. Combination stones are also available at a discount, with one grit per side.

With the exception of the finish stones, all waterstones should be submerged in water for 10 minutes prior to use. I leave mine in a constant bath except in a freezing shop. To secure a stone during use, I place it on a thin, rubber, non-skid mat, which works better than any other stone holder I've tried in my career.

155

avoid creating a hollow in the stone that will distort the back of the chisel. As a slurry of dislodged stone particles develops, check the chisel for a consistent scratch pattern that will indicate you're done with this grit. For the most aggressive cutting, wash the slurry from the stone, making sure to re-dress the surface if necessary to flatten it.

Once you've created a consistent scratch pattern across the endmost 1½" or so of the chisel, continue to rub it for a bit on the slurry, which serves as an intermediate grit between the #220-stone and the next finer grit you'll use. Wipe the metal clean and dry, then scrutinize it under strong light and magnification to make sure the surface is worked evenly, with no neglected areas or deep individual scratches. Don't worry if the back is rounded along the cutting edge from previous abuse; you can grind that away later.

Next, with a freshly dressed #800-grit waterstone, maneuver the chisel aggressively in the same fashion, again working the entire surface of the stone. After a slurry builds up, wipe the chisel dry and then check for a consistent scratch pattern under bright light and magnification. You may be able to correct a neglected area with further work on the #800-grit waterstone, but it may be more efficient to reprise your work on the #220-grit waterstone. To make any waterstone cut more aggressively, wash off the slurry or spritz some more water on it. Make sure to re-dress the stone whenever necessary to flatten it.

When you're done on the #800-grit stone, repeat the processes on a freshly dressed #1,200-grit stone. With this stone, you really want to finish up by working the metal aggressively into the finer-grit slurry because next you jump up to a considerably finer grit on your finish stone. When you're done with the #1,200-grit stone, the back should show the beginnings of a polish. Now you're ready for the final polishing on the finish stone.

Spritz your freshly dressed finish stone with water and press hard as you rub the back, keeping it flat on the stone. A gray/black slurry of stone and

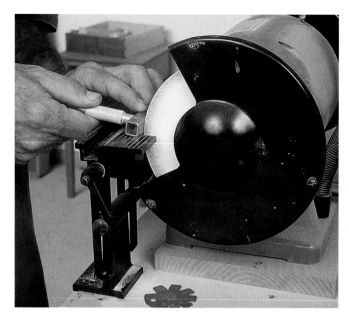

A diamond-faced dresser, such as the one shown here, cleans and trues the face of the wheel for quick, accurate grinding.

Grind the edge straight and square to the chisel sides using light pressure and moving side to side as you cut. Check your progress occasionally with a small machinist's square.

When grinding the bevel, pinch the chisel firmly, using the second section of your index finger as a fence against the rest. A finger placed lightly on the back of the blade helps direct the grinding pressure against the wheel.

Proper grinding technique results in the blunted end of the blade gradually and consistently narrowing in width until it's gone. Remember to maintain the same grip throughout the process.

metal particles will begin to build up immediately on the stone as the chisel back starts to show a polish. When friction starts to prevent rubbing, spritz the stone with water. If you need to clean and dress the stone for more aggressive cutting, spray it clean rather than dipping it into your stone bath, where it can become contaminated with coarse particles from the other stones.

The stone really starts blackening up quickly as the metal starts to shine. The back should now have a very fine scratch pattern with a near-mirror polish. Stop when it won't polish up any more. You should never have to go through this entire process again because you should only ever touch the back to your finish stone during future resharpenings.

Get Straight and Square

The next step is to grind the edge straight and square to the chisel sides, while removing any nicks or a badly rounded section at the cutting edge. As for grinding equipment, you can use a typical high-speed (3,450 rpm) grinder with a gray wheel, although you risk burning the steel unless you use a well-dressed wheel and a very light touch. A much safer bet is to use a "half-speed" (1,700-1,800 rpm) grinder with an #80- or #100-grit aluminum oxide wheel.

Like waterstones, the particles on these soft-bond wheels break away in use, exposing fresh, sharp particles for quicker, cooler cutting. Before grinding, dress your wheel if necessary to clean and true it to remove any gullies or lodged metal particles. You'll also need a solid, adjustable grinder rest, which you can buy as an aftermarket accessory because most stock grinder rests are nearly useless for accurate sharpening.

Set the grinder rest at about 90° to the face of the wheel, then very slowly press the blade against the wheel, moving it side to side as you grind. Check your progress occasionally with a machinist's square. Don't apply so much pressure that you risk burning the steel. As long as the wheel is throwing sparks, it's cutting. If the metal turns blue, it won't hold an edge in that spot because you've ruined its temper.

Grinding the Bevel

To grind the bevel, many sharpeners adjust the rest to the appropriate angle, then lay the chisel on it for grinding. I don't like this approach because the friction of so much metal on metal prevents the easy side-to-side grinding motion that is so critical to creating a consistent, evenly ground bevel.

Instead, I lay the tang of the chisel against the front edge of the rest, guessing as best I can where the bevel should contact the wheel to grind an angle of about 25°. I then pinch the tang between my thumb and index finger, with the second section of the finger against the edge of the rest to serve as a fence. This reduces metal-to-metal friction to a single point on the edge of the rest and allows very easy side-to-side movement.

Maintaining that grip, I turn on the grinder and lay the bevel against the wheel, sliding the chisel side to side without leaning it left or right. When I have created a facet about 1/8" wide, I check the bevel angle using a brass angle checker disk sold for the purpose. If I need to readjust the bevel angle, I slide my grip up or down the tang as necessary to change the lean of the chisel against the wheel. Then I take a

few more swipes across the wheel before checking the angle again.

If it becomes hard to identify the most recent facet on a bevel full of facets, wipe the bevel with a wide felt marker, then try again. Once you have established an angle of approximately 25°, lock your grip and don't move it until you're finished grinding the bevel.

A finger placed lightly on the back of the chisel helps control downward pressure and serves as a good heat sensor. When the metal gets uncomfortably warm, let it cool to avoid destroying its temper. I avoid quenching it in water when the blunted edge is less than about 1/64"-wide because quenching can cause minute cracks in a thin cutting edge.

As you grind (which may take 15-20 minutes when removing a lot of metal), the most important area to monitor is the very end of the chisel. Make sure the blunt area narrows consistently in order to ensure an evenly ground bevel. This may take some practice, but it's well worth the effort because a neatly ground bevel makes the subsequent honing a lot easier. Keep grinding until the once blunt area is just a hair's width.

to jig or not to jig

Honing jigs will hold a chisel at a steady angle when honing the bevel. Although there is no dispute that these jigs work, there is some disagreement about the wisdom of depending on them. Those in favor argue correctly that a jig will prevent you from rounding over a bevel if you have trouble maintaining the honing angle freehand. On the other hand, there is no denying that the honing process goes quicker if you don't have to mount and adjust your tool in the jig before honing. Of course, in the latter case, you do have to invest the time into learning to hone freehand, which I recommend and describe here. But if you prefer to use a honing jig, that's perfectly fine. I don't argue religion, politics or sharpening.

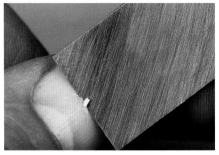

If a blade is truly sharp, it will take a light shaving from your thumbnail. This magnified shot, which shows the #8,000-grit scratch pattern, is the same polish seen on the restored chisel in the photos on page 154, but viewed from straight on.

Honing the Bevel

Begin honing the bevel using a freshly dressed #1,200-grit stone. Place the bevel down on the farthest end of the stone because you'll first pull it toward you. With the sides of the chisel pinched between the fingers of your dominant hand, and the chisel oriented at about 45° to the length of the stone, apply strong downward force behind the bevel with the index finger of your opposite hand. Make sure the toe and the heel of the bevel make firm contact against the stone. The other fingers of your dominant hand should curl under the blade and tang to simply hold the chisel at the proper angle, applying only enough lift to keep it from falling. The farther forward you keep your hands and the more downward pressure you apply at the bevel, the more you'll prevent the tool from rocking and rounding over the bevel in the process.

Now, with your wrists locked, pull the chisel toward you, maintaining firm pressure over the bevel. Afterward, hop the chisel back to the far end of the stone, and repeat once or twice. These initial pull strokes smooth out the grinding scratches at the very edge, making your upcoming pushes of the chisel much easier and reducing the chance of friction-induced rocking during pushing. After these first few strokes, you should now be able to hone easily with back-and-forth stokes the full length of the stone for efficiency. Remember to keep the cutting edge of the chisel oriented diagonally to the stone to help prevent rocking.

As soon as the newly honed facet runs all the way across the cutting edge, you're done with the #1,200-grit stone. At this point, take some time to check your progress under magnification. Then spritz water on a freshly dressed finish stone, and work the bevel on it in a similar manner until the facet is evenly polished.

The final quick task is to remove any fine wire edge created in the sharpening process. To do this, lay the chisel on its back at the far end of the stone, then pull it toward you applying a lot of downward pressure at the bevel. This initial pull stroke, instead of a push stroke, prevents trapping a wire edge under the chisel. Work the chisel back and forth three or four times, then flip it onto the bevel again for a few strokes. Finish with a few final strokes on the back and you're done.

If you've done your job well, at this point you should be able to shave your arm hair or pare just a whisper of a shaving from your thumbnail, as shown at top. You can also welcome a new member to your family of tools.

honing freehand

Front view: The secret to successful freehand honing is to concentrate all of your attention at the business end of the chisel, applying strong downward pressure above the bevel with your left hand. Use your right hand to power the chisel, pinching its sides between your index finger and thumb, as shown here.

Side view: Curl the remaining fingers under the blade, applying just enough lift to keep the handle from falling (Lefties, simply reverse all these directions.)

modifying stock chisels

BY LONNIE BIRD

In articles on cutting dovetails I have stated that the process of creating dovetails is simply sawing and chiseling to a line. And it is. But like any hand-tool process, you'll achieve the best results and have the greatest personal satisfaction if the tools are sharp and in tune. I'm sure that you've read articles on the importance of tuning hand planes. Most chisels need tuning, too. But I think you'll find the process of tuning chisels to be less time-consuming than tuning a plane. Best of all, the quality of your work will improve. Read on and I'll explain the problems with many chisels and how you can quickly and easily modify them before tackling that next set of dovetails.

Signs of a Good Chisel

A good chisel should be a well-balanced extension of your hand. When chopping (such as when removing the waste between dovetails), the chisel is held vertically (or nearly so) and struck with a mallet. The extra force of a mallet is required to push the chisel edge through tough end-grain. But just because a mallet is used doesn't mean that chopping is a crude process made with brute force. On the contrary, the force of impact should be precise and controlled. And for the greatest control, the chisel should be gripped not by the handle, but on the shaft with the hand braced on the work, just as you grip a pencil.

(Try gripping a pencil at the eraser end and signing your name; you can't get the control that you normally do.)

But what does the grip have to do with fine-tuning the chisel? It has more than you might think. Unfortunately, many chisels are too long and heavy for effective chopping; the extra mass and length make the chisel top-heavy and difficult to control. Although long chisels are an important part of a wood-worker's tool kit, they're for paring, not chopping. Besides, most of today's chisels are too short for effective paring; but more on that in a minute.

Compounding the length and balance problems is that the ends of the handles on many chisels are excessively rounded. When chopping, as the mallet strikes the round surface, it has a tendency to glance off. The solution is to change the shape; the end of the handle should be slightly crowned, not rounded. A crowned end will absorb the impact of the mallet and direct it to the cutting edge.

Now let's examine the other end of the chisel, adjacent to the cutting edge. Like many chisels that were manufactured years ago, most of today's chisels are bevel-edged. In other words, the sides of the chisel are chamfered. The reason for the beveled edges is so that you can easily cut into an acute corner, such as the space between dovetails. However, the problem with many chisels is that the sides are not beveled

Grinding down the side bevels on a stock chisel is a quick process when using a motorized grinder. Set the tool rest close to the wheel and work the first 1" of the tool. Quench the blade to avoid overheating the steel.

nearly enough. To be effective the sides should be beveled to almost a knife edge. Examine the chisels from your kit closely and you'll most likely see that a square portion of the sides remains. As a result, each time that you make a cut next to a dovetail, the corners of the chisel crush the adjacent surfaces and spoil the crisp appearance of the joint.

Fortunately, the excessive length, rounded ends and square sides are all easily corrected. And it takes just a few minutes to tune the tools and fix the problems. The results are well worth it, too. After modifying a chisel you'll be surprised at how much easier it is to use. In fact, your skill level will seemingly jump up a notch or two. First let's address the problem with the excess length.

Fixing Excessive Length

Years ago, many chisels were available in two lengths: The long length was for paring; the shorter length was for chopping with a mallet. For more than 20 years I've used the Stanley No. 750s. These venerable socket chisels were manufactured by the thousands up until the late 1960s. The short length, around 9", and light weight make them perfectly balanced. And remember, balance is the key. In addition, the leather-tipped ash handles were slightly crowned so that a blow from a mallet landed squarely on the end.

At the same time Stanley was producing the No. 750s it also made a longer version, the No. 720. The extra length of these chisels make them ideal for paring long, thin shavings. Yet, most

Most chisels today are the wrong length for chopping or paring. Above, the short chisel (left) is the right length for chopping. The long chisel (right) is the right length for paring. The Marples chisel (middle) isn't a good length for chopping or paring.

Cutting off the extra handle length dramatically improves the balance of the chisel.

buying chisels ready for woodworking

Lie-Nielsen socket chisels (right) are based upon the old Stanley No. 750s.

No doubt most every woodworker is familiar with Lie-Nielsen planes. Thomas Lie-Nielsen has taken a number of old Stanley designs, such as the esteemed Bed Rock bench plane, and made significant improvements. The result is some of the best planes available today.

Now he's at it again. This time he has developed a line of chisels based upon the old and long-discontinued Stanley No. 750s. Like the No. 750s, the Lie-Nielsen socket chisels are short, lightweight and have perfect balance. And with just a bit of honing and polishing, the Lie-Nielsen chisels are ready to use. Unlike the old Stanleys, there's no need to further bevel the sides; they come ground to a thin, almost knife-like edge. The chisels come equipped with hornbeam handles sans the leather washers on the end. But in my experience there is no need for the leather cap; the hornbeam is tough. In fact,

I've used my chisels for months and the handles appear as new. Rosewood handles are also available for an extra charge; but Lie-Nielsen recommends the hornbeam if you intend to use the tools with a mallet.

If you're interested in the Stanley No. 750s there are still plenty of old ones available. Of course many are ground down from years of use. But it's not uncommon to find them with most of the original length remaining. Similar to any old tool, the collectors drive up the price on the chisels in pristine condition. But those that exhibit minor wear and discoloration can be had at a reasonable price. Once you have your hands on a set you'll still need to tune them by beveling the edges further, but you'll be rewarded with perfectly balanced chisels at a price lower than most new chisels.

chisels that are manufactured today are too long for controlled chopping and too short to gain the leverage often needed for paring. The exception is the Lie-Nielsen chisels (see "Buying Chisels Ready for Woodworking" at left).

The solution is to cut off a portion of the handle. I know that sounds drastic, but it dramatically improves the balance of the tool. (And I'll admit, the sawed-off handle won't look pretty either, but your dovetails will.) After sawing off the excess with a hand saw, use a file to shape a small chamfer around the perimeter and slightly crown the end. This will ensure that mallet blows land squarely on the end rather than glancing off. If you grimace at the thought of such a radical modification to your prized chisels, then I suggest you purchase an inexpensive set of plastic-handled tools and dedicate them specifically for chopping.

Grinding the Sides

The next step in the tune-up is to grind the sides of the chisel to nearly a knife edge. There's no need to bevel the entire length of the blade; 1" is enough to reach inside of most dovetails. You don't need an expensive wet wheel grinder for this step – an ordinary dry grinder with 6" wheels works fine. To prevent burning the steel, I use a pink aluminum oxide wheel and stop often to quench the tool in a can of water. I usually use the factory bevel as a guide and just slowly grind away the excess steel. Use care and don't grind into the back of the blade. As I'm grinding, I pause periodically to cool the steel and inspect the edge. The entire process usually takes just a minute or so. Finally, don't forget to polish the back and hone the bevel.

For more information on sharpening hand tools, see "Sharpening Plane Irons" on page 25 and "Sharpen a Chisel" on page 31. For information on restoring vintage chisels, see "Resurrecting Chisels" on page 153.

Now give the newly transformed chisel a try. I think that you'll be pleasantly surprised with the results.

Carefully ground sides (left) look like a knife edge. This helps you produce cleaner, tighter dovetails.

Using the proper grip and having a tool with narrow side bevels adds control to the dovetailing process.

YOU DON'T HAVE TO OWN A LATHE TO **MAKE REPLACEMENT HANDLES** THAT WILL FEEL LIKE AN EXTENSION OF YOUR HAND.

32

make your own chisel handles

BY ROGER HOLMES

A few months ago I had to face the unpleasant truth about my chisels. Given to me years ago by my father, my trusty old set of Marples bevel-edge chisels had run out of steel. Ground and sharpened to stubs, they had to be replaced.

A little research into the chisel market revealed a surprisingly large selection. The important consideration, it seemed to me, was performance — which blades would take the keenest edge and hold it longest. But when I'd plowed through a stack of reviews (not being a tool steel expert, I relied on the tests and experience of others) and narrowed the field, I found I'd overlooked a second important consideration: handles.

No matter how marvelous the cutting edge, if the tool feels like a billy club in your hand it's of little use. Several of the top-performing chisels had clunky handles, while the handles I liked best were attached to chisels that didn't rate so high. Marples chisels,while not at the top of the league performance ratings, were a good value for money. But instead of the leather-washered, well proportioned ash handles of my old set, they come today with rather billy-clubbish handles of composite or ash. In the end, I found myself buying several chisels as much for their handles as for their steel.

Handle
ILLUSTRATIONS BY MARY JANE FAVORITE.
Ferrule seat
Ferrule
Tang
Bolster
Neck
Blade

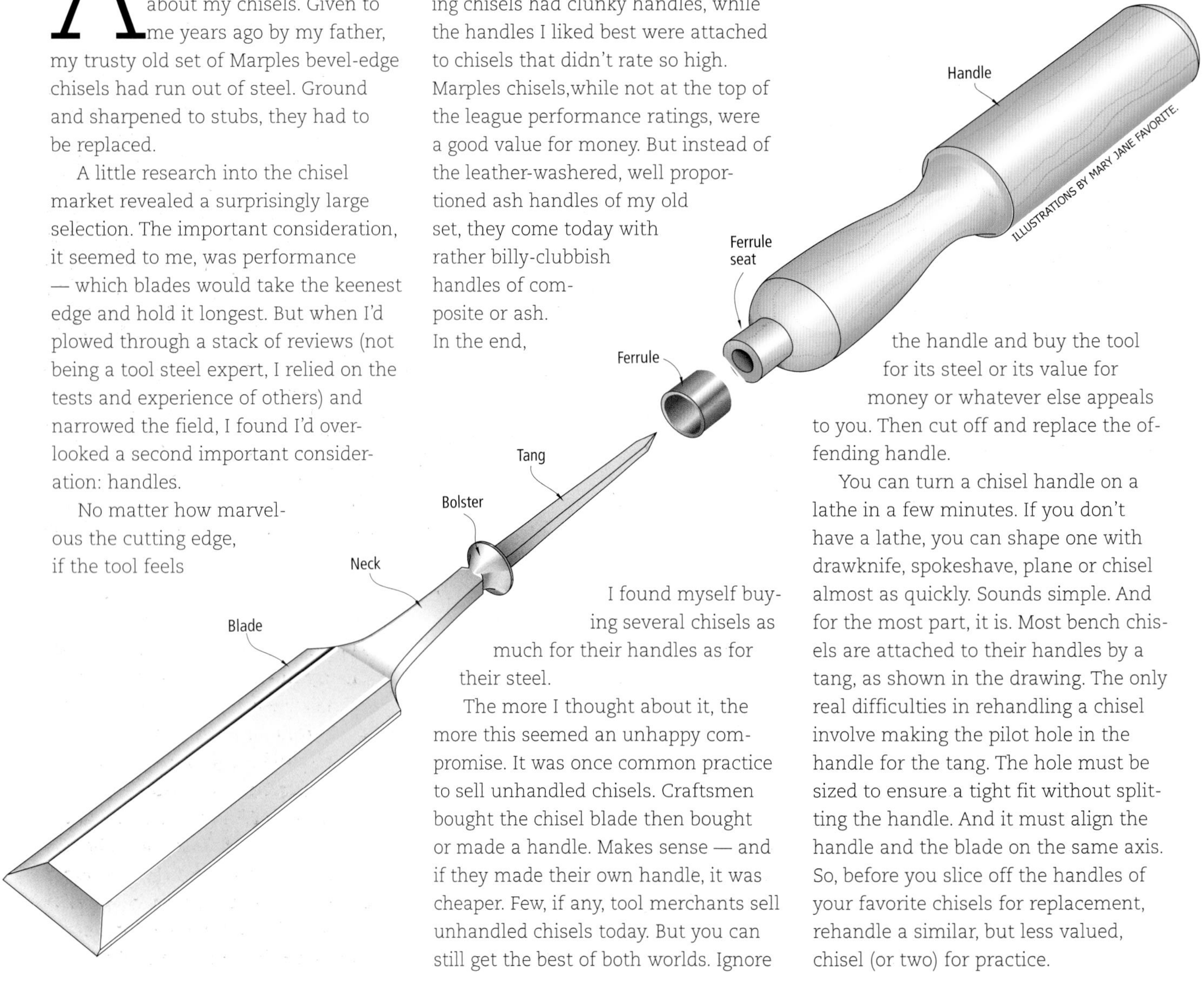

The more I thought about it, the more this seemed an unhappy compromise. It was once common practice to sell unhandled chisels. Craftsmen bought the chisel blade then bought or made a handle. Makes sense — and if they made their own handle, it was cheaper. Few, if any, tool merchants sell unhandled chisels today. But you can still get the best of both worlds. Ignore the handle and buy the tool for its steel or its value for money or whatever else appeals to you. Then cut off and replace the offending handle.

You can turn a chisel handle on a lathe in a few minutes. If you don't have a lathe, you can shape one with drawknife, spokeshave, plane or chisel almost as quickly. Sounds simple. And for the most part, it is. Most bench chisels are attached to their handles by a tang, as shown in the drawing. The only real difficulties in rehandling a chisel involve making the pilot hole in the handle for the tang. The hole must be sized to ensure a tight fit without splitting the handle. And it must align the handle and the blade on the same axis. So, before you slice off the handles of your favorite chisels for replacement, rehandle a similar, but less valued, chisel (or two) for practice.

Saw off the top of the old handle with a hacksaw—you won't damage the saw teeth if you hit the tang by mistake.

After making saw cuts at the top of the ferrule in to the tang, split a wooden handle away from the tang.

Off With the Old

Before you can put on a new handle, you have to get rid of the old one. First, mark the estimated length of the tang on the handle — 2" or so should do — then cut off the top of the handle above that point. I cut both composite and wood handles with a hacksaw. If I've miscalculated the tang length, I won't ruin the teeth of my nice backsaw.

If you're removing a wooden handle and you want to reuse the ferrule, next make a few saw cuts just above the ferrule down to the tang. Then split away the remainder of the handle, using another chisel as a wedge. You may now be able to drive the ferrule off the tang with a hammer and cold chisel. Or you may need to bore out some of the wood from inside the ferrule to loosen it. If you don't want to keep the ferrule, just cut through its length with the hacksaw and pry it off the tang.

The process is similar for a composite handle, which is cast in place around the tang. Using the hacksaw, I cut off the end of the handle. Then I make lengthwise cuts down to the tang to quarter the remainder of the handle, which makes it easier to split.

Tang Types

Tangs on my old chisels are four-sided and tapered to a point. Some are irregu-

To remove a composite handle, saw lengthwise down to the tang in three or four places, then split the remains of the handle from the tang.

lar and bear the marks of forging. They are seated in the handle in a stepped pilot hole, as shown in the drawings on the following pages.

Tangs on some of my newer chisels are different. Those for wooden handles are faceted on four sides, but not tapered. They seat in a single pilot hole. The corners of tapered and faceted tangs dig into the wood to make a tight, torque-resistant fit.

Tangs for my composite handled chisels are cylindrical, with small raised "fins" along their length to key them into

the composite material formed around them. Driven into a wooden handle bored to the same diameter as the tang (or slightly smaller), the fins might be enough to ensure a tight fit, particularly for a light-duty chisel. I ground facets on the tang and sized the pilot hole accordingly to be on the safe side.

To ensure that the edges of the tang dig into the wood, the pilot hole should be smaller than the tang. For a square-section tapered tang, the larger of the stepped pilot holes can be the same diameter as the diagonal across the tang

The chisel blade in the center has a forged, four-sided tapered tang. The other blades have cast tangs. The left one, for a composite handle, is cylindrical, with small "fins" along its length. The right blade, for a wooden handle, has four faceted faces but no taper.

Ferrules

These short cylinders of brass or copper bind the handle just above the bolster of the chisel. The bolster and ferrule work together to prevent the handle from splitting when the chisel is driven by a mallet. Chisels and gouges used only with hand pressure need no ferrules. But most chisels have ferrules even if they're intended for fine paring work; some carving tools do not. For many chisels, the greatest risk of splitting the handle comes when fitting the handle, so a ferrule is a good precaution regardless of the tool's intended use. Chisels and gouges subjected to heavy banging are often fitted with a metal hoop at the top of the chisel to prevent splitting at that end.

The size of the tang and bolster largely determine the size of the ferrule. If you're replacing a wooden handle,

as measured about one quarter the length of the tang from the bolster. (The bolster is the flared section between the chisel's narrow neck and the tang; it seats against the end of the handle.) Take the measure for the smaller hole about three-quarters of the length of the tang from the bolster. For an untapered faceted tang, make a single

pilot hole of smaller diameter than the tang's diagonal measure. The difference in the size of the hole and the tang can be larger in softer woods than harder woods, which have less give and will split more easily.

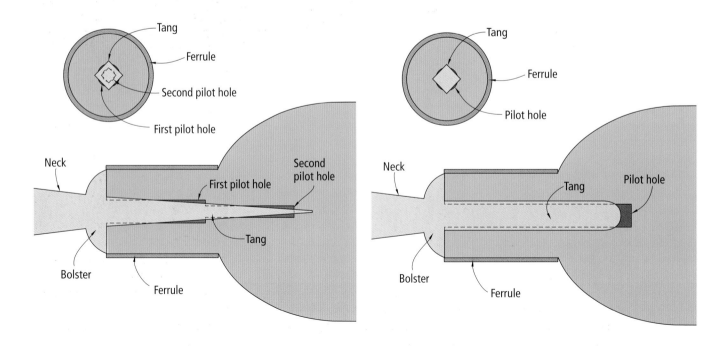

You can make handles in a wide variety of shapes quickly and easily on a lathe.

Grind flat facets on a round cast tang made for a composite handle to ensure a tight fit in the new wooden handle.

you can reuse the ferrule or use one the same size. If you want to fit a smaller ferrule or you're replacing a composite handle, make sure there will be enough wood inside the ferrule to accommodate the tang. In general, the diameter of the ferrule must be at least that of the chisel's bolster.

If you don't reuse a ferrule, you can make your own from copper tubing sold at hardware stores. Or you can buy brass ferrules for a few cents apiece from Lee Valley Tools. These come in a wider range of diameters than are available in copper tube. You need to fit the handle to the ferrule, so always have the ferrule you intend to use before you make the handle. Some chisels are fitted with leather washers that slip over the tang and seat between the bolster and the end of the handle. I think they're intended somehow to cushion mallet blows, but I can't say I feel a difference in use. I like them anyway, so I cut them out of a piece of shoemaker's sole leather and put them on.

Making the Handle

This is the fun part. You can make any kind of handle you can imagine. Turning handles on a lathe is quick and easy—you can make and discard half a dozen before you find the one you want and still be done in an hour. Shaping handles with drawknife, spokeshave, plane or chisels takes longer, but can

Bore the tang pilot hole on the lathe using a machinist's drill mounted in a chuck on the head stock. Feed the handle into the spinning bit with the feed wheel on the tail stock.

produce handle shapes — faceted or flattened for example — that are unobtainable on a lathe. And you can combine turning and hand-shaping. If you want to rehandle a chisel but don't want to make the handle, you can buy a classic boxwood pattern in several sizes from Lee Valley.

Commercial handles are commonly made of ash, beech or boxwood. But any reasonably hard wood will do. I'm looking forward to making some handles of osage orange, a native species here in Nebraska that has tight grain, a lovely orange color, and is tough as

nails. Firewood suppliers are excellent sources of ash, maple, birch and other local woods that make fine handles. If you can split handle blanks from the log, you'll ensure that the grain will run parallel to the handle's length, the strongest orientation.

On the Lathe

Turning is the easiest way to make a handle. Whatever shape you choose, it is important to fit the ferrule snugly to one end. It needn't be a forced fit, but it shouldn't rattle around on the wood, either.

165

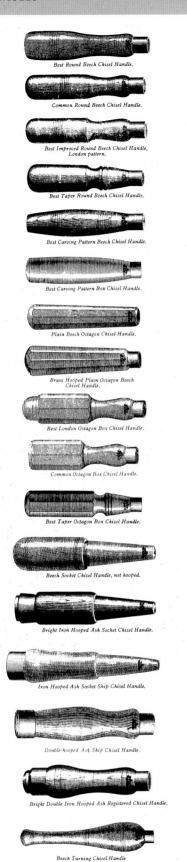

Different chisel handles as shown in R.A. Salaman's *Dictionary of Woodworking Tools* (Astragal Press), an excellent resource on the identification and history of hand tools.

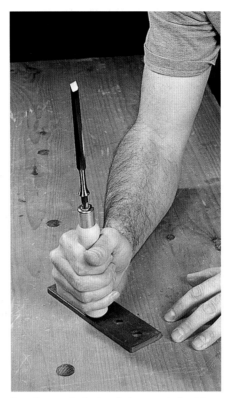

Seat the tang in the handle by repeatedly striking the end of the handle against an iron plate or machine table.

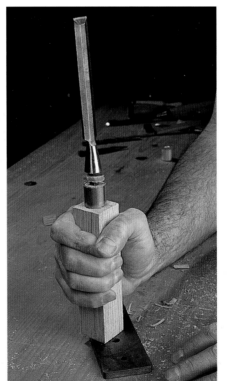

If you're uncertain about the alignment of the tang pilot hole and handle, you can assemble the blade to the handle blank.

After making cuts at the corner to prevent splitting along the handle's entire length, form the ferrule seat with a chisel.

The great advantage of a lathe is in boring the pilot hole for the tang. I mount a chuck and bit on the head stock and feed the handle onto the bit by turning the tailstock's dead-center wheel. This bores a hole right on the handle's axis, ensuring that the chisel blade and handle will be properly aligned.

Use machinist's bits — the tapered nose makes a neater, easier entry than a brad point or other spur bit. Complete the handle's shape (and rub finish on the spinning handle with a cloth if you wish) before you bore the hole.

Assembly

To join chisel and handle, slip the ferrule in place on the end of the chisel handle, add a leather washer if you want one and start the tang in the pilot hole. You can fix the chisel in a vise and drive the handle on. I prefer to upend the chisel and handle and bang the end of the handle on a machine table or other heavy piece of iron. Done this way, the blade's own weight drives the tang into the handle and I don't have to worry about the blade slipping in the vise. It takes a while, but unless you've badly underestimated the size of the pilot hole, the bolster will eventually seat snugly against the end of the handle. Even if the hole is a bit too tight, splits are usually contained by the ferrule.

Hand-Shaping a Handle

If you don't have a lathe, or you want a faceted handle, it is easy to shape one by hand. The tricky part is boring the pilot hole in the handle so that the blade and handle will be aligned. A blade that skews off the handle centerline can be very awkward to use. I think the easiest method is to bore the hole in a square handle blank before shaping the handle. With a drill press the hole can be bored very accurately. Or the blank can be held firmly in a vise for hand drilling. Set a square or two up to gauge the angles.

Next, form the seat for the ferrule. Make saw cuts in at each corner to prevent splitting beyond the ferrule seat. Then pare carefully with a chisel until the ferrule fits the seat snugly. If you're confident that the pilot hole is well centered along the length of the blank, you can shape the handle, then assemble it with ferrule and blade as described previously. If you're uncertain about the orientation of the pilot hole, you can assemble the handle and blade, then shape with drawknife and spokeshaves, as shown in the photos. This can be a bit awkward in spots, but it allows you to make adjustments in the handle to offset an off-center pilot hole.

Rehandling a chisel or gouge is very satisfying. A homemade handle may not be stronger or more durable than one from the factory. But it is certainly more personal and is worth doing for that reason alone.

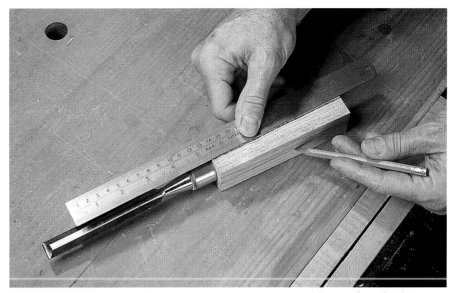

With the blade assembled to the handle blank, draw lines on the handle along the axes of the blade (top). Then shape the handle parallel to the axes to ensure good blade-handle alignment.

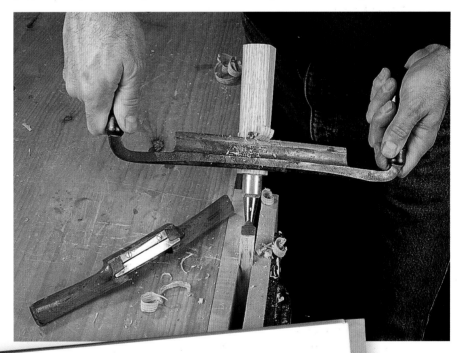

Supplies

Lee Valley Tools
800-871-8158
leevalley.com

Octagonal Boxwood Chisel Handles available in 5¼" lengths to 6¼" lengths. Priced from $6.95 to $8.25 each.

Brass Ferrules available with interior dimensions from .312" to 1½". Prices range from 15 cents to 96 cents each.

33

DESIGNED FOR PIERCING WOOD AND LAYING OUT MARKS, SOME AWLS ARE BETTER THAN OTHERS.
LEARN WHICH ONES ARE BEST SUITED TO YOUR STYLE OF WORK.

the essential awl

BY PAUL SELLERS

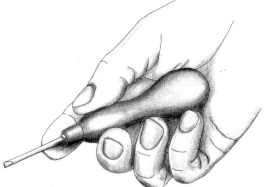

See the difference between the oval wood and the triangular-shaped piece of plastic. Bulbous, oval handles better distribute pressure.

Many tools seen for the first time express their full function by their very existence. They need no explanation. Hammers, a saw and a vise are such tools. There is an informal aesthetic working that delivers the tool's function and technique to the observant viewer. This aesthetic immediately conveys all the information without explanation. Awls are that type of tool.

With one glance a woodworker knows an awl's function. Piercing awls (sometimes called brad awls) pierce wood. Scratch awls (also known as marking awls) are used for laying out projects and joints. Here I discuss how to identify, use and maintain three types of piercing awls and the scratch awl.

The aesthetics of an awl are complete when the awl "looks" as though it will fit the hand and do the work. There are two ends to an awl, the business end and the handle. Both are important. Good awls have bulbous handles that serve to distribute the pressure needed to push the awl into the wood over a wide area of the heel of the palm of the hand. Use an awl with a handle that is too narrow all day long and you'll see my point – no pun intended.

Not 'Awl' That Common
A few years ago while I was demonstrating at a national woodworking show, a couple of young men came by my demonstration area and caught the tail end of my presentation. When I had finished, they joined the usual crowd, traced their fingertips over the handles of my hand planes and saws, and said, "Man! Where did you get all these old tools?"

However, while looking among the scattering of tools, these men didn't pick up or even notice one of my piercing awls –a birdcage awl – which is still fairly uncommon in the United States. I bought it, along with my other tools, as a young man earning my modest wage of the English equivalent of $4.50 for a 52-hour week. Though the awl's real value compared to planes and saws lay somewhat obscured to the men's cursory glances, I have grown to depend on my square-pointed birdcage awl more than any other type of awl.

For the most part all awls are fairly underestimated tools. Mention awls to most woodworkers and they will likely stare back at you blankly and wonder what you are talking about, that is until they hinge a few doors and box lids.

The true appreciation of this unobtrusive little tool comes only when, with swift, single-handed dexterity, you locate the sharpened point in the center of the hinge hole, press and twist, and there you have the most perfectly tapered hole, ready to receive the likewise tapered screw threads of even the smallest of screws. Hand tools such as these only become truly appreciated when they have fulfilled their function time and time again, year after year.

All Awls Aren't Created Equal
Awls once came in a wide variety of shapes and sizes. R.A. Salaman, in his comprehensive *Dictionary of Woodworking Tools* (Astragal Press) describes 14 different types of awls including the brad awl, upholsterers awl, flooring awl, sprig awl, scratch awl and marking awl. In the United States it's common to term any of the more specific awl names under the singular heading of "awl." But not all awls are created equal. In fact, they can be quite different.

Generally, we use awls for two purposes: piercing wood or scribing wood surfaces for layout. Most people put awls in two categories: brad awls (also called sprig bits) and scratch awls (or marking awls). However, a brad awl is just one kind of piercing awl – many different types of piercing awls exist.

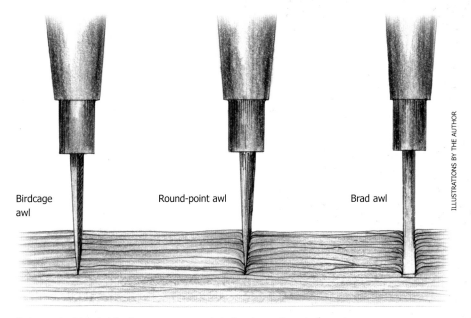

Birdcage awl

Round-point awl

Brad awl

ILLUSTRATIONS BY THE AUTHOR

Awls may be intended for the same purpose, but all awls aren't created equal.

all about ergonomics

With its wide, oval-shaped bulbous handle designed to resist slippage and to fit up against the heel of the palm, my favorite brad awl was ergonomic long before anyone ever heard the word.

Comfort, fashioned by a man's hand, had little to do with the kind of economy that concerns us today. It was more a sense of commonplace frugality and carefulness because the very tools a man worked with were intrinsic to his life as a craftsman. Tools handed down through centuries of work still serve as perfect examples of true craftsmanship because the qualities of the man were reflected in the tools he made and were passed on to those of us who follow. The tool shown here tells its own story.

The awl is old and English in origin. Economy was of little consequence to its maker, except that he respected time and so used the best materials at hand. The heavy-gauge brass ferrule he used was a scrap found and saved as treasure in the till of his tool chest. The steel awl gently tapers up to the bolster that intersects the square, hammer-drawn tang. The brass-securing pin barely protruding through the shoulders of the handle prevents the tang of the awl bit from twisting in the handle.

But above all, don't overlook the oval-shaped, English ash handle. It never twists or slips under torque. When all the raw components were shaped into a tool to fit his own hand – one that would serve him for six decades or more – this tool meant more to him than gold. His heir would one day find this tool and honor it with a replica made from similar scraps. The replica would soon allow the original to rest in its corner of the tool chest jusat as this one did.

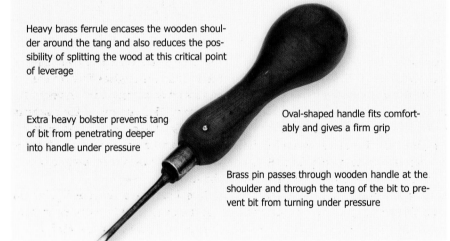

Heavy brass ferrule encases the wooden shoulder around the tang and also reduces the possibility of splitting the wood at this critical point of leverage

Extra heavy bolster prevents tang of bit from penetrating deeper into handle under pressure

Oval-shaped handle fits comfortably and gives a firm grip

Brass pin passes through wooden handle at the shoulder and through the tang of the bit to prevent bit from turning under pressure

'Awl in Awl,' What's the Difference?

The most common use for piercing awls is to pierce wood fibers for starting screws or nails. All piercing awls are used the same way with a push-and-twist-of-the-wrist action back and forth to the required depth. There are definite differences between each of the three types of piercing awls, even though

Here I discuss three types of piercing awls (the screwdriver-shaped brad awl, the square-point birdcage awl and the round-point awl), and the scratch awl.

their objective while in use and the end result are always the same.

All planes plane wood. Some are dedicated to straightening boards whereas some merely smooth surfaces. Others create shapes and still others fit parts. But all of them remove shavings. So, too, piercing awls are used to pierce wood fibers in some way. It's how they pierce wood and what the result of that piercing is that has a bearing on which type of piercing awl you choose.

To show the difference between the three piercing awls, moreover, to feel the difference, I suggest that you cut

some strips of wood about $\frac{1}{8}$" thick by $\frac{1}{2}$" wide by 10" long. Pine, maple, cherry or walnut will work fine, or you can use craft sticks as shown.

Take a round-point awl and, about $\frac{1}{2}$" from the end of the stick, press and twist the awl through the wood. Inevitably the awl will split the wood along the grain. It will do this in almost all wood types.

Now try the same with a screwdriver-shaped brad awl. The wood will usually split, though not quite so quickly or automatically as with the round-point awl, provided you begin penetrating the fibers with the screwdriver point initially placed across the grain as shown in the illustration at right, and then pushing and twisting the awl as it penetrates the fibers.

This twisting technique accompanied an intentional design feature of the tool. The problem was that nobody passed on the technique with the tool. The idea is that the cross-grain positioning of the flat blade acts something like a chisel to first cut the fibers and prepare for deeper penetration with subsequent pressure as you twist and push deeper through the fibers.

Now take a square-point birdcage awl and use the standard technique of twist and push continuously but carefully as you continue through the craft stick. You should have a perfectly round hole all the way through to the diameter of the corner-to-corner measurement of the awl.

Notice how the birdcage awl acts more like a reamer with the sharp, angular corners of the awl cutting the wood fibers instead of parting them and splitting the wood. Because round-point awls have no way of cutting the fibers, they instead serve only to compress, force and bruise the wood. The round point only parts the fibers and this inevitably causes the fibers to split.

In some situations, compression isn't bad. Sometimes it's good to leave all the fibers in place, such as in a large door stile or door frame where there is enough mass surrounding the hole to support the pressure given by the awl.

But for more delicate situations, such as near the ends of wood pieces, the birdcage awl finds its true value as a craftsman-designed tool. Though we no longer use the birdcage awl for its original task (more about that later) this tool has this main advantage: It will make large or small holes to receive large and small screws as needed. Another advantage is its convenient size, which makes it much handier than a conventional hand drill or even a screw gun because of its single-handed simplicity, weight and compact size.

Now let's take a closer look at the three piercing awls described above as well as the scratch awl.

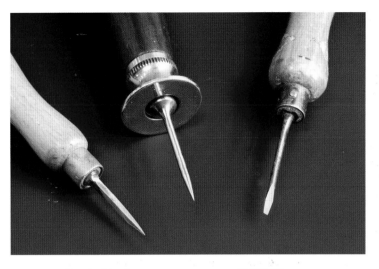

From left to right: birdcage awl, round-point awl and brad awl.

The Birdcage Awl

The square-point birdcage awl also is known as the square awl or a sprig bit. Any one of these names will do, but the two true names are birdcage awl and square awl.

The term "birdcage" identifies and isolates the tool to its original application rather than its more common function in our modern woodworking era – creating simple holes. At one time, country woodworkers made all types and sizes of birdcages for catching, transporting and keeping birds. The cages were made from wooden frames within which wood, bamboo cane or metal bars were fitted to contain the captive birds.

Cages for all types of poultry as well as exotic and singing birds were common throughout the world, and so this tool found its greatest use for boring fine, medium and large holes in rails of wood to build bird enclosures and all types of cages. Simple six-sided boxes and ornate, multilevel palace cages came from the craftsman's hands to entertain and decorate peasant homes and royal households alike. In fact, birdcages predate metal screws by many hundreds of years.

In reality the birdcage awl was the only awl capable of producing a round hole in wood by actually removing material from the hole by its reaming action. Other awls, such as the brad awl, might come close but the birdcage awl could produce round holes more efficiently than any other tool of its

Round-point awl

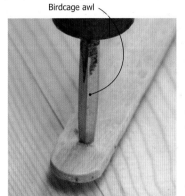

Birdcage awl

Press and twist different types of awls into the ends of craft sticks and you can easily see the different ways different types of awls pierce wood.

type and in locations that no other awl could.

The birdcage awl will not do what the screwdriver-shaped brad awl will do because it's square along the whole length of the bit. So when you turn the birdcage awl in the woody fibers it automatically reams out the whole length of the tapered hole rather than the periodic bypassing action that you can do with the screwdriver-shaped brad awl. Of course if you simply push and waggle the birdcage awl as you would a round-point awl and refrain from the twist-and-turn action, the birdcage awl will leave all the wood fibers in place.

The Round-Point Awl

The round-point awl is simply pushed into the wood to the necessary depth. The advantage of this awl is that, particularly in soft-fibered woods, the fibers are compressed rather than cut or reamed away.

When the awl is removed, the compressed fibers spring back so that when you screw into the parted fibers of

the hole with a wood screw, you have retained all the original fibers of the wood to then surround the threads of the screw. Also, because of the elasticity of the compressed wood fibers pressing against the wall of the screw's main body, you add even more security to the screw.

The downside of the round-point awl is its tendency to split the wood rather than cut the fibers. It's a handy but sometimes restrictive tool.

The Brad Awl

Again, the name "brad awl" is a generic term meant for a pointed tool used primarily for piercing and separating wood fibers to receive screws and small nails. Woodworkers are typically called on to work with other materials such as cloth or leather. So for many years this tool also has been employed as a support tool for furniture makers undertaking upholstery or boat builders working with sail cloth and other canvas awning fabrics.

Most woodworkers use the screwdriver-shaped brad awl until they

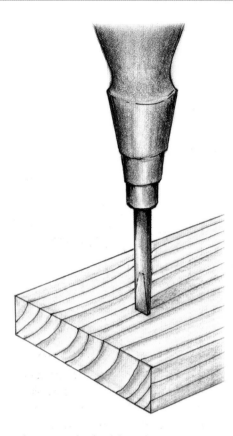

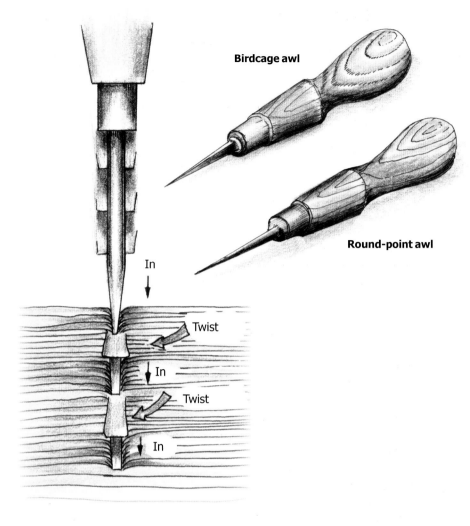

Birdcage awl

Round-point awl

In

Twist

In

Twist

In

When using a brad awl, begin by penetrating the fibers with the screwdriver point initially placed across the grain as shown above, and then push and twist the awl as it penetrates the fibers (right).

discover the birdcage awl or the round-point awl. Discovering these other two awls, how to use them, sharpen them and how they effectively work the wood fibers, will exponentially change your perspective of awls.

Both the brad awl and the birdcage awl will achieve similar results. You can use them to simply separate fibers, or you can use them to ream out the fibers and bore clean, clear and round holes with a simple twist of the wrist back and forth.

Although the screwdriver-shaped brad awl can be used both with or across the grain, we generally enter the wood cross-grain so that the leading edge of the awl performs an action similar to a dull chisel, severing the cross-grain fibers rather than simply parting the wood fibers to create a pointed hole. By repeatedly pressing and turn-

ing the awl alternately back and forth to deepen the hole, the awl parts the fibers and then reams the next section of fibers below.

This action of successive twisting and pushing keeps more of the fibers intact on either side of the spade bit. As the point first forces and compresses the fibers apart, and then rips the fibers below, we effectively create a "compression, rip, compression, rip" effect to the depth of penetration. This makes it a hybrid of the birdcage awl and the tapered cone point of the round-point awl. (See the illustration above.) Alternatively, pushing the brad awl into the wood with its spade point in line with the grain, the brad awl will simply part the fibers only, performing more like the round-point awl.

My Favorite Piercing Awl

I prefer the birdcage awl followed quickly by the brad awl. I'm often working in more dense, hard-grained woods, and birdcage awls clear a passage for the main body of the screw while allowing for the screw threads to actually bite into and thread the wall of the hole as I drive the screw home. Hardwoods have more of a tendency to split because many of them have a brittle nature. The reaming function of the corners of the birdcage awl creates a tapered round hole, which is the ideal shape for traditional wood screws.

I didn't arrive at my conclusion by some conscious decision after discovering each successive awl to be better than the previous one. I simply realized that after 40 years I always reach for the same awl every time and so the birdcage awl, for me, became the better awl.

Finding a Piercing Awl

There are several ways to acquire your first square-point birdcage awl. They are relatively inexpensive to buy, but you can also make one yourself by simply filing an inexpensive round-point awl or screwdriver to a square tapered point. I once did this when I misplaced mine and I am still using it today (see the photo below). However, many awls have hardened steel bits that are harder than the teeth of a file and so will easily ruin the file for further use. Test it first at a less important part of the file to make sure the awl is soft enough to sharpen.

Lee Valley also sells a square awl (800-871-8158 or leevalley.com, #35N13.01, $15.95) that is made in England using traditional methods, and it has a turned rosewood handle, solid brass ferrule, and a forged and ground steel bit. The bulbous handle fits my hand well and allows me to give full pressure to the tool.

An awl unique to Veritas is its own "chisel point" brad awl (# 05N60.01, $15.50) designed to efficiently bore through the wood fibers using the typical twisting action associated with awls. Veritas hybridized the traditional brad awl with the birdcage awl (see illustration above), which resulted in another well-thought through, finely crafted tool so typical of Veritas engineering.

The Scratch Awl

One other awl in R.A. Salaman's *Dictionary of Woodworking Tools* (though in a completely different category) is a longer version of the round-point awl that goes under the more modern title of

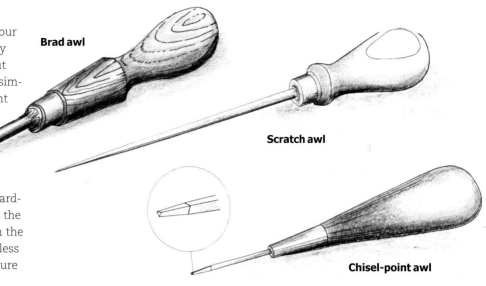

Brad awl

Scratch awl

Chisel-point awl

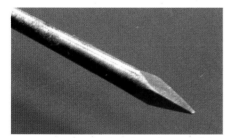

You can easily make your own birdcage awl by filing an inexpensive round-point awl or screwdriver to a square tapered point. I made the awl shown here after I misplaced mine.

"scratch awl." The scratch awl is self-descriptive and is simply used by carpenters and joiners to mark or scratch the shoulders of tenons, dovetails and the positions for parts of furniture and various other woodworking projects.

Though it does scribe the surface fibers by either cutting or indenting the wood, this tool is not as definitive as the layout knife and is therefore used more for carpentry work, timber framing, and making farm implement parts, wheels and so on. The pencil actually replaced the awl for many preparatory steps because it allowed temporary marking without permanently marking the wood in readiness for subsequent permanent markings with the knife, or the marking or mortise gauge for instance.

Its secondary use for most, and maybe its true value, comes when the nozzle of my glue bottle gums up, or when I have some caulking to do and I need to pierce the silver foil seal inside the nozzle of the tube.

I ordered a scratch awl from Lee Valley (#50K06.01, $9.95). The scratch awl is typical of most scratch awls, except that instead of simply providing a round handle, this tool has two flats on either side so that the awl stays in place wherever you lay it down. The 5"-long hardened carbon steel point is hardened to Rc 55, which means it will keep its edge, yet it can be readily resharpened as needed.

Replacing an Awl Handle

All too often the twisting action wallows out the walls of the hole and there is no substance there to securely hold the tang of the awl. At this point you can either fill the hole with two-part epoxy and push the tang back in place or replace the handle.

As a beginning craftsman, I repaired many a tanged tool with a replacement handle. That was how I acquired many of my first tools. Hot coals from the heat stove quickly turned the tang bright yellow and pushing the point into the center of the handle was like pushing a hot knife into butter. Stopping just short of the bolster of the bit bottoming out at the tang shoulder, withdrawing the hot tang and quenching it, and then driving the bit home into the handle resulted in a well-held bit.

Sharpening Awls

Woodworking tools deteriorate through extended years of use and awls are no exception. I simply sharpen my birdcage awl with a fine single-cut file on all four faces working from the wider flat areas of each face and along toward the point. I find a fishhook sharpener works great for sharpening round awls. To sharpen brad awls, simply lay each of the flat faces on the bench stone and rub the faces back and forth until they are flat. Trim the flat point with a file.

the striking knife

BY ADAM CHERUBINI

The striking knife was a tool frequently found in the tool kits of early woodworkers. Though it's extremely useful, it is a surprisingly uncommon tool to encounter today.

As preposterous as the notion seems, the historical record suggests cabinetmakers working in dim shops with hand tools were able to produce fine furniture with great speed. Despite the superiority of our modern tools and shops, few can match their productivity. So modern woodworkers are left with this question: How were they able to work efficiently with hand tools?

In this chapter I shall attempt to do what my 18th century counterpart swore not to do: Reveal the once secret "arts and mysteries" of working quickly and efficiently with hand tools.

My Favorite Tool: The Humble Striking Knife

Do you have a favorite tool? It may be a tool that fits your hand well or does a fine job. Or it might be a tool that simply appeals to you. Well I certainly do. It's a tool not much used anymore called a striking knife. A striking knife is a double-ended marking tool with a skewed chisel-like blade on one end and a scratch awl on the other. My striking knife came to me in a parcel of old Sheffield brace bits purchased from an English auction house. It appears to have been made from a thin, fine-toothed file. Some striking knives have wooden scales (handles), but not mine. Two carefully placed and well-smoothed indentations are all its maker offered to comfort those who have used it.

I understand those who would question the striking knife's relevance. The 0.5mm mechanical pencil is indeed the fine woodworker's friend. And while I accept the accusation that I am a traditionalist – even a Luddite in my preference for wooden bodied planes – I defend my use of the striking knife as an important and helpful tool. As a marking tool, it leaves exactly the line you want. It's like a pencil that can lay a different thickness line depending on the situation. But unlike the pencil, the striking knife leaves a physical feature that is not only useful, but responsible for fine craftsmanship. Allow me to explain.

Awl Marks With the Grain & End Grain

Many marking knives currently available don't have awl ends, which is unfortunate. The awl side seems crude but it's quite helpful. Marking with the grain, even on rough-sawn surfaces, is simple with the awl side of the tool (the

blade end can catch the wood's grain, pulling the edge and line astray).

Begin the long grain mark by laying the awl's point in the corner made between the work to be marked and your straightedge. The point of the awl should hang off the workpiece as you begin the line. Keep the upper end angled back toward you and pitched slightly away from the straightedge. Drag the point onto the work and along the straightedge. Use a light touch and several passes to make an acceptable line. In fine-grained woods, you needn't make a deep line. Your line will be difficult to find in nearly every species of oak.

When planing to a scratched line (or even a gauged line) you can see where the plane has met the line from the top. The edge of the board becomes slightly narrower as you reach the scored line. Even the shavings emerging from the plane will reveal this.

I also use the awl end of the tool to mark end grain. Unlike awl lines, I

are there really arts & mysteries in woodworking?

The phrase "Arts and Mysteries" was typically used in contracts between masters and apprentices. Some modern scholars consider it merely a term of "art," and open to interpretation. I interpret the phrase literally to mean that there are tricks and trade secrets that were passed on from master to apprentice. Each apprentice swore to keep these secrets. The fact that not a single English language text was written on the subject during the whole of the 18th century attests to the seriousness with which the oath was taken.

Marking parallel to long grain requires a sharp tool and a light touch. Begin the mark with the tool hanging over the end of the work. The striking knife must be angled down (toward you) and slightly away from the straightedge as shown.

It's difficult to accurately mark end grain. Pencil lines across sawn end grain of dark woods such as black walnut, are nearly invisible in anything but direct light. A scratched line is much better, especially in the raking light typical of all workshops. Here, the striking knife offers an extra benefit: Its slender awl end reaches into tight places like these tiny "London pattern" dovetails.

can't see knife lines in freshly sawn end grain, and I prefer not to plane end grain just to see my marks.

The long thin awl end is especially helpful when marking dovetail pins. There is an advantage to making the pins very small and the tails very wide, but the trouble with this approach is the marking. The long awl end of a striking knife fits into tiny spaces well.

Knife Marks Across the Grain

Making cross-grain marks is where the striking knife excels. Hold the knife using a pencil grip with the tool nearly vertical. Lay the flat side of the knife against a try square's blade or a straightedge. Place the center of the blade on the corner of your work and make a deep nick. Draw the knife slowly towards you, cutting lightly with its tip. To keep the knife firmly against the square or straightedge, rotate the knife to steer the blade toward the square. Just before you reach the near end, roll the blade down to mark the near corner with a deep nick. If you want a deeper line, make another pass. Never force your knife. That will only cause inaccuracies. Remember: The slow knife cuts best.

Those nicks at the beginning and the end of the line offer four important advantages:

1. Positioning your try square: When you wish to make an accurate crosscut, it's helpful to mark the face and both edges. After marking the face, place your knife back into the nick in the corner from your first mark. Reposition your square to the knife to then mark the edge of the board. Repeat this process each time you move your square.

This is an accurate way to mark multiple faces. If you are working rough stock and the corners aren't crisp, this technique is especially helpful. But I also appreciate it because my nearsight vision is failing. Pencil lines, you see, force you to align your square by eye. At least some of my woodwork is done in the evening when my eyes are weary. This technique allows me to continue doing

Marking cross grain begins with a nick in the far corner. Notice the angle at which the knife is held. Because most of the wear happens at the tip of the blade, the middle of its edge stays sharp. Draw the knife toward you in one smooth motion. A light touch is all that's needed here. Notice the knife is still nearly vertical. The grip is relaxed. The wrist is straight.

good work hours after I should have hung up my shop apron. It may also help explain how such good work was possible in poorly lit period workshops.

2. Guiding saw cuts: Not only is the mark accurate, but it guides my saw or chisel. The teeth of my crosscut-filed backsaw jump into the knife mark. By keeping a relaxed grip on the saw, I've found the saw will find the mark, again sparing me from straining my eyes.

3. Fixing wayward saw cuts: Many beginning sawyers quickly learn to track the line on the face of the stock, but they lose square in the thickness. I do as well. In that case, and provided you are off on the heavy side, you can easily pare away the excess with a chisel. The marked line is most helpful for

Here, the wrist is relaxed and still quite straight. For softer woods such as this poplar, a single pass is usually sufficient to leave an acceptable mark. The mark is finished with a near side nick. This is easily made thanks to the low skew angle of the blade.

The striking knife is easy to overlook. This has no doubt led to its near extinction.

this operation. I prefer this approach to planing end grain, which is difficult.

4. Preventing breakout: Having a knife mark all around your stock also helps prevent tear-out when using a crosscut saw. This is especially helpful if your stock has already been planed.

Having both ends on a single tool is handy when both types of marks are required for a job. Marking a tenon comes to mind. I use a marking gauge to lay out the cheeks, but the awl end marks across the end grain. Obviously the knife end defines the shoulders.

Beyond marking (it is my favorite tool!) I find my striking knife helpful for pencil sharpening, dovetail paring, slic-

ing drips of gelled hide glue and clearing shavings from my planes' throats.

Characteristics of a Good Knife

Old striking knives aren't common. It would be easy to overlook one. There's little wonder you don't see them in tool shops, or even in period inventories of tools. They are among those once-ubiquitous items such as pencils or chalked string lines that would have been accounted for under the catch-all heading: "smalle things forgotten." The famous Benjamin Seaton tool chest includes a striking knife under the heading "marking awl."

The old knives look far less like craft knives than modern marking knives do. The blade end has dramatically less skew, maybe 15° or 20° off square. While this forces you to hold the knife nearly vertically, I find this a distinct advantage. When marking the near corner, you must roll the knife down toward your body. If you hold the knife as you would a pencil, that last roll can be a wrist breaker.

For right-hand use, the left-hand side should be flat. For southpaws, the

right side should be flat. I've used, but don't love, the V-shaped knives, which are supposed to work either handed. The problem I have with them is that the angle at the point is either too steep or exactly double what I would prefer it to be. I've never sharpened one, but it seems like it would be a touch more work to hone. Still, a bad knife is better than no knife.

A striking knife would make a great addition to any shop. I love mine, but maybe not solely for the reasons I've stated thus far. You see, the striking knife, like this article, offers the attentive craftsman the chance to learn important lessons about woodworking quickly and efficiently with hand tools. For if you think this article is about how to use a striking knife, you're only half-right. Read it again, but this time forget about learning how to use a striking knife and concentrate instead on learning the lessons it wants to teach you. Consider the ramifications of its use. Only then will you understand my first lesson to working quickly and efficiently with hand tools … and it has nothing whatsoever to do with the striking knife.

finding a striking knife – or someone who will make one for you

It's possible but rare to find striking knives "in the wild." Most folks don't know what they are. Knowledgeable tool dealers or tool-collecting organizations may be helpful. British tool dealers seem to be more familiar with the tool and may actually have one or two to sell from time to time.

Failing that, I recommend seeking a blacksmith accustomed to making tools or knives. The striking knife can be forged from high-carbon steel; its hardness should be that of a chisel. An old file would be a good place to start. The dimensions in fig. A are for my knife. The dimensions in fig. B are for a knife owned by Christopher Schwarz.

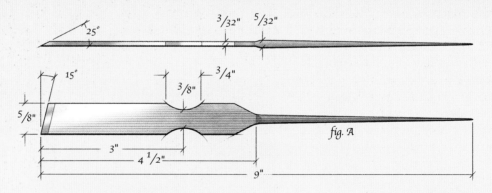

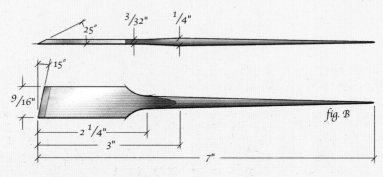

ILLUSTRATIONS BY MATT BANTLY

Old striking knives have incorporated decades of practical experience. Their form is a reasonable starting place for craftsmen unwilling to reinvent every wheel. Surely improvements can be made, but why not start where our forefathers left off?

35

using a marking knife

BY CHRISTOPHER SCHWARZ

I f you've ever been upgraded from coach to first class on a flight, then you already know what it's like to upgrade from a pencil to a marking knife. Suddenly, a task that was once frustrating (a cross-country flight or marking out a dovetail) is accomplished with surprisingly great ease.

Marking knives are the trick to getting a piece of wood to end up exactly the size and shape you intend it to be. They cut a predictable fine line that tells your tools exactly where to start and stop their cutting.

Despite their great usefulness and long history (they show up in several inventories of early woodworking tools), marking knives are uncommon in the modern workshop. Many woodworkers graduate from the carpenter's pencil to a sharp writing pencil to a mechanical pencil. Then they stop there. All woodworkers, regardless of their skill level, will benefit by matriculating one more time to the marking knife.

Accuracy at a (Fair) Price

Of course, this upgrade isn't entirely free. You need to learn to sharpen marking knives reasonably well, and the small bevels of the tool can be intimidating to the beginning sharpener. I struggled with these tools for years myself until I stopped trying to sharpen them as keenly as a plane iron. This level of sharpening is simply not necessary, even for fine work. They just need to be sharp enough to sever the wood fibers cleanly. Any more than that is wasted effort.

Once you accept this notion, sharpening your knife becomes a simple affair. I have a dozen sharpening stones I could use for this task, but I've devised a simple and effective alternative. I've stuck four grits of adhesive-backed sandpaper (#100, #150, #240 and #320 grit) to two small and flat blocks of wood. Now whenever I need to touch up a knife, I pull these from below my bench and quickly tweak the tool.

Once you touch up the two bevels, you still need to remove the burr on the backside of the tool by stroking it once or twice on your finest grit of sandpaper. (Note: Most quality marking knives come from the maker with the back completely flat and polished. If yours is not, you should flatten it first on a diamond stone. A flat back will register accurately against your square or straightedge – an important point.)

Basic Principles of Use

A marking knife is ideal for marking across the grain and OK for marking end grain. To mark out a tenon or a crosscut, secure your try square against the jointed edge of your workpiece. Then, using your dominant hand, place the flat backside of the knife against your square. Score the far corner, drag the knife toward you and score the near corner. Some practitioners instead register the knife's bevel against the square, arguing that this positions your arm free of your torso. I've never been comfortable using this technique, but it is a valid method among respected craftsmen.

Paired with a steel straightedge, a marking knife is capable of directing your tools to make precise cuts. In addition to marking out dados, I'll use my knife to fit doors and drawers in their openings. With the door in place in its opening, I'll knife in on the door exactly where I want the reveals (the gaps between the door and cabinet). Then I use the straightedge and knife to connect the knife marks. If there's a lot of long grain, I might switch to an awl to con-

After years of messing around with sharpening my knives on stones, I switched to sandpaper stuck to small (but flat) scraps. These do the job well and are convenient to keep at the bench so you can sharpen and get back to work. One scrap has #100-grit and #150-grit paper. The other scrap has #240- and #320-grit paper.

After you touch up the bevel, feel the back of the knife for a slight burr. Then remove that burr by stroking the back on your finest grit paper. It should take only one or two strokes.

A steel straightedge and marking knife allow you to mark out any line you please. One hand controls the straightedge; the other controls the knife. Keep the flat side of the knife against the straightedge, though some craftsmen work with the bevel against the straightedge.

Spear-point knives are bothersome to sharpen because you have two narrow bevels. The trick is to always keep the bevel flat on the sandpaper. For the left bevel, I put my thumb on the blade and my forefinger on the handle (as shown here) to control the blade.

Marking knives are great for marking across the grain and OK for marking end grain. (Awls work better for marking with the grain.) For marking out a tenon, a dado or a line for a crosscut, place the flat end of the tool against your square and draw the tool toward you. Mark the far and near corner more heavily. This allows you to carry your line around corners.

Score here first   Then score here

Begin marking out your dovetail joint by making a deep score at the far corner then the front corner. Now mark down the face grain. Bring your knife back to the rear corner and mark the end grain. If you struggle with this (it takes practice) try using a scratch awl.

nect the marks. Then I hand plane the door or drawer to the line.

Marking knives are also my favorite tools for marking dovetails, despite the fact that most of the marks for this joint are along the grain or across end grain. A light touch and steady hand keep your marks true.

Begin marking the dovetail by scoring the far corner of the work, then the near corner. Then swiftly bring the knife down to your joint's baseline. Now bring your knife back up to your far corner and mark the end grain.

Once your tails are cut, use your knife to transfer the tails to the pin board. If you like the look of tight tails, you're going to want to purchase a thin marking knife. Thick knives simply won't reach into the tails.

Make Your Own Knife

It is simple to make your own knife. I've never been much of a toolmaker; I've always thought it took me away from what I really enjoy: woodworking. But making a marking knife – once you know one trick – is embarrassingly easy.

Buy a spear-point spade bit. A $^1/4$" or $^3/8$" Stanley or Speedbor 2000 bit is perfect. These bits are the correct length (about 6"), are made from hardened steel and the shape of the tip is already a spear. All you need to do is grind a 25° or 30° bevel on both sides of the spear, polish the back and hone the bevels. If you want a wooden handle, drill a hole in the end grain of a block of wood, epoxy the bit in place and shape the handle.

So now there is little excuse for not owning or using a marking knife. No matter how little money or time you have, you should be able to get a knife working in the hours between breakfast and lunch on a Saturday. And so for once, we can all go first class.

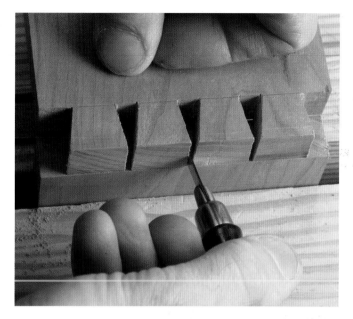

For tightly spaced dovetails, a thin knife is the only tool that will navigate between the tails to mark out the mating pins.

A thick knife is not suited for tightly spaced tails.

These marking knives were Stanley-brand spade bits in a former life. I purchased them at a flea market for a quarter each. Five minutes on the grinder and a little honing produced exactly the knife I like for my woodworking.

the mystery of try squares

BY ADAM CHERUBINI

Traditional try squares were made by the craftsman who was going to use them. By making your own try squares you can unlock some of the mysteries of 18th-century woodworking.

Furniture makers in the 18th century used shop-made wooden try squares. Though subject to wear and seasonal movement, these squares produced some of the world's finest woodwork. We've learned time and time again that if we want to do good work, it's important to have the right tool for the job. If you are setting up a table saw blade, an all-metal engineer's square may be the right tool. But if you are marking tenon shoulders and you want that joint to be tight, you'll need a wooden square. Wooden try squares feature a level of accuracy unlike all other squares currently available. Making a few for your shop is a great way to spend an afternoon.

Making the Square

Eighteenth-century craftsmen would not have had detailed project plans. A few critical dimensions and a good sense for proportion were all that were required. The dimensions and proportions I've listed (illustration at right)

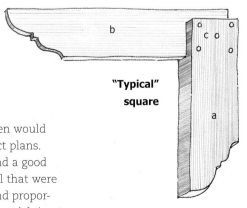

"Typical" square

ILLUSTRATIONS BY THE AUTHOR

and below are based on a scant few examples, but the result is good enough for museum work!

a) Handle – The length of the handle is typically $5/6$ of the length of the tongue (b). Both handle and tongue are typically $1\frac{1}{2}$" to 2" wide. The handle is sometimes decoratively scrolled as shown, drilled for a hang hole or both.

b) Tongue – The thickness of the tongue should be $1/8$"- to $1/4$" and planed to match the width of a chisel in your set. This facilitates the execution of the saddle joint (d) that joins the handle and tongue. A thick tongue gives the tool a club-like feel that I find objectionable.

c) Pegs – The handle and tongue are held with glue and three to five $1/4$"- wooden pegs.

d) Saddle joint – Earlier periods probably used a double-tenon joint as Joseph Moxon described in *Mechanick Exercises* (1678).

e) The thickness of the handle should be roughly three times the tongue thickness, and $5/8$" minimum to facilitate the marking of boards with rounded edges. I find thicker is better, $7/8$" not being too much.

f) The tongue should protrude $1/4$" to $1/2$" from the top of the handle to allow easy adjustment of this surface later.

Begin the construction of your square by finding some good straight-grained stock. You want a stable wood with fine grain. I've seen 18th-century squares in beech, birch, maple and mahogany. It's best to choose material with growth rings perpendicular to the wide face. You don't need to buy special quartersawn stock for this. You can simply rip a thin slice from thick rift-sawn stuff.

Planing the thin tongue flat is the first challenge. You may find this more difficult than it seems. It's not likely you will start with perfectly flat and

This is why I don't recommend metallic planing stops or bench dogs! Though it seems to defy logic, I prefer a plane with a curved iron to achieve the flatness I desire. A curved blade lets you take off material precisely where you need to.

I'm using my carcase saw for this joint. The trick is carefully marking and then sawing the lines out.

A firming chisel, perfectly sized to fit the joint, makes paring the waste particularly easy. Like all good "square sided" firmers, the sides of this chisel are ever-so-slightly beveled like a mortise chisel.

Carefully chisel in from each side. Undercutting the middle is the natural desire of the chisel and beneficial in this instance.

Strike a line with your striking knife on a piece of scrap wood.

Flip the square over and fit the blade to the previously struck line. Though you can't see the line in this picture, the top of the blade is touching it and there is a gap at the bottom. My striking knife is pointing to the line at the bottom. There's less than an $1/8$" inch gap there. So, on my first attempt, I'm out of square about $1/16$".

parallel stock. Set your marking gauge to the width of a conveniently sized chisel. You'll later use this chisel to cut the saddle joint. Carefully work to your gauged lines, but don't sweat it too much. A little gap isn't the end of the world. The handle needn't be planed as carefully. Get the thickness you want and make it pretty. Finish squaring up the handle and tongue by carefully planing their edges parallel.

I've seen squares with twin-tenon joinery. I find this difficult to execute (because the mortise is so short) and not worthwhile. So I'm just going to saw

a saddle joint into the stock and glue the blade in. Because I'll be using hide glue, I prefer a rough-sawn surface to maintain the bondline. This adds a bit of pressure to the sawing. Remember to saw down at an angle, working each corner out in turn. It would be extremely difficult to put the saw in the end grain and try to saw down with the saw held level with the floor. This is a simple joint but it requires precise work. I'm guessing this could be done quickly with a machine. But this is a quick job with a hand saw and a chance to practice your technique. If you make a mis-

take, you can easily start over, or later fill in any gaps with glue.

With the joint complete and tight, the next challenge is to get the blade square with the stock. Prepare a scrap board by straightening its edge with a long plane. Lay the square against the straightened edge and knife a line (a pencil line is too thick).

Reverse the square, and compare the difference between the struck line and the blade. Chisel the saddle carefully and repeat by striking a new line and flipping the square over and comparing. Continue this process until the blade, when flipped over, matches the struck line. Use this same technique to check other squares in your shop. You may be surprised by the results!

Use hot hide glue or epoxy to attach the blade to the stock. Both hot hide glue and epoxy will fill small gaps and form inflexible bonds which will help maintain the accuracy of your square for years to come. It's important to ensure the blade is fully seated in the saddle. Don't worry about squeezing all the glue out of the bottom of the saddle. The end grain won't provide any strength to the joint.

Glue the pegs in after the glue in the saddle joint is dry. If you use one of those no-good electric drills, be sure you clamp your handle to a scrap board to prevent fiber breakout on the back side of the hole.

when your square isn't

Like even the best machinist's tools, wooden squares need regular maintenance to remain at their very best. Since you made the square, you will easily be able to correct it. Though your square may move weekly or even daily in some seasons, you needn't correct it that often. You can simply strike a line, flip the square over, strike another, then eyeball a square line between the first marks and the second.

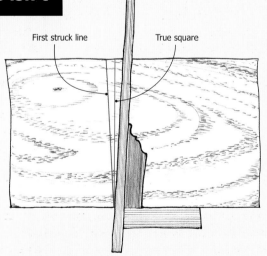

First struck line   True square

This isn't helpful only when you suspect your square isn't square enough, but whenever you need to mark across a wide panel, where even a slight error can be magnified with the panel's width.

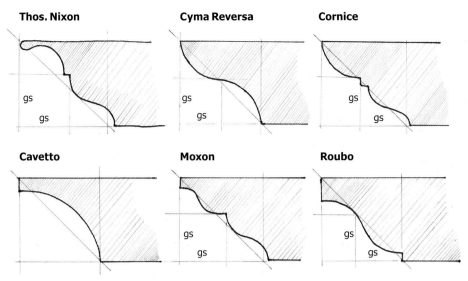

Thos. Nixon

gs
gs

Cyma Reversa

gs
gs

Cornice

gs
gs

Cavetto

Moxon

gs
gs

Roubo

gs
gs

All the end trims are basically cut on a 45° angle. The shapes within the trim are without exception comprised of ellipses and are divided using the golden section (gs= .618).

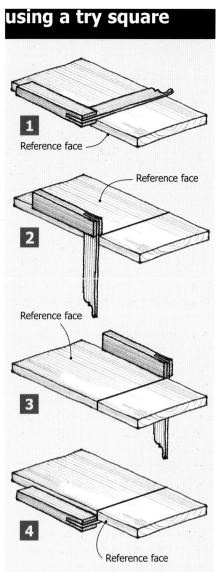

using a try square

1
Reference face

2
Reference face

3
Reference face

4
Reference face

When you work with hand tools, your squares never leave your bench. They are needed almost continuously and they are much too delicate to throw into a drawer. I know you are anxious to start using your wooden try squares, but take a few extra minutes to make them beautiful. Doing so reveals an important truth about them, and at the same time forms a wonderful connection with the past.

As woodworking became a full-time occupation, woodworkers began to see their tools less in terms of utility and increasingly as the essential instruments of their newly elevated occupation. As such, they reflected the evolved aesthetics of their makers. While we may think the end trims and delicate proportions are arbitrary or superfluous, the 18th-century woodworker probably saw such adornments as indicative of the tool's importance, and the complexity of its design and construction.

Though it is entirely speculation on my part, Thomas Nixon's squares, which all feature the same end trim, may indicate that unique end trims were used to help identify the ownership of tools that few woodworkers would willingly lend.

Using the Square

Striking is the process of using a try square to make a mark perpendicular to a reference face. The trick to striking accurately is always using the same two sides of the square (typically the inside of the handle and the outside of the tongue) and the same two reference faces of the board. This eliminates any errors associated with inaccuracies in your square or stock preparation.

Trying is the process of using the two inside or two outside edges of the square to check the edges of boards or joints. In period work, this function is typically less important than striking. The scale of furniture carcasses or drawers for example, is typically beyond the capability of any square. For such assemblies, a string can be used to check diagonal lengths with greater speed and accuracy than any square can.

Checking a board's edge is rarely critical since period-edge joinery is usually accomplished by match planing both edges simultaneously (a process where the actual angle of the edge produced is irrelevant).

Conclusion

So the trick to making a good wooden try square is understanding that only two edges really need to be square (the inside of the handle and the outside of the tongue).

The trick to using a wooden try square is understanding that your work will be more accurate if you only use two reference faces on any board. Never

trust that your boards are straight and their surfaces are parallel.

You probably know by now that the "level of accuracy unlike all other squares currently available" means wooden squares are terribly inaccurate. But knowing that forces you to use them carefully. With a wooden square you have no choice but to use only two sides of the square, and two faces of the work.

You may think buying an expensive square is a better solution. That may be true. But sloppy technique reduces the accuracy of your expensive square and leaves you with joinery that looks like you used a cheap square. So if you want your work to show the accuracy you paid for, work with your try square like it is a wooden try square.

37

HAVE MODERN GLUES AND CLAMPS RENDERED THIS **ANCIENT JOINERY TECHNIQUE** OBSOLETE? ABSOLUTELY NOT.

drawboring resurrected

BY CHRISTOPHER SCHWARZ

Drawboring is a simple and fundamental skill that will radically transform your joinery. The few extra steps it requires will virtually eliminate gaps in a mortise-and-tenon joint – even if the wood still needs to reach equilibrium with its environment. Plus, drawboring reduces clamping and the need for a perfect fit.

Drawboring is one of the simple reasons that so much antique furniture survives today, some of it as sound as the day it was made.

What is drawboring? It's a technique that greatly strengthens a mortise-and-tenon joint, transforming it from a joint that relies on glue adhesion into a joint that has a permanent and mechanical interlock. In essence, you bore a hole through both walls of your mortise. Then you bore a separate hole through the tenon, but this hole is closer to the shoulder of the tenon. Then you assemble the joint and drive a stout peg through the offset holes. The peg draws the joint tight.

Drawboring offers several advantages compared to a standard glued mortise and tenon:

■ The joint will remain tight. A common problem with mortise-and-tenon joints is that the joint can open up and develop an ugly gap at the shoulder. Sometimes this is caused by the wood shrinking as it reaches equilibrium with a new environment (such as your living room with its forced-air heat). Sometimes this gap is caused by simple seasonal expansion and contraction, especially with woods that tend to move a lot, such as flat-sawn oak. The peg in a drawbored joint keeps the tenon in tension against the mortise during almost any shrinkage.

■ The joint can be assembled without clamps. Drawboring is excellent for unusual clamping situations. Driving the peg through the joint closes it and clamps are generally not needed. Chairmakers use drawboring to join odd-shaped pieces at odd angles. It's also an excellent technique when your clamps aren't long enough. Or when you don't have enough clamps. Drawboring also allows you to assemble a project one piece at a time if need be.

■ The joint can be assembled without glue. There is good evidence that drawboring allowed early joiners to assemble their wares without any glue. This is handy today when you're joining resinous woods (such as teak) that resist modern glues or when you're assembling joints that will be exposed to the weather, which will allow water to get into them and destroy the adhesive.

■ The joint doesn't have to be perfect. The mechanical interlock of drawboring means that your tenon's cheeks don't have to have a piston fit with your mortise's walls. In fact, you might be surprised at how sloppy the joint can be and still be tight after hundreds of years. Drawboring requires you to be careful only when fitting the tenon's shoulder against your mortised piece. The other parts of the joint are not as important. And while I never argue against doing a good job, drawboring ensures that every joint (even the less-than-perfect ones) can be tight for many lifetimes. For this reason, I think drawboring is an excellent basic skill for beginning woodworkers.

So why has drawboring become an almost-lost art? It's a good question, and one that I cannot fully answer. I suspect that modern glues and machine-made joinery made the technique less necessary, particularly for manufac-

drawboring basics

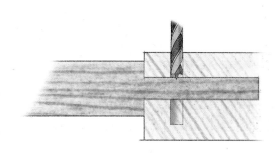

1 Bore $^1/_4$"-diameter hole through both mortise walls. The center of the hole should be $^3/_8$" from the edge of the mortise.

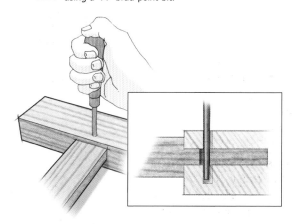

2 Assemble the joint. Mark the hole's center on the tenon using a $^1/_4$" brad-point bit.

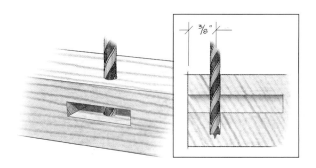

3 Remove the tenon and shift the mark closer to the tenon shoulder – $^1/_{16}$" to $^3/_{32}$". Use the same bit to bore a $^1/_4$"-diameter hole through the tenon at the offset mark.

4 Reassemble the joint. Twist the drawbore pin into the joint to check the fit. Ensure there are no gaps in the joint.

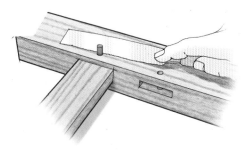

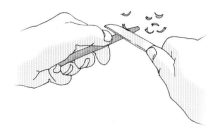

5 Whittle the end of a $^1/_4$" peg to about $^1/_8$" diameter at the tip. Add glue to the joint and peg. Assemble the joint and hammer the peg through the offset holes.

6 Saw (or chisel) the protruding peg material flush with the work.

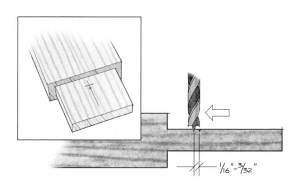

tured furniture. Drawboring does require several extra steps, and the benefits of it – particularly the long-term durability of the joint – is not something that is apparent to a customer.

Another reason the technique has fallen out of favor, I suspect, is that manufacturers have stopped making drawbore pins. These tapered steel tools allow you to temporarily assemble the joint to check the fit and to ease the path that the wooden peg will later follow. You can drawbore without drawbore pins by relying on the peg (and luck) alone. But once you use a proper set of drawbore pins, you will wonder why they are not in every tool catalog. Fortunately, you can make your own set of drawbore pins inexpensively. The sidebar on page 186 shows you how.

Joint Details

I have drawbored many joints during the last five years or so and have found the methods described here to be highly effective. My method is based on historical descriptions of the process from the 17th century and from my own work.

The first detail to tend to is the size and location of the hole through the

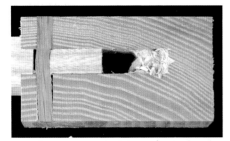

I sawed apart a completed drawbored joint to show how the oak peg bends through the offset hole. This was a $3/32$" offset in ash.

mortise. I have found that a $1/4$"-diameter hole is good for cabinet work. For larger-scale work (workbenches, doors and windows for homes) a $3/8$"-diameter hole is better because the peg is stouter. In general, place the hole $3/8$" from the opening of the mortise in furniture work and $1/2$" in larger work. Make the hole as deep as you can. Usually this requires boring it through the entire assembly, though the hole can be stopped in thick stock. The goal is to ensure that the untapered part of the peg passes into the other wall of the mortise.

Historically, many of the drawbore pins I've encountered are a diameter that's best suited for a $3/8$"-diameter hole and peg. Entryway doors and large windows are appropriate for this larger hole and peg. I have encountered (and own) a set of old pins that work with a $1/4$"-diameter hole, however, so this approach is historically accurate.

The next thing to consider is how much to offset the hole in the tenon. The bigger the offset, the sounder the joint, but the bigger the risk that you'll destroy the tenon or peg during assembly.

The traditional joiner was advised to offset the holes by the width of a shilling, according to Joseph Moxon's *Mechanick Exercises*, a 17th-century how-to book on woodworking. I had difficulty locating a shilling from the middle to late 17th century (I did try), but according to one knowledgeable collector of English coins, a 17th-century shilling would be about $1/16$" thick.

An offset of $1/16$" will indeed almost always work and is easy to assemble. But I've found that it's sometimes not enough to get the job done. Some of the joints I assembled with this small offset

Making your own drawbore pins is easy using an inexpensive alignment pin and a scrap of sawn (or turned) hardwood.

were just a bit wiggly. For furniture-scale work, I prefer a $3/32$" offset. For big-scale work, I'll push that offset to almost $1/8$" if the parts of the joint are large and the wood is a tough species, such as ash or elm. Experience will be your guide. Begin with small offsets in a sample joint and gradually increase them. You'll know when you've found the sweet spot.

Marking the offset on the tenon must be done with a bit of care because small changes can make a significant difference and cause the tenon to split in fragile woods, such as cherry. If you mark the offset with a slightly dull pencil, it can shift your mark by $1/32$" or so. I recommend you use a sharp mechanical pencil or (even better) a knife.

The shape of the peg is important, too. I whittle mine so the last $1/2$" tapers to an $1/8$" tip. In almost all cases, I use straight-grained white oak for my pegs. It must be completely dry; wet pegs will shrink in time and allow the joint to loosen up. Typically I'll split out my pegs from some dry oak using a pocketknife and mallet. This is called "riving," and it is a technique used by chairmakers to produce durable chair parts. Wood that is shaped by riving is stronger because it splits along the

make your own draw-bore pins in one hour

Proper drawbore pins are absolutely the key to successfully and consistently executing a drawbored joint. The pins allow you to work with bigger offsets, to know exactly how the joint will fit before final assembly and to pave the way for your peg by slightly distorting the hole through the tenon.

You can purchase traditional pins from dealers of antique English tools, though you will spend $45 to $80 for a pair, and you must sometimes search for the smaller-sized drawbore pins. I've had good experiences with two dealers: Tony Murland's Antique Tools (www.antiquetools.co.uk) and Classic Tools (classictools.co.uk). Both British dealers that sell to the United States.

The other option is to make your own. It's easy and takes only about an hour once you have the materials in hand.

The metal part of the tool is easy to find. Machinists, bridge builders, mechanics and anyone who works with metal has a set of tools they use that are much like drawbore pins. They're sometimes called drift pins, alignment tools or line-up tools. And they come in a wide variety of sizes and tapers.

To make your first set, I recommend you buy a set of alignment tools from Sears (sears.com, 800-349-4358 or visit your local store). The company sells an eight-piece set of punches and alignment tools under its "Companion" brand name. The set, which contains two alignment tools for our purposes, costs $6. The model number of the set is #30130.

One of the alignment tools in the set has a $5/32$" tip that tapers to almost $3/8$"

wood's grain lines. Sawing cuts across the grain lines, which can create a more fragile peg in some cases.

I then whittle the pegs round or roughly octagonal. Another option is to pound them through a steel plate with the correct-size hole bored in it. When pressed for time, I'll use dowel stock, which I

over a span of almost 4". This is a decent tool for furniture-scale work, though it will be much easier to navigate the offset if you grind the tip a bit smaller. The other alignment tool has a 3/16" tip that tapers up to a bit shy of 1/2" over a span of 45/16". This is a good size for larger work.

The first thing to do is to sand the black paint off the tapered section of the tool, which will come off on the wood eventually. Then you need to set the alignment tool into a wooden handle. Drawbore pins must be twisted in and out of their holes to work properly in my opinion. (Striking them is not a good idea.) I prefer a traditional tapered octagonal handle, which is easy to twist in and out of the holes. However, a lathe-turned handle will work nearly as well.

First bore a hole straight into the end grain of a 1 1/4" x 1 1/4" x 6 3/4" scrap of wood that will accommodate the hex-shaped end of the tool. For the smaller tool, use a 1 3/32" bit for the hole (this is why you bought that fancy set with so many bits!) For the larger tool, bore a 17/32" hole. If your bit isn't long enough to go deep enough, finish up the hole with a long auger bit that is a bit undersized (3/8" or 1/2").

With the holes bored, shape the handle to your liking. I tapered my handles to 7/8" or 1" square at the small end.

Now comes the fun part. Get a propane torch and heat up the hex shank of the tool for a minute or two. Then knock the handle onto the tool. The heat will char the wood as you insert the steel and prevent the handle from splitting as its driven on. Allow everything to cool down and then add a couple coats of wiping varnish to your handle. Now you are ready to explore this ancient joinery technique for yourself.

1. Bore a hole vertically into your handle blank. The hole should be slightly undersized compared to the largest dimension of the steel pin.

2. Taper the handle using your band saw. Be sure to keep the hole in the center of the blank.

3. I have a clever chamfer attachment for my Veritas block plane that's sold by Lee Valley Tools. You can also do this operation freehand.

4. Use a simple propane torch to heat the pin. Heat it up for two minutes. It will not change color.

5. With the pin still in the vise and hot, drive the handle onto the pin. When the handle is fully seated, the sound of the mallet hitting the handle will change.

This tapered octagonal handle is the perfect shape for the twisting action needed when inserting the tool in the joint.

have found to be satisfactory as long as I choose dowels with straight grain.

When you knock the peg home, you'll sometimes create a small gap between the hole and the peg as the peg leans heavily into one side of the mortise as it makes its twisty path through your joint. If this gap is unsightly, try a different strategy on your next joint. Whittle your pegs slightly larger in diameter and switch to an octagonal shape. A bit of practice in a couple of sample joints will help you get it right.

Despite everything I know about drawboring, I still glue most of my joints and even coat the peg with glue before driving it in. It cannot hurt. But I do take great satisfaction in knowing that when that modern glue has given up, the peg will still keep everything in place so the joint will be just as tight as the day I made it.

38

ONCE AVAILABLE IN DOZENS OF PATTERNS, THE RASP HAS
ALL BUT DISAPPEARED. BUT THE STAGE IS NOW SET FOR A COMEBACK.

return of the rasp

BY CHRISTOPHER SCHWARZ

One of the most useful wood-shaping tools – the rasp – is on my personal list of endangered tools.

Flip through any early 20th-century hardware catalog and you'll be astonished at the variety of rasps that were once available to the woodworker, shoemaker, farrier and even the baker (for removing burnt crust from the bottom of a loaf).

For example, a 1922 hardware catalog from the Hibbard, Spencer & Bartlett Co. in Chicago lists dozens of rasps in lengths from 6" to 16", in three different tooth patterns and a variety of shapes.

But until recently, modern woodworkers had few choices when buying rasps. Nicholson makes a couple quality tools, the #49 and #50. There are imported rasps from Europe and China. And then there's the Microplane – a tool invented in 1990 that's really in a class by itself.

But 2004 turned out to be a good year for rasps. Auriou, a French company that has been making rasps by hand since 1856, has begun importing its huge line of tools to the United States. These are premium rasps – a single cabinetmaker's rasp costs between $67 and $96. But the big bonus with the line from Auriou (pronounced "are-you") is it offers tools that haven't been sold new in this country for years.

Because of this influx of high-quality tools, I decided to look at what's available today, compare the tools and try to reacquaint woodworkers with this historically useful class of tool.

Why Use Rasps?

Among some woodworkers, rasps have developed a bad reputation. For the hand-tool purist, rasps are viewed by some as cheating. Real woodworkers, the thinking goes, use edge tools, such as spokeshaves, for curved work. And among the power-tool crowd, rasps are

Shaping complex and compound surfaces – such as the bow to this Welsh stick chair – is child's play for a decent rasp. I can't imagine a router jig that could make these cuts.

Shown are a few rasps on the market. From left: an Auriou modeler's rasp, an Auriou cabinetmaker's rasp, a Microplane, the Blundell and the Belotta cabinet rasp with an aftermarket handle.

seen as just another vestigial tool of the pre-router revolution.

Both groups are wrong. Rasps are an indispensable shaping tool that will greatly expand the scope of your work and the ease at which you can accomplish things that are difficult or impossible with other hand and power tools.

The true beauty of rasps is that you can create any shape or curve you desire without specialized cutters. The work proceeds quickly if you select the correct tool. And rasps are easy to master.

The Basics

While it's still possible to find vintage rasps at flea markets, most of the ones I've unearthed there are dull or damaged. The one excellent source of vintage tools I've found is Slav's Hardware Store in Chicago. Slav Jelesijevich haunts old hardware stores and buys up files and rasps that have been languishing in the basements of stores for more than 50 years.

The tools he sells have never been used (many are new in the box) and Jelesijevich's prices are reasonable. See the Supplies list on page 191 for details.

For the majority of us, however, we need to look at modern versions. Among the modern tools, there are two

Here you can see some structural differences: The Blundell (left) has hand-cut teeth but a blunt point, the Auriou has hand-cut teeth but a sharp point, and the Belotta has machine-cut teeth with a blunt point.

basic types: machine-made and hand-made. With the machine-made tools, the machine-cut teeth are quite uniform across the face and the point of the tool is blunt. With hand-made tools, the teeth are spaced irregularly across the face. And with the Auriou rasps, the tool comes to a point, which allows you to cut precisely into corners.

This makes a difference. With the lower quality machine-cut teeth, the perfectly lined-up rows of teeth plow perfectly lined-up grooves in your work. With well-made hand-cut teeth, the

One side advantage to rasps is you can modify your tools to fit your grip. Here I'm shaping the bun and handle of a Norris-style smoothing plane kit from Shepherd Tool so it feels like an extension of my arm.

finish of the wood is much smoother thanks to the random tooth pattern. (Note that the high-quality machine-cut rasps have teeth that simulate hand-cut teeth.)

Rasps are available in a variety of shapes, but there are three basic shapes that are useful to most woodworkers: half-round, rattail and rifflers. The half-round tools have one face that is flat or just slightly convex and a second face that is curved. These two profiles allow you to shape flat edges plus concave and convex curves.

The rattail shape – essentially a long tapered cone – is useful for enlarging holes and shaping their rims. The rattail is also a mainstay of trim carpenters when cope-cutting inside miters.

The riffler is for detail work. It is a bar of steel with complementary shapes at either end. Sometimes a riffler is the only tool that can get into tight spaces.

With the exception of the rifflers, rasps have a tang for fitting a handle. A handle makes the tool easier to control and safer – the tang can puncture your palm.

In addition to the different shapes, there are different degrees of coarseness to the teeth. Most new rasps for sale are patternmaker's rasps, which have a

fine tooth, are used for final smoothing and are needed for high-end work.

I also recommend you buy at least one cabinet rasp, which will quickly shape wood with a minimum of effort. (Cabinet rasps are further divided into those with bastard, second and smooth cuts – essentially really coarse, coarse and a bit coarse.) Then you come back with a patternmaker's rasp to clean up your work.

Think of this process like you would sanding. You wouldn't start sanding a rough board with #220-grit paper. Let the coarse tool do the heavy lifting and leave the finer tools for the finesse work. Your work will go faster and your tools will last longer.

When using a rasp, you should cut with the grain and approach the work with the tool at an angle. Some texts recommend a 40° angle, but I find that the angle varies with the user and the speed of the work. As with using a scraper, your body and hands will find the best position with a little practice.

Cut only on the push stroke. Applying pressure on the return stroke will dull the teeth. After a few strokes, tap the tool against the bench to dislodge shavings from the teeth. Periodically clean the teeth with a stiff-bristled brush. Some recommend a wire brush, but I don't find it necessary.

Comparing Different Tools

For the last five months, I've been using a selection of rasps for a variety of tasks, from shaping the bow of a Welsh stick chair to cutting wide bevels on tabletops to forming the handle and bun of an infill smoothing plane.

Let's start with the tools that do the initial hogging of material, the cabinet rasps.

The Spanish-made Belotta cabinet rasp is reasonably priced, but it cuts slowly like a patternmaker's rasp. And its machine-cut teeth left a deep scratch pattern. I don't recommend it.

The inexpensive tool that surprised me was the Czech-made Blundell, which has hand-cut teeth and a black plastic handle. From the looks of it, I wasn't expecting much. However the tool impressed me. It cut smoothly and left a decent finish. My only complaint was the teeth required more cleaning

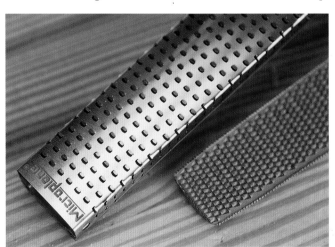

The Microplane is in a class by itself. The teeth cut like small razors instead of saw blades.

than the other tools and I don't like plastic handles. If I were going to use this tool every day, I'd replace the black plastic job.

For rapid material removal, I preferred the Microplane offset-handled rasp. I was ready to dismiss the tool as a gimmick, but I found it in my hands constantly when I needed to remove material in a hurry. Because the tool's teeth are like razor blades instead of saw teeth, the resulting surface is different than with a traditional rasp. Though the resulting surface looks cleanly cut instead of abraded, it's faceted. After using the Microplane I'd follow up with a patternmaker's rasp and found the facets easy to knock down.

Microplanes come in a variety of profiles and have replaceable blades. After months of use, the Microplane has become my favorite modern tool for shaping.

With the cabinet rasp's work complete, the patternmaker's rasp gets its turn to finish the job.

For many woodworkers the Nicholson #50 rasp is the go-to tool. It cuts smoothly and leaves a pretty good surface behind. I've always thought it was a bit expensive, but it always outperformed the inexpensive imports.

But then there are the Aurious. These tools will spoil you. After working with the other rasps for a couple weeks I'd eventually switch back to the Aurious and never want to go back. They cut smoothly and leave such

a nice surface behind that you don't mind paying the extra money (I paid it out of my own pocket).

Plus the sharp point of the tool allowed me to go places the other rasps wouldn't. My only complaint was the handle, which I considered to be rough for a tool that performs at this level and commands this price. You can, of course, finish the handle to your liking.

The only difficulty with the Auriou rasps is picking the right ones for your work. For general work, I used a 9"-long cabinetmaker's rasp with a rated 10 "grain." Unlike other brands, the Aurious are graded by "grain." The grain is the fineness of the teeth on a scale of 1 to 15, with the finer grades between 9 and 15 being common for woodworkers.

The other Auriou rasp that was useful was the 4" modeler's rasp with a 14 grain. This tool was great for getting into tight curves and difficult spaces, such as a saw handle, that the other tools couldn't deal with. I also tried out an Auriou riffler and a rattail rasp and those were equally nice.

If I were to purchase one additional Auriou for my toolbox, I'd get a 7"-long cabinetmaker's rasp with a 12 grain. There are many different shapes and sizes of tools available, including a selection for powered rotary tools. Also note that many of the tools are available with the teeth cut for either a left- or right-handed user.

The Verdict

If you've never used a well-made sharp rasp, you're in for a shock. And here's how to get started: Buy a Microplane for initial shaping tasks – be sure to get the one with the offset handle recommended in the Supplies box. Or call Slav's Hardware Store and order some vintage cabinet rasps.

And I recommend – without reservation – that you give the Auriou rasps a try. The high quality of these handmade tools is a rare find these days. You'll cringe a bit when you pay the bill, but you'll quickly forget what you paid and just be glad you own a tool that works this well.

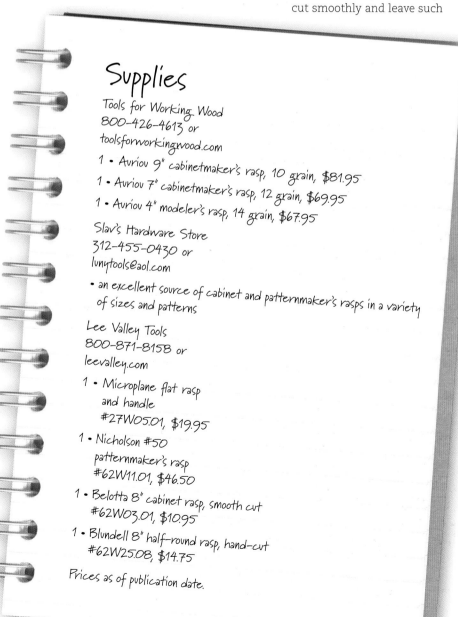

Supplies

Tools for Working Wood
800-426-4613 or
toolsforworkingwood.com

1 • Auriou 9" cabinetmaker's rasp, 10 grain, $81.95
1 • Auriou 7" cabinetmaker's rasp, 12 grain, $69.95
1 • Auriou 4" modeler's rasp, 14 grain, $67.95

Slav's Hardware Store
312-455-0430 or
lunytools@aol.com

• an excellent source of cabinet and patternmaker's rasps in a variety of sizes and patterns

Lee Valley Tools
800-871-8158 or
leevalley.com

1 • Microplane flat rasp and handle
  #27W05.01, $19.95
1 • Nicholson #50 patternmaker's rasp
  #62W11.01, $46.50
1 • Belotta 8" cabinet rasp, smooth cut
  #62W03.01, $10.95
1 • Blundell 8" half-round rasp, hand-cut
  #62W25.08, $14.75

Prices as of publication date.

wooden spokeshaves

BY DON MCCONNELL

Spokeshaves excel at shaping curved surfaces and can be either pushed or pulled over the work. Wooden tools, such as the one shown here, can be constructed easily yourself, or you can purchase a vintage one.

Many woodworkers might find the traditional wooden spokeshave invaluable for working curved and shaped surfaces. But many others often overlook this useful tool, despite its having undergone something of a revival among Windsor chairmakers during the past several years.

The wooden spokeshave's association with a fairly specific type of work (spindles, spokes, etc.) may help explain this oversight, but I suspect it's mostly because of some uncertainty about how the tool is supposed to function and wondering how to sharpen and tune it.

I hope to dispel some of the mystery surrounding wooden spokeshaves and encourage you to discover that they can be ideal for shaping and cleaning up a wide range of circular and curved work.

Chairmakers can use them to shape their spindles and chair seats. Cabinetmakers can use them to fair curves or shape complex work, such as cabriole legs. In short, any woodworker who does any curvilinear work will find them useful.

How a Spokeshave Works

Though it has some unique features, the spokeshave has a key characteristic that identifies it as a type of plane, albeit a very short one. Namely, it has a blade secured in a wooden stock (the body of the tool) and the stock regulates the cutting action.

Many of the tool's more unique features are fairly obvious and require no additional comment. But the significance of some aspects of the blade and its relationship to the stock may not be quite so apparent.

At first glance the lower face of the blade appears parallel, front to back, with the mouth plate, or sole of the shave. In fact, it could be mistakenly assumed that the lower face of the blade is intended to function as the rear sole of the tool. However, my examination of little-used older spokeshaves reveals that the lower face of the blade is slightly canted (I've observed 5° to 9°) from the sole of the shave (see the drawing below).

This slight cant provides a clearance angle for the blade, which is required of every plane. There is a slight compression of the material being worked under the focused pressure of the cutting edge. The spring-back just behind the cutting edge would tend to push the blade up off the material if there were no relief angle. While learning to use a spokeshave, it is helpful to be conscious of registering the sole, rather than the blade, on the material to maintain this relief angle.

This orientation of the blade also means it has a low cutting angle – roughly equal to the amount of cant, or clearance angle, plus the angle of the cutting bevel on the blade. This unique feature results in a very sweet cutting action when working with the grain, especially on end grain. Predictably, this is less than ideal for working against the grain or if there are unpredictable grain reversals.

Wooden spokeshaves come in a variety of sizes and configurations. From the top are: a traditional shave with square tangs set into a wooden stock; a shave with a blade that is adjustable by the thumbscrews on the top; a shave with a traditional wooden stock; a new user-made shave with a piece of persimmon inlaid in front of the blade; a vintage shave with a brass-wear plate.

Luckily, in doing curved work, grain direction is generally more pronounced and the direction you are working in can be adjusted. Because the spokeshave can be used by either pushing or pulling you can accommodate these changes in grain direction without having to change position or turn the work around.

Buying a Vintage Spokeshave

If you decide to look for an older spokeshave to use, you will discover a number of variations. The majority of older spokeshaves were made from beech, though boxwood also is common. Spokeshaves also come in a variety of sizes for different types of work.

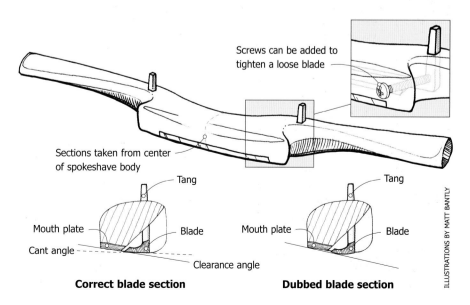

Screws can be added to tighten a loose blade

Sections taken from center of spokeshave body

Tang

Tang

Mouth plate

Blade

Mouth plate

Blade

Cant angle

Clearance angle

Correct blade section

Dubbed blade section

ILLUSTRATIONS BY MATT BANTLY

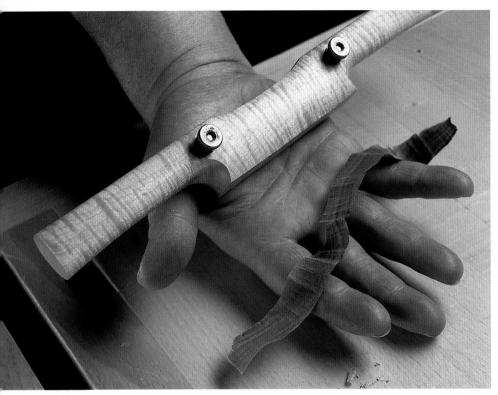

Wooden-bodied spokeshaves have a very low cutting angle, which excels at slicing end grain. Shown here is a ribbon of unbroken walnut end grain taken with this shave.

Sharpening the blade is much simpler with it secured in a handscrew clamp. The metal rib behind the hollow that's forged into the blade helps guide your slipstone as you hone the bevel.

The earliest form (which endured throughout the period when wooden spokeshaves were commercially produced) has simple tapered tangs that wedge into holes bored into the stock. These require some finesse because adjustment is achieved by hammer taps. If overdone, the stock can split or the fit can become too loose to secure the blade in the needed position. The latter can be remedied with slivers of veneer or blunted set screws inserted from the front of the stock (see the illustration, previous page). When looking for an older shave, it's best to avoid examples that are already loose or showing signs of splits in the tang holes.

Other spokeshaves have threaded tangs that are held and adjusted with captured thumbscrews at the top of the stock. These seem more user-friendly, though you have to watch for thumbscrews with noticeable wear where they are captured in the brass plate. Wear allows the blade to shift during use, resulting in erratic cutting action.

Some older spokeshaves have straight blades while many, if not most, have a slight bow, or curvature, along the blade. The purpose of this bow isn't immediately obvious, but it may be to ensure that extraneous areas of the sole don't interfere with the function of the shave on irregular surfaces.

Another feature of older blades is the hollow forged into the upper bevel, reminiscent of old straight razors. This provides guidance for honing the bevel while minimizing the amount of steel needing to be moved.

Finally, older spokeshaves may have a brass mouthplate. It is assumed this was intended to reduce wear, though brass doesn't seem to be a great choice for this purpose. Indeed, wear can be an issue for wooden spokeshaves because they are often used on narrow surfaces,

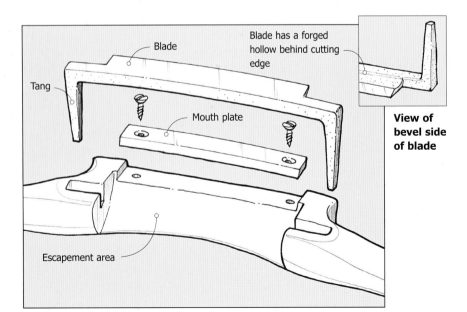

Blade

Blade has a forged hollow behind cutting edge

Tang

Mouth plate

View of bevel side of blade

Escapement area

which tends to localize and accelerate wear. People making their own wooden spokeshaves today often prefer to use a small piece of hard, dense wood instead.

One unfortunate result of this unique blade arrangement is that the working portion of the blade is shortened with repeated sharpenings. This inevitably leads to the opening of the mouth, which can't be corrected simply, though one occasionally runs across an older spokeshave that has had a new mouthplate installed to address this condition (and possibly to fix a shave where the stock has worn away from use).

Often, older shaves have seen hard use, with the sole or mouthplate showing significant wear and the blade all but used up. While this is ample evidence of past utility, it's better to find a little-used one. There are still enough of these around that a little patience is usually rewarded.

Many people today are making their own spokeshaves. Though not identical to the older ones, there are new blades suitable for wooden spokeshaves that are available; and the process of making one is an enjoyable and instructive experience.

The Trick to Sharpening the Blade

If you've acquired a wooden spokeshave to use the next task is to sharpen it. Obviously, the two tangs limit your options and you'll need to work around them.

If the blade is straight, it's possible to lay your sharpening stone on edge, providing clearance for the handles while you hone on the stone's edge. Or you can elevate the stone on another stone or block of wood so you can hone on its face. At this point, you'll appreciate the advantages provided by the forged hollow because it guides your honing.

If your blade is bowed, however, the bevel face will be slightly concave. That means you can't hone on the flat edge or face of a bench stone. The best method I've found for this is to trap the blade, bevel up, between the jaws of a handscrew – which, in turn, is being held in my bench vise. This brings it up to a comfortable working height and provides good visibility while I hone with a slip stone.

Honing and polishing the lower surface of the blade is mostly straightforward. But it's important not to "dub over" or round over the blade front to back in an effort to speed the process. This would quickly compromise the slight relief angle provided by the relationship of the blade to the sole.

Unfortunately, this is an ongoing issue. The bottom surface, just behind the edge, comes in for a fair amount of wear. So while you will probably do your primary honing on the bevel, some secondary honing of the lower face usually needs to be done. It will be tempting to concentrate your honing efforts toward the edge, which, if you're not careful, could easily result in dubbing it over.

As to setting the blade for use, people doing spindle/spoke work seem to prefer cocking their blades so that one side takes a heavier cut than the other. For general curved work, I find a uniform set to be more useful.

Whether you decide to buy or make a new spokeshave or refurbish an older one, I believe you'll find it a satisfying and versatile addition to your woodworking.

Sources

Older wooden spokeshaves:
Auctions, flea markets, antique dealers, yard sales, etc. Also, don't overlook national and regional tool collectors' association meetings where members often have tools for sale.

Make your own wooden spokeshaves:
New blades:
Hock Tools
16650 Mitchell Creek Drive
Fort Bragg, CA 95437
888-282-5233 or hocktools.com

Instructions:
John Gunterman's online tutorial: www.shavings.net/teachshave.htm

New wooden spokeshaves, kits and blades:
Dave Wachnicki
Dave's Shaves
P.O. Box 980
North Conway, NH 03860
603-356-8712 or ncworkshops.com/index.html

40

LIKE EVERYDAY LIFE, BENCHES HAVE BECOME COMPLEX AFFAIRS. BUT ARE THEY BETTER?
WE BUILD A 230-YEAR-OLD EXAMPLE AND FIND OUT.

roubo-style workbench

BY CHRISTOPHER SCHWARZ

After 250 years of refinement, workbenches have actually developed into good-looking pieces of furniture. Many of them have nice lines, a top with an attractive overhang and a useful set of drawers and shelves in the base.

And this is a bit of a problem.

Many workbenches today are designed to please our sensibilities or to take on additional workshop tasks (such as storing tools) when they should be built with a singular purpose. That is, to support and hold the work with little fuss.

I work on and have built a wide variety of benches. To hold my work, I've used benches that are drilled with dozens of dog holes, equipped with all manners of vises (from a shoulder vise to a patternmaker's vise) and that feature numerous ingenious stops and hold-downs. But with every passing year, I found myself removing these accessories and changing the configuration of my bench at work. And after shifting the bench's top so its front edge was flush with the bench's front legs (a radical act), I thought I was done.

But there was one more step, and I had to travel to New York City to take it. Last year I visited Joel Moskowitz, a Manhattan tool collector, woodworker and owner of the Tools for Working Wood store. Moskowitz has an impressive tool collection, but even more amazing is his library of original and reprinted woodworking texts.

The highlight of the evening was paging through a copy of Jacques-Andre Roubo's enormous *L'art du Menuisier* (*The Art of the Woodworker*, 1769-1775). Roubo was a professional woodworker and educated man, and his four-volume work on the craft is considered one of the seminal works in the field. (Someone really should translate and reprint

One of the key features of a workbench is its location in the shop. Placing the workbench near a window gives you a great advantage when trying to spot surface defects in your work, such as tear-out, sanding scratches or plane tracks. And the extra illumination allows older eyes to remain keen, even when working into the evening hours.

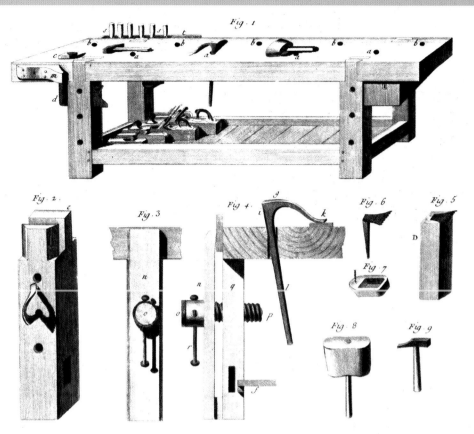

A detail of plate 11 of Jacques-Andre Roubo's *L'art du Menuisier* Vol. 1.

these four volumes for contemporary woodworkers – but I digress.)

As I was paging through volume one, I came across plate 11, which shows a workbench for joiners. A light went on in my head. My bench at work had been evolving to resemble Roubo's. When I returned home I began investigating the details of Roubo's bench. After much thought, I concluded that this simplest of benches solved almost all of my frustrations with my own workbenches and others in our shop.

Here are the key differences between Roubo's bench and some modern benches:

1. Size and mass: Roubo specified that a workbench's top should be thick and long – as much as 6" thick and between 6' and 12' long. The thickness adds weight, provides strength to the base (more on that later) and makes the top stiff so you don't have to have an apron supporting it.

Why is this important? Aprons can get in the way of your clamps when you secure anything to your bench. If you've ever used a bench without an apron,

A moisture meter is an excellent tool that will save you from making some serious mistakes. For this project, the moisture meter will help you segregate the wet boards from the dry ones and help monitor your lumber as it reaches equilibrium with your shop.

you know how liberating this feature is. As to the length, make your bench as long as your shop permits. A long bench lets you assemble at one end and work at the other. And you can work on long mouldings. As to the width, you want to easily clamp across the width of your bench; wide tops interfere with this feature. Similarly, a bench narrower than 18" can be tippy.

2. Position of the top: The legs and stretchers are flush to the front edge of the benchtop – there's no overhang

Mark the direction the grain is running on each edge as you pick your four boards for each top section. This also will make life easier when (or if) you true up the top with a hand plane.

at front or back. This is important so you can use your bench's legs and stretchers as a clamping surface. When working on anything wide – such as mortising a door's edge – you can secure it easily to the legs or stretchers.

3. Simple work-holding: To work on the edge of a board, Roubo offers a wooden hook (also called a "crochet," which is French for "hook"). The crochet stops the work from shifting sideways; holdfasts and scraps support the work below (as shown on page 196). When working on the face of a board, Roubo shows holdfasts and a single planing stop. When used with battens, the holdfasts and stop can secure a board for planing.

4. The legs are tenoned into the top: This feature seems like a wood-movement problem. After all, when the top contracts and the base doesn't, it will distort the base. However this actually is an advantage. This distortion turns your base into a stable A-frame structure when the top shrinks. Plus, unlike a dining table, most of this bench's strength emanates from the top, not from the joints in the base. So distorting the base and its joints isn't a big deal.

5. Two French gizmos: In addition to the basic bench shown in the plate, Roubo suggests adding a removable leg vise, which assists in working small parts. And in another plate he shows a sliding deadman. This gives you one more place to clamp and support your work.

Deciding to build Roubo's bench was easy. Figuring out how to do it simply and economically was another. After some work with CAD, the answer to every difficult question with this bench turned out to be Southern yellow pine, sometimes called longleaf pine.

Why Longleaf Pine?

Southern yellow pine is a construction material typically used as joists or, when treated with preservatives, for decks. It's common in the South and Midwest, though you can find it elsewhere, too. (The product locator at southernpine.com is an excellent place to start.) If you live in the West, look instead for hemlock, fir or "hem-fir," which can be either or both species. These woods have many characteristics of longleaf pine, except that they're sold a bit wetter, which is OK. If you can't find these species, poplar would be an excellent alternative, though it is more expensive.

Here's why longleaf pine is a good bench material: It's heavy, dense and resinous, though it's relatively easy to work. It's inexpensive. I bought the wood for this bench (with a fair amount left over) for $222 at Lowe's. And it's

In this assembly you can see how the board on the left is bowed. Position the concave side of the bow toward the inside of the assembly. Clamp pressure in the middle of this assembly will flatten the entire board against its neighbor.

You want a thin and consistent film of glue on the face of the board. Pour a line of glue down the board and spread it (quickly now!) with a piece of cardboard and then immediately stack it on its neighbor. This trick gives you a little more time to get the clamps on.

No matter how nice your circular saw is, don't try to make this cut by starting with a full-depth pass. Make the finished cut in two or three passes; you'll get less burning and it will be easier to clean up the ends.

sold a bit wetter than hardwoods. The moisture content of longleaf pine in equilibrium in our shop is about 10 percent. The stuff from the store is as wet as 17 percent. But the wetness of the wood is an advantage in building this bench. If you select wetter boards for the top and legs, those parts will shrink on your tenons, which should have a lower moisture content than the other parts. This will keep the joints tight and will slightly distort the base's shape as described earlier.

At the lumberyard, take your time when picking your boards, and take your moisture meter, too. It will guide you in picking dry boards for the stretchers in particular. If you don't have a moisture meter, a good way to judge wetness is the weight of the board in question. Wetter boards weigh quite a bit more.

Another good piece of advice is the wider the stock, the clearer and straighter it will be. Don't buy 2 × 4s; they will be knotty and twisted. Stick to 2 × 12s and 2 × 10s, and rip them to size.

Simple and Stout Joinery

This bench is simple enough for a beginner to build. There are but 12 joints and nothing is complex. In fact, you don't have to cut a single tenon when building this bench – though it is entirely mortise-and-tenon construction. All of the tenons on the legs and stretchers are created when laminating the boards together. The longer boards in the lamination become the tenons. The shorter boards act as the tenons' shoulders.

All of the joints are drawbored. This early and almost-forgotten technique will make your joints stouter and prevent gaps at the tenons' shoulders, even after the legs shrink. For a detailed look at this venerable technique and its tools, turn to page 184.

But most of the work in this bench is in gluing up the boards to create the top, legs and stretchers. I'd start by buying a gallon of a slow-setting glue, such as Titebond Extend, and making sure your planer and jointer are tuned up.

The tenons on the legs and stretchers are formed during the lamination process. This saves you from having to cut tenons on the end of a 5'-long stretcher – a real trick.

Make the 1/2" x 1/2" chamfer on the long stretchers by simply ripping it on the table saw. Using a chamfer bit in a router is much slower.

Good Stock Preparation

This project can be built with a typical 6" power jointer and 12" portable planer. Make sure your planer is clamped down to your bench and your jointing will be easier if you have a roller stand by the infeed table. Begin by ripping all your boards to the sizes you need for your laminations. I ripped them 1/4" oversized to allow for trimming after glue-up.

Then plane and joint all your boards to a finished thickness of 1 1/4". I recommend gluing up the top in sections, four boards to a section. This allows you to then clean up each completed section with a 6" jointer and planer.

Because you're going to machine these sections after assembly, make sure all the grain is running in the same direction in the boards. The other thing to watch for is which way the boards bow. Some of the boards are likely to have a small bow. Plan your

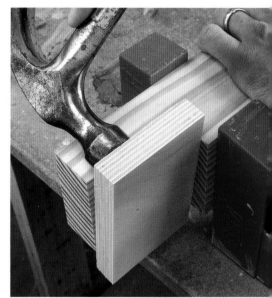

As soon as the clamps are tight, rap the spacer with a hammer and then clean out any glue in the area where the laminations create the tenons. It's easier now than it will be later.

sections so the bow faces the inside of the assembly.

Tricks for Gluing the Top

Gluing up longleaf pine can be a challenge. The wood is dense and resinous, so it resists glue penetration more than other pines. You can remove the resin at the surface by wiping the resinous areas with acetone right before applying glue. The way to get around the density issue is to allow each assembly to stay in the clamps for four hours. This isn't overcautious – it's the recommendation of a technical

a versatile bench

You don't have to add all the bench accessories shown to create a working bench. In fact, you might want to try this bench in its purest form first: a crochet, planing stop and holdfast holes. You can accomplish every major workholding task with this setup and a single clamp.

The leg vise and sliding deadman are nice additions, too. The leg vise helps hold small work. And the deadman offers quick and flexible support when holding wide boards or doors on edge. Two upgrades that aren't shown are adding a shelf between the stretchers and a bench hook, which is a standard bench accessory. A bench hook allows you to easily crosscut boards without a bench vise.

Working on Wide Panels: The batten by the planing stop is for wide panels. It's not necessary for securing narrow boards.

Working on Faces: Holdfasts and battens keep the work from skittering around on your benchtop.

Working on Edges: Holdfasts in the legs and a scrapwood ledger support the work from below. The crochet wedges the work against the benchtop and legs.

Working on Ends: You can use the crochet to hold work for tenoning and dovetailing. Holdfasts and scraps support the work from below. For really wide boards, a clamp can hold the far end to the benchtop (something you need even with quick-release vises).

specialist at Franklin International, which makes Titebond.

Apply clamps every 12" or so on each top assembly. Start at the middle and work out to the ends, pushing and pulling your boards into alignment as you go. After all four top assemblies are complete, joint and plane them to clean up the faces and edges. Keep them as thick and as wide as you can. Then arrange them as they'll appear in the finished assembly and joint all the edges to get airtight joints.

If you are skilled with a hand plane, you'll find this a task for a jointer plane. Two of my three joints for the top needed to be tuned with a hand plane. It might seem a daunting task because the edge is so big, but that actually is an advantage because your plane won't tip off the edge. I also did some further tweaking with a block plane.

When your top is complete, trim the ends using a circular saw and a straightedge guide. You'll need to cut from both the top and the bottom of the completed benchtop.

Making Tenons Out of Nothing

The next task is to glue up the legs and stretchers. These laminations are easier than the top pieces because they are shorter, but there is another challenge. You're going to leave some of the individual boards longer so they'll become tenons.

You might be asking yourself how you'll get a perfect tenon with these laminations sliding around as you're clamping. Relax. We found an easy way to get perfect tenons.

NO.	ITEM	DIMENSIONS: inches (millimeters)						MATERIAL	COMMENTS
		Thickness		Width		Length			
1	Top	4	(102)	24	(610)	96	(2438)	Pine	
4	Legs	5	(127)	5	(127)	32	(813)	Pine	2" (51mm) TOE
2	Long stretchers	$2^1/2$	(64)	$3^3/4$	(95)	61	(1549)	Pine	$2^1/2$" (64mm) TBE
2	End stretchers	$2^1/2$	(64)	3	(76)	19	(483)	Pine	$2^1/2$" (64mm) TBE
1	Deadman	$1^1/4$	(32)	8	(203)	$22^1/2$	(572)	Pine	$5/8$" (16mm) x $1^1/2$" (38mm) TOE
1	Leg vise	$1^3/4$	(44)	8	(203)	$33^3/4$	(857)	Ash	$3/4$" (19mm) x $3/4$" (19mm) chamfer, 3 edges
1	Vise handle	1	(25)	1	(25)	15	(381)	Ash	Octagonal
1	Vise's parallel guide	$1/2$	(13)	3	(76)	17	(432)	Ash	Drilled with $3/8$" (10mm) holes
1	Planing stop	2	(51)	2	(51)	12	(305)	Ash	Friction -fit into 2" (51mm) x 2" (51mm) mortises
1	Crochet	3	(76)	4	(102)	13	(330)	Ash	

Key: TOE = tenon one end; TBE= tenon, both ends

roubo bench

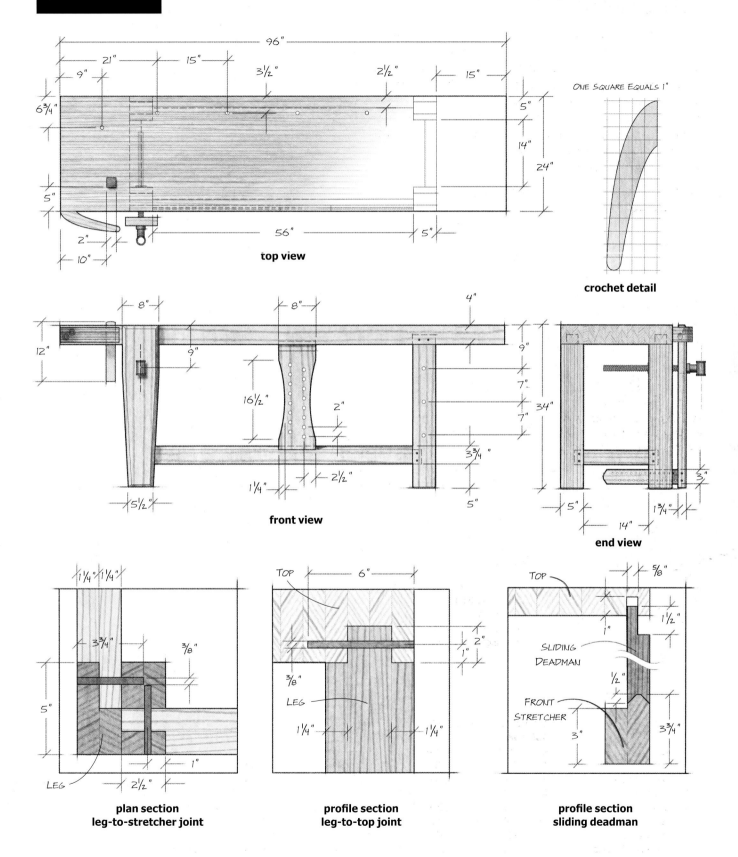

ONE SQUARE EQUALS 1"

top view

crochet detail

front view

end view

**plan section
leg-to-stretcher joint**

**profile section
leg-to-top joint**

**profile section
sliding deadman**

TOP

LEG

TOP

SLIDING
DEADMAN

FRONT
STRETCHER

LEG

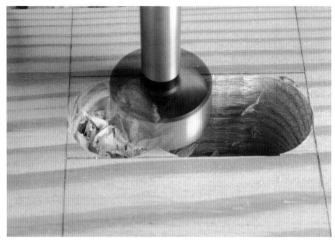

Begin the mortise by defining the beginning and ending of the joint with your Forstner bit. Then clean up the waste between. Now clean up the little triangles of waste along the long-grain walls of the mortise. Keep cleaning up the triangles. You're done when you can put the bit in the joint and it slides freely left to right in the mortise.

With all the legs and stretchers complete, I dressed the glued-up edges on the powered jointer and then used a hand plane. This is what the completed tenons look like on all the parts.

First, make sure all your pieces are crosscut square. Now get some scrap plywood – anything thicker than $1/4$" is fine. Cut it so it's as long as your tenons (2" long for the leg tenons; $2^{1}/2$" long for the stretchers). And cut it so it's wider than the assembled lamination (7" wide for the legs; 6" wide for the stretchers).

Before you glue up your legs and stretchers, nail one of these boards to the pieces that will form the tenon's cheek. Now glue up the legs and butt the outside laminations against these plywood spacers.

To keep the leg parts in alignment during glue-up, put a couple clamps along the length of the leg to align the pieces lengthwise. This guarantees a well-formed tenon. As soon as your clamps are set, knock the spacer off the assembly. You don't want it to get glued to your leg.

Before you glue up the stretchers, you need to decide if you want a sliding deadman on your bench. If the answer is yes, then cut two $1/2$" × $1/2$" chamfers on the long edges of the board that will face the outside of the bench. The deadman will slide on this track.

Making Massive Leg Mortises

The mortises in the legs are large. As a result, you won't be able to (easily) use a mortising machine. And making these

A corner chisel is an expensive tool, and they are a trick to sharpen. But when you need them, it seems worth the hassle. This operation can be carried out with a standard bench chisel, but it just takes a little longer.

mortises by chisel alone would be more work than necessary.

The best solution is to drill out the mortises and clean them up with a chisel. If you have a drill press and a $1^{1}/4$" Forstner bit, you're golden. If you are using a brace and bit with an expansive bit, that also will work – just be sure to use a brace with a large swing – 14" is about right.

The first step is to mark out the locations of all the mortises on the legs. Measure up 5" from the bottom of the legs and then use the tenon itself to lay out the mortise.

If you're going to drill out these mortises with a Forstner bit, set your

The less you measure, the more accurate you will become. Using the tenon to mark out your mortises reduces the chance of a measuring error. And it is faster, too.

drill press for 1,200 rpm (or in that neighborhood). That's a good speed for clearing chips, reducing burning and getting the job done. When I make mortises with a Forstner, I make many overlapping holes, to the point where I only have the corners to clean up. I do everything I can to avoid chiseling the long-grain walls of the mortise. This is where some of the joint's strength comes from and chiseling it almost always introduces error.

Make the mortise a bit deeper than needed. This is an asset because it gives a place for excess glue to go during assembly. To complete the joint, square up the corners with a chisel.

Details on the Legs

Before you dive into assembly, you need to take care of a few details. First, plane a $1/4$" × $1/4$" chamfer on the bottom edge of all the legs. This prevents your legs from hanging up on something in your floor and ripping out some grain when you drag your bench to a new location.

The notch for the vise is 1/2" wide, 4" long and runs through the entire leg. The best way to cut it is to saw out the cheeks (I used a band saw) and then use a mortise chisel and mallet to pop out the waste. This is both easy and fun.

When drawboring, a scrap in the mortise reduces tear-out when you drill into the mortise cheek.

A try square helps ensure your holes are straight into the underside of the top. After drilling three of these mortises, you'll have the confidence to do the fourth without it.

Remove the tenon and mark the location of the peg hole in the tenon. It should be closer to the tenon's shoulder. Reassemble the joint and twist the drawbore pin into the joint. Check the fit.

Yes, even at 350 pounds, you can move this bench around.

Next is an important decision. If you're going to install a leg vise in your bench, you must cut a big notch in the front left leg for the guide that keeps it parallel. I really like the vise's ability to secure small parts and I find it as stout as many metal-jawed vises. You also should drill the 1 1/4" hole in the leg for the vise's screw. Its location is shown in the construction drawing.

The other detail is to drill holes in the legs for your holdfasts. Before you do this, you need to decide on their diameter, and that depends on which holdfasts you purchase. Lee Valley (leevalley.com) offers one of the best modern examples (they call them hold downs) that I've tried.

Assembling the Base

The base is assembled by drawboring the joints. With the joint disassembled, drill the 3/8" holes through the mortise. Assemble the joint and mark the hole's location with a 3/8" brad-point bit. Remove the tenon and drill the hole for the peg closer to the tenon's shoulder – 3/32" to 1/8" will do. Pick the larger offset if your legs are particularly wet.

Assemble the joint without glue and twist a drawbore pin into the joint to align the holes and check the fit of the shoulder. If you see any gaps, investigate what's interfering with a good fit and chisel it out now.

When the joint fits, reassemble it with glue and whittle the ends of two 3/8" × 4" oak pegs so they look like elongated pencils.

Twist a drawbore pin into a hole and then drive a wooden peg into the other hole. Remove the steel pin and drive the other peg in. Trim the pegs flush with a saw and chisel.

And You Thought the Leg Mortises Were Big?

If you've ever built a table before you're probably concerned about how the top

connects to the base. Your first reaction might be that this design detail is simply the product of an 18th-century woodworker who didn't understand seasonal wood movement. After all, the top will expand and contract but the base will not. It seems like a disaster waiting to happen. But it's not.

By tenoning the legs into a top that is on the wet side (as yours undoubtedly is), the bench's design is counting on the top shrinking and wracking the base a bit, making it slightly wider at the bottom than at the top and more stable.

If you're skittish about this design detail, here's an option: Make the two mortises for the rear legs an 1/8" wider than necessary to allow the top to move without wracking the base. By widening the mortises for the rear legs only you'll keep the front edge of the top flush to the front legs, a critical detail. If you take this route, you'll still drawbore all four leg joints.

The original bench had the tenons passing all the way through the top. If you're confident enough to attempt this, do it. I decided to make the tenons go halfway through the top and then drawbore them to the base without

Mill the groove for the deadman using an upcut spiral bit in your plunge router. An edge guide makes this operation a snap. This groove is deep to allow the deadman to be removed or modified.

Here you can see the proper grain direction for a crochet. The grain direction and the shape of the crochet allows it to grab your work and wedge it against the benchtop. It is surprisingly effective.

glue. This accomplished the same mechanical integration offered by the original. And yes, this is an authentic Roubo detail. Volume 3 of his book shows a bench with blind tenons (it's plate 279).

Lay out your mortises on the underside of the benchtop by using the base itself. Bore out the waste using a $3/4$" auger bit. If you use an electric drill for this operation, use a corded one. You can cook a cordless drill with this operation.

Clean out the waste with a mortise chisel and use a combination square to confirm that the mortise walls are both square and deep enough to accept the leg tenons. You don't want to fit these joints any more than you have to.

If you've opted for the sliding deadman, you'll need to mill a $5/8$"-wide × 1"-deep groove in the underside of the top.

I drawbored the top to the base without glue. If I ever need to remove the top, I can drill out the $3/8$" pegs to dismantle the assembly. Follow the same drilling and pegging procedure you used to drawbore the joints in the base. The only difference is the length of the pegs; these are 6" long.

Turn the bench onto its feet. Stand on it. Park a car's engine on it if you like. This bench is up to any task. Before adding any gizmos to hold your work, take an hour or so to flatten the top. A jack and jointer plane are the most effective tools for this operation.

Workholding Details

If you're going to add the crochet to the front left, make sure that the grain direction runs straight from the tip to the far corner – this is stronger than making it parallel to the benchtop's edge. I made the crochet by face-gluing three pieces of 1"-thick ash. I cut the shape out on the band saw and then cleaned up the tool marks with a spokeshave and scraper. Drill clearance holes

To cut the trench on the bottom edge of the deadman, mark out the shape on the front edge, then set your table saw's blade to 45° and line things up with your marks. Make one pass, turn the deadman around and make a second pass to finish the cut. Clean up the work with a chisel.

in the crochet for $1/2$" x 6" lag bolts and $1/2$" washers. Drill pilot holes in the benchtop. Attach the crochet to the benchtop with the end of the crochet flush to the end of the benchtop. I centered the crochet on the top's thickness. If you use a plow plane in your work, lower it so your plow's fence will clear the crochet.

The planing stop is one of the most important parts of the bench. It is simply a piece of 2" × 2" × 12" ash that is friction fit into a 2" × 2" through-mortise in the benchtop. You knock the planing stop up and down with your mallet. Roubo shows two kinds of planing stops. One is wood only, and the stop has a slight bevel on the four edges of the top. This is an important detail. If you leave it flat you'll damage its edges with your mallet eventually. The slight dome shape ensures your mallet blows will land on the center of the stop.

The other kind of planing stop has a toothed metal stop embedded in the wooden block. The teeth grab the end grain of your work. I'm experimenting with different stops made for me by blacksmiths and have yet to form an opinion.

The leg vise is simple to make. The vise comes with a threaded metal collar that you screw to the inside of the leg, centered on the $1^1/4$" hole you drilled earlier. The jaw has a coffin shape as indicated on the construction drawings. And I planed a chamfer on three edges to soften the look. The chamfer on the top edge is the only critical one. It allows better access to your work when working at an angle with a plane, chisel or rasp.

The vise's parallel guide is tenoned and pegged into the jaw. It is the part of the vise that is most unfamiliar to modern eyes. The parallel guide is drilled with two offset rows of $3/8$" holes on 1" centers. By placing a $3/8$" peg in a hole in front of the leg and advancing the bench screw, the peg will then rest against the leg and pivot the jaw against your work at the top. The only downside is that you have to move the peg around for different thicknesses of work. It's a small price to pay for the small price of the bench screw.

I made my own vise handle with a piece of 1" × 1" × 15" leftover ash. I planed it to an octagonal shape and then secured it in the bench screw by driving $3/8$" pegs through at each end. Then I asked Senior Editor Bob Lang to carve the year into the vise jaw. The font, by the way, is authentic. We took it from a clock face made circa 1780.

The sliding deadman is another gizmo that you can add now or wait on. You

a word on bench height

The one thing you will want to customize with this project is the height of the bench. There's a lot of advice out there, and I've experimented with many heights. Here's what I've concluded.

I like a 34"-high bench. With my arms relaxed at my sides, the benchtop is where my pinky finger meets my hand. For me, this is an effective height for working with metal-bodied planes and it is the same height as my table saw, which has some real advantages.

A high bench (36" to 38") might prevent you from stooping over and will keep the work close to your eyes. But you'll wear yourself out when hand planing. A high bench requires you to use your arms more than your body weight to push a plane.

If you use wooden planes in your work, you might want to consider a low bench (32" or so). Wooden planes have

A 34"-high bench grazes the knuckle where my pinky meets my hand. This height is a good place to start when deciding how high your bench should be.

a thick body and keep your hands higher up than if you use metal planes.

But no matter what you decide, don't be afraid to experiment with different heights. You can cut down your legs with a handsaw. Or you can prop your bench up on a sled foot.

might not find your work needs it. It is simple to fabricate. Plow out the triangular trench on the bottom edge of the deadman using your table saw. Then cut the $5/8$" × $1^1/2$"-long tenon on the top. Tweak the tenon's thickness and shape until the deadman fits up into the groove and then onto the track below.

Once the deadman fits, cut the curved shape on the long edges. The curve allows you to get your hand between the deadman and leg when the deadman is pushed up against the leg. Then drill the two rows of offset holes on 2" centers. You can make a dedicated peg for these holes or you can make the holes the same size as the shaft on your holdfast and use one of those to support your work.

Finally, you want to drill the holes in the top for your holdfasts. Their location is not arbitrary and requires careful thought. The hole near the planing stop is positioned so I can put a batten in front of the planing stop and secure it with the holdfast, which allows me to plane wide panels against the batten.

The holes along the back edge allow me to secure battens up against the

long edges of long boards, as shown on page 200 of this chapter. My advice is to drill these few holes and add more when needed. With the holes drilled, you can finish the bench if you please. I applied a couple coats of an oil/varnish blend. Then I added some wax to the top to resist spilled glue.

When I completed the bench I realized something unexpected. Though building the bench was an adventure, the real journey began when I started using it. With the holdfasts, crochet and battens in my arsenal I am finding new ways to work every time I step up to the bench.

This confirms a nagging sensation I've been harboring for years now: There is much about woodworking that is still lost in the past, stuff that can help us work more effectively today. Not just with hand tools, but with routers and biscuit joiners as well (holdfasts are great at holding router templates to the bench; and battens work well with the biscuit joiner). This bench is one tool that I hope will unlock some of these secrets for me and the others who are so brave as to build this fine workbench.

41

arts & crafts tool cabinet

BY CHRISTOPHER SCHWARZ

Sometime while sawing the 60th dovetail for a drawer, when my patience was as thin as the veneer on cheap plywood, a familiar feeling crept into my body. I began to experience an understandable lust for my biscuit joiner.

It sat patiently on the top shelf above my workbench, and it watched with amusement my seemingly slow progress on the drawers. I knew that its chattering, rattling teeth would make everything about this tool cabinet proceed much faster. But I resisted, mostly because I had the words of a Victorian social reformer, art critic and part-time madman ringing in my head.

The writings of Englishman John Ruskin (1819-1900) were a cornerstone of the American Arts & Crafts movement of the last century. In his essays and books, Ruskin decried the worst parts of 19th century industrialism. He promoted craft, pensions and public education when there was little of those things for the poor.

And in his book the *Seven Lamps of Architecture, The Lamp of Memory*, which was published in 1849, he wrote a passage that all woodworkers should read. It's a bit long and a bit dramatic, but it has stuck with me just the same.

"When we build, let us think that we build forever. Let it not be for present delight nor for present use alone. Let it be such work as our descendants will thank us for; and let us think, as

we lay stone on stone, that a time is to come when those stones will be held sacred because our hands have touched them, and that men will say, as they look upon the labor and wrought substance on them, 'See! This our father did for us.'"

The biscuit joiner stayed on the shelf. I continued to saw, chop, pare and fit my joints. Ruskin, I hoped, would have approved.

From the Book of Tolpin

While Ruskin kept me going through this long and difficult project, I really have a 20th century craftsman and author to thank (or blame) for my obsession with building a fine tool cabinet. Since it was first published in 1995, *The Toolbox Book* (Taunton Press) by Jim Tolpin has become the most-thumbed book in my library. I've studied every page, toolbox and drawing between its maroon cover boards (the dust jacket is long gone).

Years ago, I resolved to build myself a cabinet that might rival some of the examples in *The Toolbox Book*. Last year, I gave it my best shot. Since early 2004 I've spent many spare moments doodling on graph paper and on my computer to come up with a design that satisfied the three things I wanted from a cabinet: It had to hold a lot of tools, look good and be built to last. After studying my work habits, measuring all my tools and paging through thousands

of examples of Arts & Crafts casework, this is what I came up with.

It's small but spacious. Have you ever ridden in an old Volkswagen Beetle? They are surprisingly roomy, and especially generous with the headroom. Somehow, the Beetle violates the laws of space and physics, and it is roomy but can also be parked between two oversized Hummers. This cabinet is designed to function the same way. The interior is a mere $11^{1}/_{4}$" deep, $22^{1}/_{2}$" wide and $31^{1}/_{2}$" tall. Yet, thanks to good planning, it holds every hand tool I need.

The cubbyholes and shelf for hand planes are carefully sized to hold all the planes needed in a modern shop. The drawers are loaded with trays of tools. Each tray contains all the tools for a routine function, such as dovetailing, sharpening or shaping curved surfaces.

The cabinet looks pretty good. I spent months thumbing through old Art & Crafts furniture catalogs and contemporary hardware catalogs for inspiration. This cabinet and its lines are a little bit Gustav Stickley, a little Harvey Ellis and a little of myself.

The cabinet will endure. No compromises were made in selecting the joints. Every major component (with the exception of the changeable, nailed-together trays) is built to withstand heavy use. Of course, when you discuss durable joints, you are usually talking dovetails, which is where we'll begin construction.

six storage solutions

Tools need to be protected, organized and easily retrieved. That's a tall order.

Here are some of the problems I've run into over the years: Hanging tools on a wall keeps them organized and close at hand, but unprotected. Keeping them in a traditional sliding tool till in a chest keeps them protected and organized, but you dig around for them endlessly. Drawers under a bench keep them protected and close at hand, but most drawers end up a jumbled mess.

Here are my solutions, and so far they work well. The cubbyholes are sized exactly to hold a full complement of hand planes. Finding the right plane and getting it down for use has never been easier.

The chisel rack puts my most-used sizes out where I can get them. And the rack is designed to hold the tools even when the door is accidentally slammed.

The saw till on the right door is the same way. These two saws do 80 percent of my work and they're always handy.

The real feature is the drawers. The smaller drawers hold tools for a specific operation. In the larger drawers, the interchangeable trays stack inside the drawers and also hold tools for a specific operation. Whenever I dovetail, I grab the top right drawer. No more making mounds of tools on the bench.

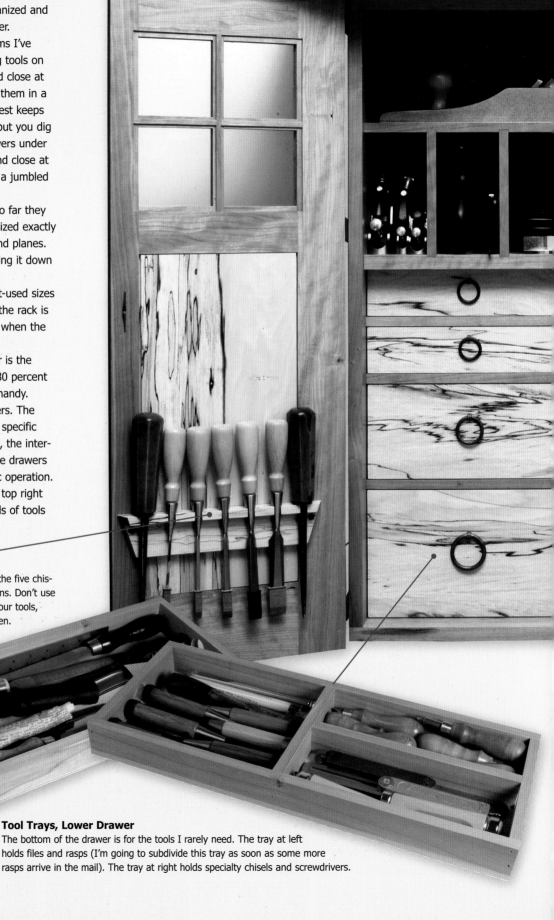

Chisel Rack
This simple L-shaped bracket holds the five chisels I use most, plus my drawbore pins. Don't use a magnetic strip; it will magnetize your tools, which makes them difficult to sharpen.

Tool Trays, Lower Drawer
The bottom of the drawer is for the tools I rarely need. The tray at left holds files and rasps (I'm going to subdivide this tray as soon as some more rasps arrive in the mail). The tray at right holds specialty chisels and screwdrivers.

Top Shelf Plane Cubby
This area isn't just what's left over from the remainder of the cabinet. It is carefully sized at 22¹/₂" wide x 5³/₄" high to hold a No. 7 jointer plane (a constant companion in my shop), plus a jack plane, panel plane and scraper plane.

Small Plane Cubbies
The cubbyholes are a magic size: 6¹/₄" high, about 3⁵/₁₆" wide and 10¹/₂" deep. This size holds all my joinery planes, my scrub plane, smoothing planes and miter plane.

Saw Till
My saw till holds the two most useful joinery saws – a dovetail saw and a carcase saw. My full-size saws reside on pegs below the cabinet.

Four Upper Drawers
Each of the four drawers holds all the tools for a common operation: one is for dovetailing, the second is for trimming and squaring assemblies, the third is for marking and measuring, and the fourth is for nailing and screwing.

Tool Tray, Middle Drawer
The lower section of the drawer holds waterstones and honing guides (make sure the stones are bone dry before putting them back in the drawer). The tray shown above holds my four spoke-shaves and some specialty sharpening equipment.

209

A Case That Takes a Beating

When this cabinet is fully loaded, my best guess is that it weighs more than any single member of our staff at the magazine (modesty prevents me from revealing what that upper limit might be). To ensure the bottom and top pieces can withstand this weight, I joined them to the side pieces with through-dovetails.

One interesting variation worth noting here is that instead of using one solid top piece, I substituted two 3"-wide rails and dovetailed them into the sides to save a little weight. Because I cut these dovetails by hand, it was simple to lay out this unusual arrangement. If you plan to use a dovetail jig, you will save yourself a headache by forgetting the rails and making your top one solid piece instead.

If you're cutting the dovetails by hand, it's faster and more accurate to clamp your two sides together and saw the tails on the side pieces simultaneously. For years I resisted this technique because it seemed more difficult, but now I know better.

A second feature of the case to note is that the rabbet for the back is a hefty 1" wide. This allows room for the $1/2$"-thick shiplapped back, plus a $1/2$"-thick French cleat that will park the cabinet on the wall and keep it there.

And then there are the stopped dados. These $1/4$"-deep joints in the side

When sawing the tails, clamp the two sides together and cut them at the same time. This saves time and effort, and prevents layout errors.

If your rabbets for the back are perfectly square, your case is much more likely to end up square, too. Clean up any imperfections with a rabbeting plane, such as this bullnose rabbet plane.

pieces hold all the dividers. Cutting these joints is simple work with three tools: a plunge router, a bearing-guided straight bit and a shop-made T-square jig that guides the whole shebang. Lay out all the locations of your dados on the sides. Park the jig so it lines up with your layout lines. Cut the dados in two passes.

Fitting all the horizontal dividers to the dados is easy. The $1/2$"-thick dividers simply need a small notch at the front to fit over the rounded end of the dado created by the round straight bit. A sharp backsaw is just the tool here.

The $3/4$"-thick horizontal divider needs a bit more work to fit in the $1/2$"-wide dado. A $1/4$" × $1/4$" end-rabbet is the answer.

The through-dados that hold the vertical dividers use the same router

jig, but with the plunge router set to make only an $1/8$"-deep cut. Laying out the locations of these parts for the hand plane cubbyholes might seem daunting. If you want the openings evenly spaced, they should each be 3.333" wide. I don't have any infinite numbers on my ruler. But it's actually child's play to lay out the cubbyholes with a pair of dividers (they look like a school compass but with two pointy tips – no pencil). You can tweak these tools until they step off the cubbyholes as precisely as you please. Dividers are one of my secret weapons.

With all these parts cut and fit, make the back of the case. I used ambrosia maple. It's cheap and looks a bit like the spalted maple I used in the doors and drawers. The back boards are joined by a $1/4$"-deep × $3/8$"-wide shiplap on each long edge.

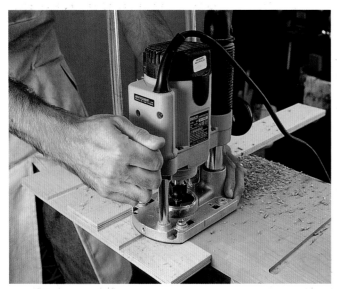

The shop-made T-square jig and a plunge router make quick work of the dados as you can see here.

Here you can see how you use the dado cut into the jig to line up the jig with your layout lines. Using a router with a flat side on its base is more accurate than using a router with a round base.

Fitting the dividers is easy with a hand plane. I merely make sure the dividers are surfaced a few thousandths of an inch thicker than where I want them to be. Then I thin them down with a smoothing plane until they slide in with just a little persuasion.

After gluing the sides to the bottom and top rails, trim the dovetails flush with a block plane. Soak the end grain with a little bit of mineral spirits to make it easier to cut. Here you can also see how I supported the case as I worked on it. The big slab holding up the side is an offcut from an old door that's clamped to my bench.

The top cap is easy. Cut the wide chamfer on the underside using your table saw. Clean up the cut with a block plane. Attach the top to the rails with screws.

You are now at a critical juncture. You can go ahead and get some quick gratification and assemble the whole case. But good luck when you go to finish it. Getting those cubbyholes finished right will be murder. The better solution is to glue up only the sides, bottom and top rails. Tape off the exposed joints and finish all the case parts (I used two coats of a satin spray lacquer). Then assemble the case. I know it sounds like a pain (it is). But the end result is worth it.

Finish the back pieces and top cap while you're at it. Now you can screw the back and the top cap in place. You are ready for the doors and drawers.

Easier Than They Look

The doors aren't too bad. The mullions and muntins that form the four lights in each door appear difficult, but thanks to a little legerdemain, it's no problem. Plus, it looks nice.

But before getting mired in those details, you need to assemble the doors. Here's how they work: The stiles and rails are joined using mortise-and-tenon joints. For mid-size doors such as these, I use $3/8$"-thick × 1"-long tenons.

Cut your tenons and your mortises, then mill a $1/4$"-wide × $3/8$"-deep groove in the rails and stiles to hold the door panel. I generally make this groove on the router table using a straight bit and featherboards. It's the easiest way to make the groove start and stop in the right place in the stiles.

The door panel needs a rabbet on its back to fit in the groove. But before you mill the panel, you should know a bit about spalted maple. Its black spidery lines are caused by the spalt fungus, which attacks the tree after it's been felled. In short, it's partly rotted wood.

It's always best to wear a respirator when dealing with spalted wood. There

Cut the rabbet on the backside of the door using a rabbeting bit in your router table. With a large tabletop such as this, it's simple work.

Glue one backing strip into the rabbet in the door on edge. Flip the door over and glue a mullion onto the backing strip. Then use spring clamps to hold everything while the glue dries.

Install the horizontal muntins the same way. First glue a backing strip into the rabbet on the backside of the door. Then flip the door over and glue the muntin to that.

are numerous accounts of people who have had respiratory problems after breathing in the dust.

Once you fit the panel, assemble the doors – the mullions and muntins are added after assembly. Once the glue cures, cut a $1/4$"-wide × $1/2$"-deep rabbet on the backside of the opening for the glass. This rabbet will hold the narrow backing strips that are built up into the mullions and muntins.

This technique is explained better in the photos above than can be done in words. Essentially, you create the T-shaped moulding that makes the mullions and muntins by gluing together $1/4$"-thick × $1/2$"-wide strips of wood. It's simple work.

What's not so simple is mounting the doors with the strap hinges. These hinges are inexpensive, beautiful and handmade. As a result, they need a bit of tweaking and bending and hammering and cursing to get them just right.

Here's my best tip for mounting the doors: Screw the hinges in place with the cabinet on its back. Then

stand it up, loosen the hinge screws and make your final adjustments. I used a block plane to make some tweaks, and a mallet for others. Let your frustration level be your guide.

Getting a Handle on Drawers

The drawers are a long slog. Even though I'm a fair dovetailer, it took me three solid days of work to get the drawers assembled and fit. But before you start listening to that lock-miter router bit whispering in your ear, remember this: The drawers are going to hold a tremendous amount of steel. And when you open the drawers during a future project, you'll never be disappointed to see dovetails.

To make things a tad easier, I built all the drawers using through-dovetails and $1/2$"-thick material for the front, sides and back. Then, with the drawer glued up, I glued on a $1/4$"-thick piece of spalted maple to the front piece. This trick also allowed me to stretch my supply of spalted maple.

The four small drawers are built a little differently than the two larger ones. Because the small drawers are shallow, I wanted to use every bit of space. So the bottom is $1/4$"-thick plywood that's nailed into a $1/4$" × $1/4$" rabbet on the drawer's underside.

Supplies

Lee Valley Tools
800-871-8158 or leevalley.com

6 • 28mm ring pulls
   01A61.28, $1.65 each

2 • 40mm ring pulls
   01A61.40, $2.45 each

2 • 50mm ring pulls
   01A61.50, $3.10 each

6 • unequal strap hinges,
   9 1/2" x 5"
   01H21.39, $8.60 each

4 • magnetic catches
   00S16.01, $1.15 each

7 • #6 x 5/8" black pyramid-head screws
   (bags of 10) 01X38.65, $1.40 a bag

Prices as of publication date.

Build the drawers with through-dovetails. Then glue a piece of $1/4$"-thick veneer to the front.

Here you can see the two different ways of installing the drawer bottoms. The bottom in the top drawer rests in a rabbet in the sides. The drawer bottom for the larger drawers slides into a groove.

The larger drawers are more conventional. Plow a $1/4$" × $1/4$" groove in the sides and front pieces to hold a $1/2$"-thick bottom, which is rabbeted to fit in the groove.

Build all the drawers to fit their openings exactly, then use a jack plane to shave the sides until the drawer slides like a piston. Finish the doors and drawers, then it's time for the fun part: dividing up the drawers, building trays for the tools and tweaking the hardware so everything works just right.

As you divide up the drawers and trays, one word of advice: Don't fasten any of the dividers permanently. Your tool set will change, and you want to be able to easily alter the dividers. I fit mine in place with friction and a couple 23-gauge headless pins. The dividers can be wrenched free when I need room for a new tool.

When you hang the cabinet, use wide cleats – mine were each 5" wide. This allows you to get more screws into the cabinet and into the studs. Also, for extra insurance, I rested the bottom of the cabinet on a 2"-wide ledger that also was screwed into the studs.

With the project complete, the voice of Ruskin was finally silenced for a short time as I assessed my work. (I for

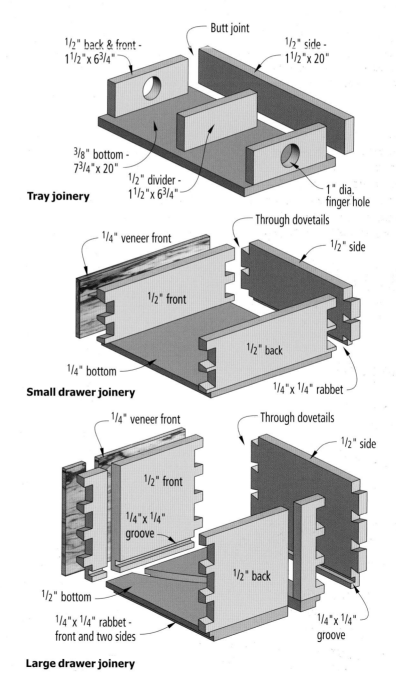

Tray joinery

Butt joint
$1/2$" back & front - $1 1/2$" x $6 3/4$"
$1/2$" side - $1 1/2$" x 20"
$3/8$" bottom - $7 3/4$" x 20"
$1/2$" divider - $1 1/2$" x $6 3/4$"
1" dia. finger hole

Small drawer joinery

$1/4$" veneer front
Through dovetails
$1/2$" side
$1/2$" front
$1/2$" back
$1/4$" bottom
$1/4$" x $1/4$" rabbet

Large drawer joinery

$1/4$" veneer front
Through dovetails
$1/2$" side
$1/2$" front
$1/4$" x $1/4$" groove
$1/2$" back
$1/2$" bottom
$1/4$" x $1/4$" rabbet - front and two sides
$1/4$" x $1/4$" groove

Install the dividers in the drawers so they can be easily removed in the future. A 23-gauge pinner is an excellent tool for this job.

Once everything is finished, install the glass using small strips of cherry ($^1/_8$" and $^1/_4$" thick). A few dabs of clear silicone and a couple small pins do the trick.

NO.	ITEM	DIMENSIONS: inches (millimeters)						MATERIAL	COMMENTS
		Thickness		Width		Length			
Carcase									
2	Sides	$^3/_4$	(19)	$12^1/_4$	(311)	33	(838)	Cherry	$^3/_8$" (10mm)-deep x 1"(25mm)-wide rabbet at back
2	Top rails	$^3/_4$	(19)	3	(76)	24	(610)	Cherry	Dovetailed into sides
1	Bottom	$^3/_4$	(19)	$11^1/_4$	(286)	24	(610)	Cherry	Dovetailed into sides
1	Top cap	1	(25)	17	(432)	32	(813)	Cherry	$^1/_2$" (13mm)-deep x 3" (76mm)-wide bevel
	Shiplapped back	$^1/_2$	(13)	$23^1/_4$	(591)	33	(838)	Maple	$^1/_4$" (6mm) x $^1/_4$" (6mm) shiplaps
1	Major horizontal divider	$^3/_4$	(19)	$10^1/_2$	(267)	23	(584)	Cherry	In $^1/_4$" (6mm)-deep x $^1/_2$" (13mm)-wide dados
1	Thin horizontal divider	$^1/_2$	(13)	$10^1/_2$	(267)	23	(584)	Cherry	In $^1/_4$" (6mm)-deep x $^1/_2$" (13mm)-wide dados
3	Thin horizontal dividers	$^1/_2$	(13)	$9^1/_4$	(235)	23	(584)	Cherry	In $^1/_4$" (6mm)-deep x $^1/_2$" (13mm)-wide dados
5	Vertical dividers	$^1/_2$	(13)	10	(254)	$6^1/_2$	(165)	Cherry	In $^1/_8$" (3mm)-deep x $^1/_2$" (13mm)-wide dados
2	Small vertical dividers	$^1/_2$	(13)	$9^1/_4$	(235)	$2^3/_4$	(70)	Cherry	In $^1/_8$" (3mm)-deep x $^1/_2$" (13mm)-wide dados
Doors									
2	Large stiles	$^3/_4$	(19)	$2^3/_4$	(70)	33	(838)	Cherry	
2	Small stiles	$^3/_4$	(19)	$1^1/_4$	(32)	33	(838)	Cherry	
2	Top rails	$^3/_4$	(19)	$2^3/_4$	(70)	10	(254)	Cherry	1" (25mm) TBE
2	Intermediate rails	$^3/_4$	(19)	$2^1/_4$	(57)	10	(254)	Cherry	1" (25mm) TBE
2	Lower rails	$^3/_4$	(19)	$3^3/_4$	(95)	10	(254)	Cherry	1" (25mm) TBE
2	Panels	$^1/_2$	(13)	$8^1/_2$	(216)	$16^3/_4$	(425)	Maple	In $^1/_4$" (6mm)-wide x $^3/_8$" (10mm)-deep groove
2	Vertical muntins	$^1/_4$	(6)	$^1/_2$	(13)	8	(203)	Cherry	
4	Horizontal muntins	$^1/_4$	(6)	$^1/_2$	(13)	$3^3/_4$	(95)	Cherry	
2	Backing strips	$^1/_4$	(6)	$^1/_2$	(13)	$8^1/_2$	(216)	Cherry	In $^1/_4$" (6mm)-wide x $^1/_2$" (13mm)-deep rabbet, glued to vertical muntin
4	Small backing strips	$^1/_4$	(6)	$^1/_2$	(13)	$4^1/_8$	(105)	Cherry	Glued to horizontal muntin
Drawers									
4	Small drawer fronts	$^3/_4$*	(19)	$2^1/_2$	(64)	11	(279)	Maple	$^1/_4$" (6mm)-deep x $^1/_2$" (13mm) rabbet on bottom edge
8	Small drawer sides	$^1/_2$	(13)	$2^1/_2$	(64)	9	(229)	Poplar	$^1/_4$" (6mm)-deep x $^1/_4$" (6mm) rabbet on bottom edge
4	Small drawer backs	$^1/_2$	(13)	$2^1/_4$	(57)	11	(279)	Poplar	
4	Small drawer bottoms	$^1/_4$	(6)	$10^1/_2$	(267)	9	(229)	Plywood	Screwed to drawer box
1	Medium drawer front	$^3/_4$*	(19)	5	(127)	$22^1/_2$	(572)	Maple	$^1/_4$" (6mm)-deep x $^1/_4$" (6mm)-wide groove for bottom
2	Medium drawer sides	$^1/_2$	(13)	5	(127)	9	(229)	Poplar	$^1/_4$" (6mm)-deep x $^1/_4$" (6mm)-wide groove for bottom
1	Medium drawer back	$^1/_2$	(13)	$4^1/_2$	(114)	$22^1/_2$	(572)	Poplar	
1	Medium drawer bottom	$^1/_2$	(13)	$8^3/_4$	(222)	22	(559)	Plywood	$^1/_4$" (6mm)-deep x $^1/_2$" (13mm) rabbet on bottom edge
1	Large drawer front	$^3/_4$*	(19)	$6^3/_4$	(171)	$22^1/_2$	(572)	Maple	$^1/_4$" (6mm)-deep x $^1/_4$" (6mm)-wide groove for bottom
2	Large drawer sides	$^1/_2$	(13)	$6^3/_4$	(171)	9	(229)	Poplar	$^1/_4$" (6mm)-deep x $^1/_4$" (6mm)-wide groove for bottom
1	Large drawer back	$^1/_2$	(13)	$6^1/_2$	(165)	$22^1/_2$	(572)	Poplar	
1	Large drawer bottom	$^1/_2$	(13)	$8^3/_4$	(222)	22	(559)	Plywood	$^1/_4$" (6mm)-deep x $^1/_2$" (13mm) rabbet on bottom edge

* Finished dimension, laminated from two pieces of wood; TBE= tenon, both ends

one was happy for the silence; Ruskin vacillated between madness and lucidity during the last years of his life.) I scolded myself for a few things: the reveals around the drawers on the left edge of the cabinet are a tad wider than the reveals on the right side. And in a couple of the dovetails at the rear of the drawers, there are a couple small gaps. It's not perfect.

But before I got too down on myself, I remembered one more quote from Ruskin that relates to handwork and the pursuit of perfection. This one deserves as much ink as the first:

"No good work whatever can be perfect, and the demand for perfection is always a sign of a misunderstanding of the ends of art."

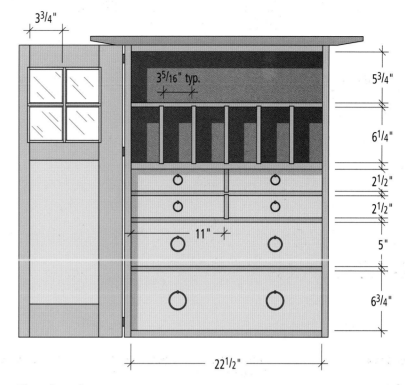

Elevation - doors open

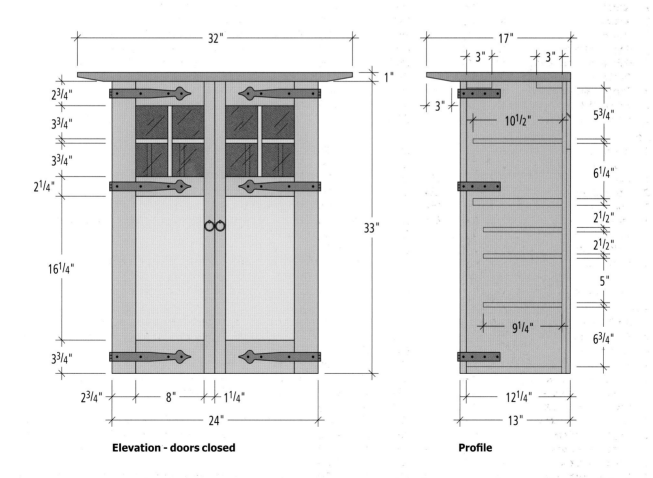

Elevation - doors closed

Profile

42

PLASTIC SAWHORSES ARE OK IN A PINCH. HOWEVER, ONCE YOU BUILD A SAWBENCH YOU WILL WONDER HOW YOU EVER WORKED WOOD WITHOUT IT.

traditional sawbench

BY CHRISTOPHER SCHWARZ

The reason sawbenches are so useful is the top. The fact that it is flat and has some width allows you to perform many operations on it. And the particular height of the sawbench unleashes the full effectiveness of full-size Western-style handsaws and panel saws.

Sawbenches are not sawhorses. Though both devices support your work, real sawbenches can be pressed to do so much more that they are worth building in a long afternoon in the shop.

The major difference between a sawbench and a sawhorse is the top. On a sawhorse, the top is generally long and skinny. It will not support anything on its own. A sawbench has a wide top: 7" is a common and useful width. And it's this detail alone that makes one worth building. The wide top allows you to cut many cabinet-sized parts using one sawbench alone. The top is also an excellent clamping surface, allowing you to secure work to it. The sawbench is a step stool for reaching up high. It's a mortising stool for hand-mortising operations – you secure the work over a leg and hold it down with a holdfast (hence the hole in the top). And then you sit on the sawbench astride or next to your work.

But, as they say on television, there's more. Much more. The shelf below holds your square and saw as you move your stock in position. The V-shaped mouth on the top – called a "ripping notch" – supports your work as you notch out corners with a handsaw or jigsaw. And the top is the traditional place for a craftsman to sit when eating lunch.

The sawbench shown here is based entirely on traditional English forms.

If you choose to alter this plan, resist changing the height of the sawbench. The 20" height is key to using the bench in conjunction with a Western handsaw. The 20" height allows you to use your legs to secure your work without clamps and makes the handsaw work efficiently. The sawbench is high enough that a 26"-long saw at the proper cutting angle won't hit the floor and the saw won't be able to jump out of its kerf on the return stroke.

Build your sawbench out of any material that is plentiful, inexpensive and easy to work. The legs and lower braces are assembled much like a trestle table: Create the through-mortise by cutting away the material before gluing the two pieces together that form each leg. If you like, chamfer all the edges of your components with a block plane or chamfer bit in a router.

Cut the ends of the legs at 10°, then cut a notch at the top of each leg that will allow it to nest into notches in the top piece. Each leg notch measures $1/2$" × $2^1/2$" × $1^1/4$". Cut your tenons on the lower braces then assemble the braces and legs. Drawbore the joints then wedge them using hardwood wedges and glue.

With the legs and braces assembled, clamp them temporarily to the top and mark precisely where they intersect the edges of the top. Take the clamps off and mark out the $1^1/2$" × $2^1/2$" notches in the top that will receive the legs. Saw out the notches and cut the ripping notch. Glue the leg assemblies to the top and reinforce the joint with a $1/2$"-diameter dowel or Miller Dowel.

Clamp the plywood top braces in place and trace the angle of the legs on the braces. Unclamp the braces and

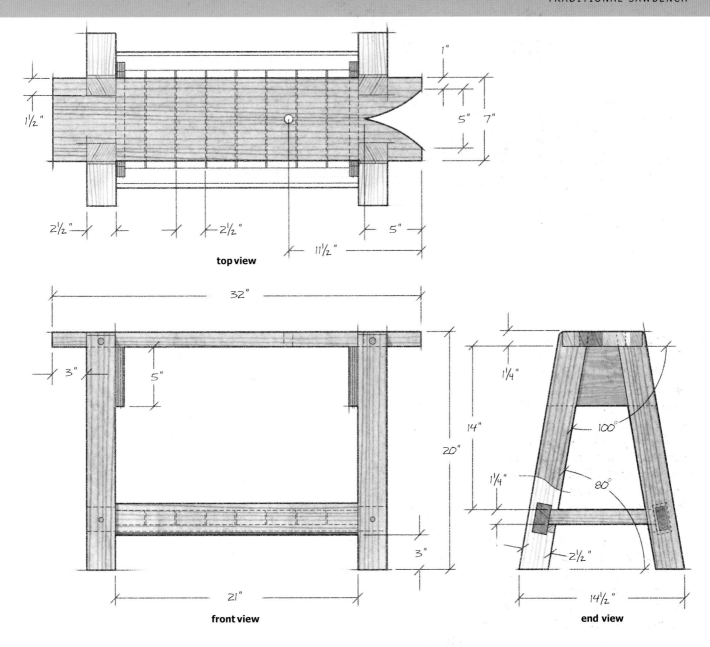

top view

front view

end view

leg joint detail

saw each one to shape. Glue and screw the braces to the legs using three #8 × 2" wood screws in each leg. If you want to add a shelf, first rip a 10° bevel on the shelf braces and cut the ends of the shelf pieces at 10°. With the saw-bench upside down on your bench, place the shelf pieces against the lower braces. Now glue the shelf braces against the shelf pieces and nail everything in place.

Bore a ³/₄"-diameter hole in the top for a holdfast or holddown. Position the hole so the pad of the holdfast will touch the tops of the legs. Mine is positioned to accommodate the Veritas hold-down.

NO.	ITEM	DIMENSIONS: inches (millimeters)						MATERIAL	COMMENTS
		Thickness		Width		Length			
1	Top	1¹/₄	(32)	7	(178)	32	(813)	Pine	
4	Legs	2¹/₂	(64)	2¹/₂	(64)	21	(533)	Pine	Includes extra length for trimming
2	Lower braces	1¹/₄	(32)	2¹/₂	(64)	26¹/₄	(667)	Pine	2⁵/₈" (67mm)-long tenon, both ends
2	Shelf braces	³/₄	(19)	⁵/₈	(16)	21	(533)	Pine	10° bevel on one long edge
8	Shelf pieces	1¹/₄	(32)	2¹/₂	(64)	9¹/₄	(235)	Pine	10° bevel both ends, cut to fit
2	Top braces	³/₄	(19)	5	(127)	9¹/₂	(241)	Plywood	10° angle on edges, cut to fit

217

43

SAWING MITERS SO THEY ARE 'JUST RIGHT' IS A PROBLEM FACED BY ALL WOODWORKERS. **HERE'S HOW TO SNEAK UP ON THE PERFECT MITER** WITH SCRAP WOOD AND A PLANE.

miter shooting boards

BY DON MCCONNELL

You find yourself in a quandary. To ensure that you don't cut a miter too short, you end up cutting it just a bit too long to fit. You wish you could trim it shorter by just a shaving or two, but the moulding is too small to plane, reliably, freehand.

If you're working with a powered miter saw, you might be able to correct this cut if the moulding is held in place perfectly, but it is easy to cut too much off and the blade might deflect during the cut, spoiling the angle. If you're working with a hand miter saw and miter box, it's difficult to get an accurate cut that's thinner than the width of the saw's kerf. This is when you should turn to a shop appliance known as a miter shooting board.

A shop appliance, you ask? Like a washing machine? No, I'm using the term "appliance" here in the more general sense: "A piece of equipment for adapting a tool or machine to a special purpose" (Merriam-Webster dictionary). In the world of hand tools, what some people might call "jigs" usually are called appliances.

In this case, the special purpose of the miter shooting board is to enable you to plane a miter in an accurate and controlled manner. Indeed, with this appliance you can quite literally correct the length and/or angle of a miter one shaving at a time.

Shop appliances have great value. If you are already working with hand

tools, you may be encountering unnecessary difficulties without the right appliance for the job. If you are not generally interested in hand tools, that may be due, in part, to not realizing their capabilities when used with appropriate and time-tested appliances.

I've chosen to focus on the miter shooting board here because it is an appliance that could be useful to almost every woodworker – even those who have little interest in hand tools.

Simple Jig; Easy to Use

The basic idea of a miter shooting board is simple. At one edge is a wide, shallow rabbet in which a plane (block, miter, etc.) rides. The bed of the rab-

bet supports the plane's cheek (sometimes called the "side wing"), and the shoulder of the rabbet guides the sole of the plane. A stop, or stops, set at 45° are affixed to the upper surface of the board. The material being planed is held against the stop while the mitered end is planed. The height of the rabbet's shoulder needs to be fairly minimal in order to make use of most of the cutting edge of the plane iron.

Build a Simple Miter Shooting Board

There are a number of ways to construct a miter shooting board. The simple version that is shown on page 219 takes only a minimal amount of mate-

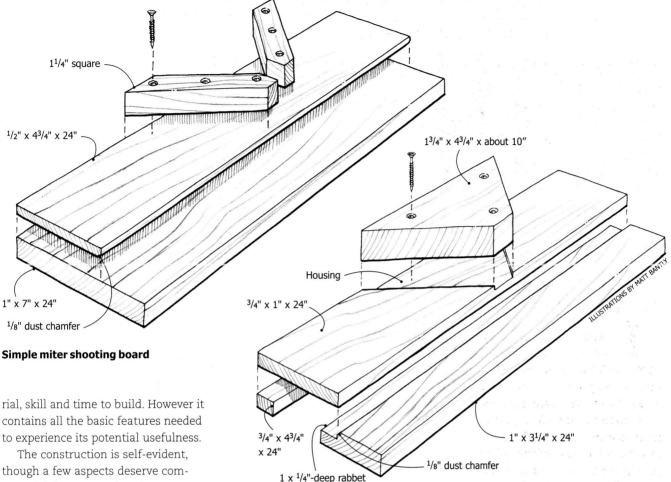

1¼" square

½" x 4¾" x 24"

1" x 7" x 24"

⅛" dust chamfer

Simple miter shooting board

1¾" x 4¾" x about 10"

Housing

¾" x 1" x 24"

¾" x 4¾" x 24"

1 x ¼"-deep rabbet

1" x 3¼" x 24"

⅛" dust chamfer

ILLUSTRATIONS BY MATT BANTLY

Improved miter shooting board

rial, skill and time to build. However it contains all the basic features needed to experience its potential usefulness.

The construction is self-evident, though a few aspects deserve comment. It's important that the stop pieces be positioned at a true 45° angle. This needs to be laid out and checked carefully with a miter square or sliding bevel you know is accurate. Using a pair of stops allows planing from both directions (a useful feature), and the placement shown allows the stops to reinforce each other against the planing stresses.

While this version can be satisfactory, there are drawbacks in the long term. First, the manner in which the two base elements are assembled provides for unequal moisture movement from the opposite faces of each piece. This can lead to the appliance going out of true. Careful material selection (quartersawn and straight-grain) can minimize this. And, within reason, it can be disassembled and the pieces re-trued, from time to time. There are other alternative forms of construction that address these issues.

Second, the means of attaching the stops to the shooting board doesn't

anchor them securely. Though this can largely be overcome by installing them in housings such as dados, the problem of cross-grain construction remains.

An Improved Shooting Board

As always, there is a better way. The stop block of the improved miter shooting board is more secure and avoids the difficulties of cross-grain construction. It consists of a single piece of wood that's mitered on both ends so that its grain orientation is identical to that of the board it's attached to.

The stop block can be planted on the face of the guide piece, but is better secured by installing it in a housing cut into the bed.

Using hand tools to obtain the accuracy required to create this housing and the guide block might seem difficult or

mysterious to some woodworkers. So I thought it would be worthwhile to touch on the critical aspects of this process.

Start by cutting the housing. It does not need to be deep (¼" at most), but the shoulders need to be accurate. This begins with accurate layout, knifing the shoulders with a reliable miter square. The space between the shoulders at the narrow end isn't critical. Primarily, it needs to be wide enough to allow passage for your tools during construction.

Establishing the shoulders could be done straightaway with a saw. But in such a critical situation and with relatively long shoulders, I prefer to saw, freehand, slightly to the waste side of the knife line. Then, after the balance of the waste is removed, clean up the shoulder through vertical paring with a sharp and wide chisel.

Mark your 45° angles using a knife. Clamp a steel straightedge against the knife line and chisel away your waste. Or pare to the line freehand.

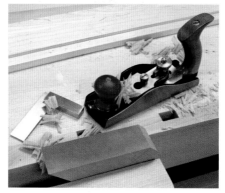

Cut your stop block as close as you dare and then plane it to a perfect fit in the triangular housing you just chopped out.

Test your stop block against your housing; plane until you have a perfect fit.

You could clamp a straight batten or metal straightedge to the board to guide your chisel, but I can better see my progress relative to the knife line if I do it freehand.

By assuming a relaxed and balanced stance, you can usually get a pretty good sense as to when you are holding the chisel vertical for this paring operation. You can check this with a small square if you are uncertain.

The shoulders need to finish accurately at 45° and with nothing to obstruct the stop block from registering solidly against them when in place. While it's good practice to aim for achieving the required accuracy the first time, in this instance you have the luxury that you can, within limits, simply knife a new line and try again.

Stop Block has Critical Angles

The material for the stop block needs to be somewhat wider than its finished width to allow you to do final trimming after arriving at an accurate fit of the critical miters.

First, mark out one of the mitered ends and saw it as close as you feel comfortable. Then, with a sharp and finely set block or miter plane, clean it up. You want to keep it fairly close to 45° (for the sake of grain orientation), but the critical factors are that it be flat and square to the face that will attach to the shooting board. Then, allowing enough space to have some width for final trimming, lay out the other miter at a right angle to the miter you've just established on the stop block.

In use, the miter shooting board is used with the plane always pointed toward the stop block.

Again, saw as close as possible and true the second miter up with your plane. This miter needs to be not only square to the lower face and flat, but at a true right angle to the first one. So, it's a little more critical. But there is some forgiveness in that you can continue to plane to arrive at the necessary accuracy as long as you have sufficient width.

Finally, test the block's fit in the housing (make sure it reads accurately) and trim so its nose is in line with the guide shoulders and perpendicular to the bed. Install the stop block with screws (no glue) and you have a very accurate and serviceable miter shooting board.

Take it for a Test Drive

A miter shooting board is simple to use. You hold the work in place against the stop block with one hand, and push or pull the plane with the other. Always work so that the plane pushes the work against the stop block.

The miter shooting board is most obviously useful when doing inside mitering. In this case, the far edge of the miter is fully supported by the stop block. While it's easy to assume that it wouldn't be as useful for planing outside miters, I believe that to be a mistaken assumption. A sharp iron set to a fine cut will minimize any tear-out when shooting outside miters.

I had been building furniture for a few years before I finally built my first miter shooting board. Though I occasionally considered it before, there was always a question as to whether it would be worth taking the time. After just a few passes with my plane in fitting up the first miter, I was amazed at the control and accuracy provided by this simple appliance. My only regret was that I hadn't made one years earlier.

ADRIA TOOLWORKS
4739 Chancellor Blvd.
Vancouver, BC V6T 1C8
604-710-5748
adriatools.com
Woodworking tools

ANDERSON PLANES
12752 208th Ave. N.W.
Elk River, MN 55330
763-241-0138
andersonplanes.com
Woodworking planes

CLARK & WILLIAMS
P.O. Box 121
Eureka Springs, AR 72632
479-253-7416
planemaker.com
Woodworking planes

DAVE'S SHAVES
P.O. Box 980
North Conway, NH 03860
603-356-8712
ncworkshops.com/index.html
Wooden spokeshaves

EUROPEAN HAND TOOLS
P.O. Box 20005
RPO Westwood
Winnipeg, Manitoba R3K 2E5
888-222-8331
europeanhandtools.com
Woodworking tools

HIDA TOOLS
1333 San Pablo Ave.
Berkeley, CA 94702
800-443-5512
hidatool.com
Japanese hand tools

HOCK TOOLS
16650 Mitchell Creek Drive
Fort Bragg, CA 95437
888-282-5233
hocktools.com
Woodworking blades and tools

THE JAPAN WOODWORKER
1731 Clement Ave.
Alameda, CA 94501
800-537-7820
japanwoodworker.com
Japanese hand tools

JAPANESE TOOLS
877-692-3624
japanesetools.com
Japanese hand tools

KNIGHT TOOLWORKS
304 SE Main, #600
Portland, OR 97214
503-421-6146
knight-toolworks.com
Woodworking planes

LEE VALLEY TOOLS LTD.
P.O. Box 1780
Ogdensburg, NY 13669-6780
800-871-8158 (U.S.)
800-267-8767 (Canada)
leevalley.com
Woodworking tools and hardware

LIE-NIELSEN TOOLWORKS
P.O. Box 9
Warren, ME 04864-0009
800-327-2520
lie-nielsen.com
Woodworking tools

POWELL MANUFACTURING
396 Washington St.
#114
Wellesley, MA 02481
781-237-4876
Sharpening stones

ROCKLER WOODWORKING AND HARDWARE
4365 Willow Dr.
Medina, MN 55340
800-279-4441
rockler.com
Woodworking tools, hardware and books

SLAV'S HARDWARE STORE
2023 West Carroll
Chicgo, IL 60612
312-455-0430
lunytools@aol.com
Woodworking rasps

TASHIRO HARDWARE
P.O. Box 3409
Seattle, WA 98114
206-328-7641
tashirohardware.com
Japanese saws

TOOLS FOR WORKING WOOD
27 West 20th Street
Suite 507
New York, NY 10011
800-426-4613
toolsforworkingwood.com
Woodworking tools, supplies and hardware

WOODCRAFT SUPPLY CORP.
1177 Rosemar Rd.
P.O. Box 1686
Parkersburg, WV 26102
800-535-4482
woodcraft.com
Woodworking tools, hardware and supplies

MORE GREAT TITLES FROM POPULAR WOODWORKING!

Authentic Shaker Furniture

by Kerry Pierce

The classic grace of the Shaker style is captured in twenty timeless furniture projects built using a combination of hand and power tools. With step-by-step photos and Pierce's clear instruction, you will discover how to build each unique creation, including:

- An armed rocker and a straight-back chair
- A drop-leaf table and a sewing desk
- Hanging boxes, bentwood boxes, clothes hangers and more!

ISBN-13: 978-1-55870-657-6
ISBN-10: 1-55870-657-7
$24.99 pb, 128p, #70607

Glen Huey's Illustrated Guide to Building Period Furniture

By Glen Huey

If you've entertained the thought of building a tall clock, a chest-on-chest, or a secretary, then this is the book for you. This book and DVD set will walk you through the building of five classic American furniture masterpieces. Learn how to shape cabriole legs, as well as mitering, sticking, and other classic techniques.

ISBN-13: 978-1-55870-770-2
ISBN-10: 1-55870-770-0
$29.99 hc, 128p, #70722

Authentic Arts & Crafts Furniture Projects

By the editors of *Popular Woodworking* magazine

This book is a collection of 23 projects in the Arts & Crafts style. Unlike many books on Mission furniture, *Authentic Arts & Crafts Furniture Projects* is filled with projects that, for the most part, are exact reproductions of historical pieces or sensitive adaptations. Stickley, Limbert, Roycroft and Greene and Green projects are included.

ISBN-13: 978-1-55870-568-5
ISBN-10: 1-55870-568-6
$24.99 pb, 128p, #70499

Building Traditional Country Furniture

By the editors of *Popular Woodworking* magazine

You'll add charm to your home and new life to your woodshop with these exciting, attractive projects. Each one is faithful to the Country Furniture tradition, mixing classic lines with straightforward construction techniques. You'll find an incredible range of designs, some simple, but clever, others exquisite and heirloom-worthy.

ISBN-13: 978-1-55870-585-2
ISBN-10: 1-55870-585-6
$24.99 pb, 128p, #70521

THESE AND OTHER GREAT WOODWORKING BOOKS ARE AVAILABLE AT YOUR LOCAL BOOKSTORE, WOODWORKING STORES, OR FROM ONLINE SUPPLIERS.

www.popularwoodworking.com